LOST MINES and HIDDEN TREASURE

LOST MINES and
HIDDEN TREASURE

by

Leland Lovelace

The Naylor Company
Book Publishers of the Southwest
San Antonio, Texas

9TH PRINTING

To the many adventure-loving youths
in the armed services, and from the farms,
the city streets, and the colleges, who have
come to me, asking for "waybills" to lost
treasures, and to the many others of the
same mind everywhere, I dedicate this
little volume, with complete sympathy
and understanding.

— LELAND LOVELACE

Chandler, Arizona,
November, 1956

Contents

vii

1

Lingard's Lost Lake of Gold

THE STORY OF LINGARD'S lost lake of gold brilliantly illuminates two principles: one, that folks are folks, wherever you find them; two, that human nature never — must I say hardly ever — changes. Even before the days of King Midas, the man who had made his first million sat up nights studying on how to make a second. And it is as natural as breathing, so it seems, to reject the notion of working for a dollar in order to hunt for ten.

In 1850 the world was thrilled by the enormous production of gold in the placer fields at the foot of the Sierras, in California. Americans, Frenchmen, Italians, Britishers, Mexicans, Chinese, and Chilenos were each panning more than a hundred dollars a day, placering in the streambeds and the river banks. All the equipment necessary was a shovel, a pan, and the river water.

Up to June of that year, the miners were satisfied with their find, taking no time out to speculate on the mother lode that was feeding the placers. They were content to keep on taking the golden eggs the goose had already laid.

They knew the gold had been washing down the mountainsides for centuries, and that it was not likely to end.

These miners had seen the diggings in Soldiers' Gulch, at Volcano, where the sand and gravel had been worked down fifty feet from the surface, equally rich from top to bottom, with nothing to indicate how much farther down lay the bedrock. It all seemed good enough and they were content.

But all this contentment vanished when the month of June arrived, bringing with it one Scandinavian named Lingard.

Lingard came into a camp where a party of miners was placering near Grass Valley. He hung around for a few days, taking note that many of the miners were panning several hundred dollars a day, while even the laziest were making a hundred dollars daily without straining themselves.

Having made the acquaintance of a few of the miners, he disappeared for about two weeks and then returned. This time he visited not only the Grass Valley placers, but also Downieville and Sierra City. In each place he told a select few of his acquaintances the same confidential tale: He had found, he said, the mother lode of all the placer fields in that region.

"The Sierras," he stated, "are full of volcanic gold that washes down the mountainsides in the rains and melting snows and feeds these placers.

"Far up in these mountains," he continued, "I have found in what was once the crater of a volcano, a lake whose shores are covered with gold nuggets in such profusion that the sand and gravel can scarcely be seen. If all this gold could be put upon the market at one time, the price of gold would go down below the price of lead or copper, and the gold market would be ruined."

Lingard's friends listened, open-mouthed, as he went on:

"I want to take some reliable men in with me, to bring out as much gold as we can; have the gold minted, and

2

then quietly invest our money without creating any stir or starting a stampede. We must keep all this a secret."

Never was there a siren song that could have sounded better to the gold miners. At placering they were making only a measly few hundred dollars a day. Why toil and moil for such a pittance, when they could, by going up into the mountain, make thousands of dollars a day, taking up gold by the shovelful?

Lingard's party made an honest effort to keep his so-called discovery a secret. But their extensive and lavish preparations for a trip to the bonanza gave the game away. They bought mules, packsaddles, a vast number of containers for ore, a huge amount of provisions, sugar, coffee, whiskey, even champagne, and many other luxuries not usually found in a miner's outfit.

When the story of the lake of gold began to circulate, it made wildfire look like molasses in January. Every gold camp up and down California was completely demoralized. Retail stores in San Francisco, Sacramento, and way stations, had such a run on hardware, leather goods, mining outfits, and whiskey, as never happened before. Supply took a severe beating at the onslaughts of demand, and prices went up past all belief.

Mules, packhorses, and burros sold for $1000 each. The price of flour, sugar, and coffee went up so high the merchants became wealthy enough to retire, in a month's time. Whiskey soared, but who cared, since they were all to be multimillionaires almost overnight.

Downieville was the outfitting point, and the streets, then unpaved, became channels of dust, crowded as they were with moving masses of miners, pack animals, and their drivers.

Every man and woman not laid up in a wheel chair was making plans and buying an outfit to go up into the Sierras hunting the lake of gold. Mining in established camps came to a standstill for want of man power, since most of the miners were on their way to stake a claim on Lingard's golden shores.

3

Though only two per cent of the popluation were women, mostly engaged in the oldest profession, nevertheless these rare birds also joined in the prospecting parties to share in the fabulous riches waiting at the lake.

"Within a month," says Major Horace Bell, writing of that country at the time, "50,000 men were penetrating the canyons and scaling the mountains in search of Gold Lake."

One historian relates that so strong was the pull toward the lake of gold that sailors deserted their ships, soldiers deserted the army, town councils ceased to sit, while they joined the many thousands dancing to the tune played by Greed-for-Gold, an air far more seductive than any played by the Pied Piper to entice the children of Hamlintown. Merchants and their clerks, lawyers, judges, and criminals, so say the pioneer writers, one and all were stricken with Gold Lake fever, for which there seemed to be no cure.

Meanwhile, Lingard with his small select party to whom he had first disclosed his secret, was moving stealthily higher and higher in the Sierras, in his endeavor to relocate the small deep lake of sky blue water whose shores were a mosaic of almost solid gold, which he claimed to have seen a few weeks earlier.

Up and over they went. Day after day passed, and still he could not find the trail back to the volcanic lake of gold. The food supply ran low. Their whiskey gave out. Their ammunition for shooting game was depleted. But they went on, still trusting Lingard to bring them at last to their goal.

The winter rains came, and at last the snow. Some straggled away from their party and were lost amid the crags and ravines. Some fell over precipices and were seen no more. Snowed in, many starved, game not being available.

At last, in hunger, exhaustion, and despair, they gave up. Lingard at last was forced to admit he could not again find the treasure he had once found. Some of his party were enraged; some said he was crazy; some believed he never had found the lake of gold. But all were agreed that if he ever had seen it, he certainly could not find it now.

4

Some historians, contemporary with Lingard, say the enraged members of his party hanged him. Others deny this and say he was among those who survived, and that he returned to Downieville.

The miners who finally reached the foot of the mountains found their old claims taken by others who were rapidly taking out the gold at the once despised rate of a few hundred dollars a day. That scale of wage must have looked rather good, after their grueling experience, flirting with death, while searching for gold by the shovelful, on the shore of Lingard's lost lake.

From an airplane, examine the high Sierras, in the region of Grass Valley, Downieville, and Sierra City. Look for the crater of a long-extinct volcano, now a lake. When you have located such a lake, find a way to reach it from the ground. Remember that in countless instances in many places on the earth, gold has been thrown to the surface by volcanic action. Consider how rich California is known to be in volcanic gold. Now, as we see it, if a volcano can toss up a small dab of gold, what's to stop it from tossing up a lot of it? Answer that one. And where would be a more likely place for the gold to fall than on the rim of the crater? This story doesn't strain our believer at all. When we consider the many mysterious forces in old Mother Earth, we can well believe Lingard's lake may not be a myth.

2

Lost Treasure at Tumacacori

EVEN AFTER MANY VISITS to the old Tumacacori mission on the Mexican border, in southern Arizona, I find it impossible to shake off the fascination of its historic lore, its alluring setting, its haunting, brooding atmosphere, and its power to stir the imagination.

Leaving the antiquated cathedral with reluctance, at each visit, I resolved to make such research into its lore as would fill a book. Almost before you could say knife, I had a huge filing-jacket overflowing with many kinds of material: legends, history, ancient documents, facts, and hitherto unpublished traditions, of such dramatic and historic quality as to give me that elation believed to be bestowed only by the possession of great riches.

Of this vast amount of fact and legend relating to the huge treasures known to be hidden in the environs of the old mission, and in the nearby hills, I am here setting forth two choice tales, as a mere foretaste of what might be available for reading pleasure, as well as suggestive for hunting treasure within certain prescribed limits. For the old mission is now a United States national monument, and — at least in theory — belongs to all of us.

1. Ópatas Stain Padres' Silver with Blood.

There are many stories of the lost and buried treasures of the old padres who lived at Tumacacori mission, teaching the Holy Faith to the Papago and Ópata Indians.

The Ópatas, now almost extinct, were less tractable than the Papagoes. They cherished an implacable resentment against the enforced labor to which they were subjected by the Spaniards, whom they never ceased to regard as nefarious interlopers.

It is often denied that the padres were actively interested in mining; but in the environs of this old mission, archaeologists and even casual, greedy, unlettered prospectors have found incontrovertible evidence, in the form of antique smelters, tunnels, timbered shafts, and other items, showing the hills roundabout the mission were rich in gold and silver, and that much mining and reducing were done under expert guidance.

In 1850, J. Ross Browne, in his report to the United States government, referring to the mission and nearby Tubac, wrote:

"Tubac . . . had probably 150 silver mines within a radius of 16 miles. They have not been worked for 50 years." Note that this would then place the abandonment of operations at around 1800.

While the Ópatas were grudgingly submissive, and made a pretense of being Christianized, they still remained Ópatas, with all their inherited traits. They had, however, not inherited a taste for working in the silver mines on the rigid schedule imposed upon them by the padres. They had learned to keep well hidden their own ways and beliefs, and under cover they kept their old pagan religion alive by a constant secret practice of their traditional rites and ceremonies.

The Ópatas were engaged in enforced labor in the mines at the time the king of Spain decreed that one-fifth of all

7

gold and silver mined in Spanish possessions should be set aside for the royal treasury and shipped to him in Madrid. This twenty per cent cut became known as the Royal Fifth. The Spaniards in the New World did not relish this decree and regarded it not unethical to circumvent it. The result was that much mining ceased, and those who continued to acquire gold and silver cached it away to await a more propitious time for using it. And this accounts for many a tale of "lost and buried treasure."

While the Ópatas were engaged in taking out the rich silver ore from the various mines, they made no secret of their unwillingness to work under such compulsion. There was one silver mine, however, in which they worked willingly, even gladly. Observing this, the padres named this mine the Ópata.

The good fathers were mystified by the sullen resentment at working in the other mines while accepting complacently the same sort of labor in this special mine, but they had no way of solving the enigma, not understanding the vagaries of the Ópata mind.

The mine called the Ópata was in a hill, the silver deposits being reached through a tunnel in the hillside. The silver was reduced to bullion, cast into bars, and because of the Royal Fifth decree, the bars were placed far back in the cave made by the excavation of ore, at the end of the tunnel. In time this cave became a large-sized room, even larger, in the opinion of the padres, who practically never entered it, than the mining operations seemed to demand.

Day by day the ! ars of silver increased in number, and yet the time when the mine would be exhausted seemed not in sight. The padres were delighted at the immensity of the treasure, and imagination suggests they often blessed the mine and the Ópata miners.

The padres did not know that in this underground chamber which they so seldom entered, the Ópatas were accustomed to gather in the silence of the night and hold their pagan religious rites, which often included the sacrifice of animals and sometimes of human beings.

These Indians had come to the Tumacacori mission from the region of the Arispe River, in Sonora, where they had contact with the Mayo tribe. Through some mystery which the Mayos never have disclosed, there were among them some members of their tribe who had white skin, blue eyes, and fine reddish blond hair. Their women so endowed were looked upon with a veneration which was practically deification.

The Ópatas had seen these rare blond Mayo women and regarded them with an overwhelming admiration, and with envy and jealousy. At the altars of the padres they had seen the figures of the Virgin Mary, and they may have deemed it more fitting to the Ópata way of life to have a living goddess than one inanimate, as their primitive minds conceived the Blessed Virgin to be. They determined to capture a white-skinned Mayo maiden and make her the goddess of their tribe.

A small number of them accordingly absented themselves from the mission, traveled swiftly to the region where the Arispe River flows southward to the Mayo country, and there they stole away a beautiful young Mayo maid, the daughter of a chief, and the promised bride of a son of a powerful subchief.

The young woman was brought by night to the underground chamber in the Ópata mine and held captive in the room with the great cache of silver, her captors unaware of her rank in the Mayo tribe.

In the mine the Ópatas guarded the maiden and worshipped her as a goddess. They gave her the richest gifts within their power and gratified her every expressed desire, except that for freedom. Her judgment was asked in all their tribal affairs, and thus, involuntarily, she ruled over them.

But after all, she was not an Ópata. To bind her to the tribe forever, they decided to wed her to their leader, so her children would be of the Ópata blood. They conveyed this plan to her and she rejected it with scorn. She had no intention, she said, of disregarding her vows to her Mayo lover.

9

All their arguments and inducements availed nothing. When the Ópatas threatened her with force, she replied she would die rather than be untrue to her bethrothed.

Enraged and vindictive, the Ópatas, realizing they had reached an impasse, decided to offer the maiden as a sacrifice. Preparations were made to hold the ceremony in the underground chamber of the mine. Above, they made an opening in the rocks to admit the rays of the sun upon a certain area within, in which was to be placed the sacrificial stone.

It was a brilliant Sunday afternoon, in the autumn of 1766. The miners were off duty for the Sabbath. The padres were enjoying a siesta. All was serene in Sunday quietude. The Ópatas were underground, preparing to carry out their barbarous scheme.

Having bound the body of the Mayo princess to the stone of sacrifice, they moved the stone so it lay a given distance from a shaft of bright sunlight shining through the aperture above.

"Consent to wed our Ópata chief and all will be well with you," a spokesman for the Ópatas told the maiden. "Refuse and you will suffer the most painful tortures. You must make your decision quickly."

The Mayo maid gave no response. After a brief interval, a huge Ópata medicine man advanced to the stone and, with a piece of sharp obsidian, made several small incisions in the girl's fair skin. Into these wounds he rubbed a poison made from yucca.

The girl had never flinched at the wounds, and she knew from traditional Indian lore that when she became heated from the concentrated rays of the sun, the poison would begin to take effect, her body would swell, her skin become suffused with blood, and the pain, racking her from head to foot, would be greater than mortal could endure. Death would then end her suffering. She watched while an Ópata placed within reach of her hand a bamboo cup containing an antidote to the yucca.

"If, before the sun reaches the center of this stone where

10

you are lying, you decide to wed an Ópata, reach out your hand and take this cup. This potion will render the poison of no avail, and you will be saved. Drink this cup and live an Ópata; refuse it and die an unwed Mayo!"

So spoke the leader, while the others grunted loudly in acquiescence, as they heavily and rhythmically danced around the stone.

The maiden gave no sign she had heard. At whatever cost to herself, she would remain a Mayo maid, true to her tribal lover. As the sun's rays moved nearer to her slender body, her torturers implored her with words and shouts to submit, save herself.

At last the yucca began to take effect. Unable to suppress her agony, she writhed in pain, with groans and shrill cries, which gave such pleasure to the dancing savages, they apparently forgot the possibility of discovery from outside, and gave ecstatic yells in an accelerated dancing fury.

With never a thought of saving herself by the medicine in the bamboo cup, the maid raised herself as far as the binding thongs would permit, and with all her remaining strength concentrated in speech, she called down the wrath of the gods in eternal rage, in a curse upon the cruel Ópatas.

She called upon the gods of fire to burn them in their house and home wherever they might be. She called the gods of water to drown them in camp and field. She called the gods of the storm to scatter them and theirs beyond all hope of reunion in a tribal state. She called the gods of lightning to strike them down in pain and terror. She called the vultures, the coyotes, and the wolves to clean the Ópatas' bones to the whiteness of snow, to be left, in hatred and scorn, unburied, upon the deserts.

She called down curses upon all the Ópata children, living and yet unborn. They shall be born deaf, dumb, blind, and deformed, racked with all manner of vile diseases, she cried. They shall be slaves, and drag out their weary days in poverty and hunger forever homeless. And may your tribe die out and become extinct, and the world

11

forget an Ópata had ever lived — wiped from the memory of man forever.

As her voice died out with the conclusion of her anathema on all Ópatas, living and dead, she sank back, gasped, and died.

While the ringing words poured from the blond goddess' lips, the Ópatas shrank back in terror. At her last breath a low moan of fear escaped from every savage breast. Then silence, as with one accord they turned and looked at a sudden apparition standing where the tunnel joined their chamber.

In the quiet of the Sunday afternoon, a padre from the mission was taking a walk in the nearby hills. Hearing a strange noise, rising and falling, he stopped to listen. He concluded it was coming from under the ground, in the direction of the Ópata mine.

He hurried to the mouth of the tunnel, and as he entered he became assured something extraordinary was going on in the mine chamber where the silver bars were stored. To avoid making any sound which would announce his approach, he advanced slowly and heard every word of the goddess' curse. As she finished and sank back in death, the padre stepped out into sight of the frightened Indians.

The tribesmen shrank against the wall, silent. The padre ordered them out into the open, leaving the white-skinned goddess upon the stone. He had taken in the situation at a glance. Moved by an impulse of self-blame, he knelt and prayed, begging forgiveness for the padres' credulity in trusting the Indians too far, and for remissness by failing to keep a check upon Ópata activity, satisfied as long as they produced the silver.

The padre and his associates that day called the Ópatas together and told them to leave the mission forever, to go back whence they came, the Arispe River region of the Sierra Madre; and if they ever returned, the padres would visit them with a devastating warfare by their hereditary enemies, the Apaches, until not an Ópata remained.

Refusing to make use of any treasure which, by remissness on their part, had been so barbarously stained with innocent blood, and fearing the curse of God upon the labors of the Ópatas, the padres, after doing penance, concluded to abandon the mine, with all the treasure that had come out of it.

They called upon their faithful Papago friends to close the aperture in the top of the mine chamber, fill in the tunnel, conceal with rock, brush, and growing vegetation the mouth of the mine, and erase all traces of mining, so the Ópata mine would never again be located. So well was the work done that the mine has not to this day been rediscovered. Abandoned in 1766, still untouched in 1850, although innumerable treasure-hunters have since then endeavored to trace the long lost silver, it eludes them, one and all.

In the early 1860's, when the French were trying to occupy Mexico, an ancient record giving a description of the old Tumacacori mines, was taken to Paris by "a personage," a relative of Madame Conde, wife of General Conde, Mexican commissioner. This record was placed in the National Museum at Paris, and copies of it were later returned to Mexico. According to this document, which carries some irreconcilable dates, the Ópata mine is halfway between the Guadalupe and the Pure Concepción mines. The Guadalupe, so says this record, is one league south of "the big gate" of the mission, probably meaning the front door, as this door faces south. From the Guadalupe to the Pure Concepción is three leagues south. The Spanish league in those days was 3:45 miles. Place the Ópata midway between them.

Go to the hills east of the mission. Then be sure you are accurate in observing the limits of the Tumacacori national monument, for inside these boundaries treasure-hunters are not welcomed by Uncle Sam's representatives who serve as sentries, and who have been known to refer to a certain inquisitive visitor as "another damned treasure-hunter."

2. The Blackgowns' Treasures are Still Safe.

In 1878, in the mineral region of Tumacacori mission, and slightly west of the old town of Tubac, Arizona, an American, named Hardwick, was keeping a little store, selling to the ranchers, miners, and Indians who frequented his vicinity.

Hardwick wasn't getting rich very fast, but he believed his occupation was more profitable than that of many a prospector who applied to him for supplies. However, he really would not be averse, he thought, to giving up the buying and selling of corn, coffee, beans, and bacon, if he could find a rich mine of the bonanza type — like the Veta Negra or the Planchas de Plata.

Many of his customers were in the habit of paying for their purchases with gold ore or nuggets, and he took it for granted that these were the legitimate proceeds of their prospecting venture. There was always a great deal of digging going on for the lost gold and silver treasures of the old mission, in the hills between Tubac and the mission, and as far away as the Huachuca Mountains, for the border had long been rife with tales of the buried treasures of the long gone padres.

Among Hardwick's customers was an aged Papago Indian. The Papago never had any money but always paid with nuggets or pure gold for whatever he bought. He was a gentle old soul, never looking for end-of-the-month sales or bargain days, and buying only the simplest necessities for himself and his aged wife.

Sometimes he came to the store when he had no gold, and Hardwick was always willing to trust him for anything he wanted, knowing that he would return in his own good time and pay his little bill with nice new gold.

Since the Papago was never known to do any mining or other labor, Hardwick often speculated upon where he got his unfailing supply of gold nuggets and rich ore. He was familiar with the fact that the Indians were taught from their earliest childhood that there must be no trafficking in

14

gold with the white man. Any Indian knows he will be punished severely by the gods if he ever gives information as to where gold may be found; for gold belongs to the gods, and the knowledge of its source must never be divulged to white men. If the Indian finds gold, that is different, for then it is a gift from the gods.

So Hardwick assumed it would be useless to ask the old man any questions; it might turn him sullen and put an end to their amicable relations, which were of long standing, and in a small way profitable to them both.

Yet he could not resist the temptation to ask the Indian where his wonderful gold mine was.

"*Está escondida*," replied the old man. It is hidden.

"He won't tell, so let it ride," thought the trader.

Several years passed, and the Papago was becoming somewhat incapacitated from the infirmities of age. He came into the store one autumn day and purchased a supply of food — enough to last him and his wife a long time. He paid with his customary kind of coin: small, clean nuggets of pure gold.

As he passed the gold over the counter to be weighed in Hardwick's scales, he gave way to a sadness which seemed to pervade his entire being. He said:

"Not many more times I come back here. I'm too old and sick. You're my friend. You've been good to me. I want you to have gold when I'm gone. I will tell you."

Hardwick saw the old man was weak and nervous. Opening the door to his living quarters back of the store, he said: "Come in here."

Seated, stiffly uncomfortable, on the edge of a rough armchair, in front of the stone fireplace, and sipping a cup of Hardwick's homemade wine, the Papago told his story, taking his time and telling it in his own way:

Many years ago, even before Hardwick's father and grandfather were born, the "blackgowns" who lived in the old mission had gold and silver mines all over that part of the country. What they wanted with so much metal the old Indian did not know, but they collected every bit of it they could lay their hands on, and cached it away under the ground, in the caves and in the tunnels of the mines. Some said they sent it away to a great chief across the big water, and to that other great chief who held the keys of heaven.

But there came a time, so the old Papago had been told, when the "blackgowns" received some very disturbing news and they hurriedly concealed all traces of their vast mass of treasure and disappeared. No one knows where they went, and no one knows when they will return, as they promised to do.

One October night, so the Papago told Hardwick, when the evening air had become too chill for comfort, the Papago, then a young man, was building a little fire to warm himself before sleeping. As he sat there idly watching the smoke curl skyward in a thin spiral, his eye caught the top of a nearby hill. On the skyline he saw a moving cloud, darker and heavier than he had ever noticed before.

The cloud kept on moving oddly down the side of the hill, and he was amazed to discover it was an immense horde of bats — millions of them. They were coming out of a fissure in the side of the hill, to consume the insects infesting the mountains and desert all through the year.

Unwilling to believe that so many bats could come out of that hillside, he ran to examine the spot. He found, as he had expected, a long, narrow fissure opening into a cave.

The Papago knew the ways of bats, though Indians hate and fear them. He knew they slept all day, hanging with their heads downward in darkly shadowed places within caves and mine tunnels, far from the light, coming out only at night on their quest for food, and returning to their homes while it was still dark.

He sat awake through the night hours until the time came for the bats to return to their home just before the break of day. He watched them all go in, and he knew there must be a huge chamber within to provide hanging space for so many of them. When the last bat was safely within that mysterious hill, his mind was made up to probe their secret hiding place.

The next day he returned to the spot, and with some sharp-edged rocks he widened the fissure large enough for him to enter. He found himself in a tunnel which, at one end, connected with a cave, high and wide. At the other end was what had once been the mouth of the tunnel opening from the side of the hill. This opening had been covered over with rock and soil and was now overgrown with a heavy stand of mesquite and greasewood, so that it was as effectually concealed as if it had never existed.

Inside, the timbers of the tunnel were in fairly good condition, but nevertheless bore evidence of great age. Where the tunnel ended in the cave, there was almost total darkness, and the stifling, foul atmosphere was better suited to a bat than to a Papago accustomed to plenty of fresh air. Air or no air, bats or no bats, the young Indian was determined to explore the cave as far as he could. It did not take him long to realize he had discovered the long lost treasures of the "blackgowns."

Against the wall of the tunnel were many ancient seats, tables, and benches, such as a modern mind would associate with churches. Upon them were lying in great profusion a number of gold images: statues of the saints, figures of the crucified Christ, and images of the holy Virgin — all of pure. solid gold. There were candlesticks, chalices, holy water stoups, crucifixes, utensils of many kinds, all made of silver and gold, some of them richly wrought, as one may surmise, in the complicated baroque style so characteristic of the work of the Spanish artificer.

Where the tunnel ended and the cave began, there were great heaps of silver and gold in bars and ingots, and a large mass of ore, selected for its richness and stored for lack of time to reduce it to purity. A few ore buckets made of skins were full of gold dust and nuggets, such as the Papago had handed over the counter in payment for the necessities to keep him alive.

The Papago was now very old; he had not long to live, and to repay the long-continued friendship of the trader, he had resolved to disclose the secret of the cave, that his friend might also share in the wealth so long hidden in the hill. The nights were getting cold now; winter would soon be here and

17

the old Indian might not live through another season. He had come to tell his secret before it was too late.

With the first frost, the bats go into hibernation, and do not come forth again until all danger of cold has passed. So he had come to tell his friend where to look for the gold while the weather was still warm enough for the bats to come out on their nightly search for food.

"Go to the third little mountain to the southwest," the Papago said. "Wait at the mountain from the early evening until you see the great cloud of bats rising from the skyline. At the point where they seem to come out, you can enter the cave."

The Papago said good-by and went his way.

Hardwick felt sure, with directions so explicit, he had the treasure just as good as within his grasp. So intense was his excitement he could not sleep.

The following day he prepared to go to the spot designated by the Papago. In the afternoon, taking enough sacks to bring back nuggets, ingots, ore, and artifacts, he set off for the third little hill.

He arrived shortly before dusk, tired, hungry, and more than ordinarily sleepy, for he had not had his usual amount of sleep the night before. He selected a spot to rest from which he thought he would be able to see the cloud of bats when they began to rise.

He made a small campfire, cooked some supper, and lay down to snatch forty winks before that twilight hour when he must begin to watch . . .

When with a start he awoke from the sleep which had overtaken him, the bats were already in the air and so far from their hillside home the point from which they had emerged could not be determined.

Hardwick returned to his store, intending to try again under conditions in which he could keep awake.

Late that day, the old Papago came again to Hardwick, in a state of tremendous excitement. He seemed to be laboring under some strong compelling fear.

18

"Have you seen the bats, and did you find the cave?" he asked in a weak whisper.

"No," said the trader. "I went to sleep just before dusk and when I awoke it was too late to see where they had come from."

"*Es bueno*," said the old Indian, with a trembling smile. "That is good. No bats will ever again come out of the hole. No one will ever find the cave. I did wrong to tell."

He then explained he did not think he was doing wrong to take a little of the gold from the "blackgowns" for himself and his wife. He didn't take very much. But to give away a secret that wasn't his own was wrong. Anyway, the grandfathers had taught the Indians they must not show a white man where gold was: the gods forbid.

Upon thinking this over, he had become conscience-stricken and immediately regretted what he had done. He had gone the next day to the hillside, and concealing himself there that night until the bats had come out again and returned to the cave, the Papago had filled the hole, unseen by Hardwick, covering it with brush and rocks in such a manner it would be impossible for anyone but an Indian to locate it.

In various places between the ancient city of Tubac and Tumacacori mission, many old hoards of bullion, ingots, and artifacts of solid gold and silver were buried by the Indian miners and by the old padres. Among the many caches are the treasures described in this story, if you are willing to accept the word of the old Papago.

If that "third little hill" lies within the limits of the Tumacacori National monument, Uncle Sam forbids any treasure-hunting or digging for it. But who knows? Maybe it is outside these limits.

3

Breyfogle's Lost Ledge

NO; the Lost Breyfogle mine has never been rediscovered. But does it not seem inevitable that the
time must come when modern methods of prospecting will
uncover it and add its great deposit of massive silver to the
permanent, if peripatetic, wealth of the world?

When this celebrated lost ledge is found, it will, according to tradition, be seen to be of a beautiful strawberry
quartz — pink, or rose quartz — full of free silver. There is
a difference of opinion, however, as to the variety of rock
in which the silver will be found.

According to the statement of a well known Southwest
treasure-hunter, the prospector who again uncovers the silver ledge will find it to be not a free silver, as the well established tradition relates, but a certain compound of silver
associated with gold.

When such detailed descriptions of ore and explicit locations and directions are given, they are likely to be pur-
posely misleading, and should be regarded with suspicion.
Every man who is prospecting after the old lost treasures, or

20

who is awaiting the day when he can renounce his cares
and set forth after the Golden Fleece, thinks:

"Why should I hand on this information and help the
other fellow to go out and get what I hope someday to get
for myself, I will tell him just enough to throw him off the
track, and in a few days I'll go after it and stake the claim
for myself."

It was May or June of 1852. A group of Mormons were
preparing for a trip from Utah to California. Their point
of departure was Mountain Meadows and their objective
was San Bernardino. Believing in the safety that is said to
lie in numbers, a few "Gentiles" had asked and received permission to join the Mormon group, as the entire journey
lay along a route much traveled by hostile Indians.

The route that had already in that early day been laid
out as the best between that part of Utah and California,
was then known as the old Spanish trail between Salt Lake
City and San Bernardino. It was fairly well traveled and
every inch of the route was definitely known. If the way-
farer could but hold off the marauding Indians, the trip
could be made in safety, if not in comfort. Grave danger lay
in wandering from the trail.

The rolling stock of the Mormons and their fellow
travelers made up a train of sixty wagons, well loaded with
goods and gear. In the caravan was a goodly number of
women and children, as some of the party were on their
way to settle permanently in Southern California.

When they were well on their way, and the novelty and
excitement of their starting had faded, they began to an-
ticipate the many hardships, dangers, and discomforts which
they knew they would be compelled to undergo before they
reached their destination. The inventive minds among them
began to study ways for shortening the journey and saving
not only mileage but time and misery as well.

The route took them to Las Vegas Springs, about thirty-
five miles from the Colorado River. To reach these springs,
the road made a big bend, adding a considerable number
of miles to the distance. Nevertheless it had always been

21

regarded as worth while for the wagons to travel these extra miles in order to have access to the water for replenishing the caravan's water-casks.

The leaders of the party finally decided to save mileage by cutting off this big bend in the road. It would be best, they judged, to leave the trail and go in what they thought to be more nearly a bee line.

When they arrived at the Armagosa Spring, having decided to make the short cut, they were unable to agree as to the better route to take. Those who had never been along this way before thought it best to take a straight cut across the desert — in those days, wild, untrailed, and uncharted. Those who were more experienced in western travel were determined to keep within reach of the river, for they knew the terrible sufferings they might be compelled to endure from excessive heat and lack of water in the interminable desert wastes.

The inability to agree or to compromise ended in a heated and bitter quarrel. Fifty of the wagons, with their human and other freight, started back to try to regain the beaten trail, with the intention of keeping, from then on, to the well-worn road. The other nine wagons followed the Funeral range of mountains between the Armagosa and Death Valley. This section is one of the hottest places in the United States, the temperature often reaching 122 degrees, Fahrenheit.

Wearily, this smaller party trudged on until they reached Furnace Creek, where they camped. In this place, another acrimonious quarrel arose.

Here they were, far off the beaten path, worn to a frazzle by the unaccustomed hardships, with nerves and tempers raw, in a totally unknown sort of country made up of desert, mountains and barren plain, and nothing in sight to relieve their weariness except the small water supply by which they were camped.

Again they were unable to agree or to compromise, blind to the wisdom of keeping all together, and ignorant of the

simple old adage that the longest way round is the surest
way home.

So seven of the nine wagons started off to the northwest,
hoping to find a way out of Death Valley in that direction.
The other two drove off to the southwest, certain that sal-
vation lay in that way; they were soon lost, without com-
pass or sense of direction, in the rough and rugged slopes
of the mountains along the edge of Panamint Valley.

In their wanderings, they came upon the Poisoned Spring,
which had evidently been visited by travelers before them.
Around this spring, they found the skeletons of three men.
Many bones were scattered around upon the ground which
could be identified as the bones of cattle and of the wild
animals in which that rugged and virgin country abounded.
They recalled stories they had heard of the poisoned waters,
and refrained from taking any for their nearly empty water-
casks. The bones were proof enough that the stories were no
myths.

In the group of fifty wagons which had turned back
to find the well-worn road, were three men who figured
that, with all the quarreling, back-tracking, and continual
discord that prevailed, they could do better by themselves.
They were known as Farley, Towne, and Cadwallader.

Pleasant companions are as good as a coach, in California
as in Rome. They knew they would never arrive anywhere
with satisfaction, accompanied by so much bickering and
quarreling. So, to speed up their progress and get rid of dis-
agreeable companionship, they purchased from some of the
wagoners a small supply of jerked beef and a few other of
the smaller articles of food, such as they could compress
into a little space and conveniently carry on their backs.
Accoutered in this manner, they said good-bye to the party
and briskly started off by themselves.

The three companions took a course a little north of
west. For several days they trudged on into the wilderness,
in the intense heat of the summer sun and through a great
stretch of arid desert plain. Their sufferings were extreme,
but their determination was equal to their distress.

Only those who have experienced it can know the misery and anguish of being lost in the desert, with the hot sun drawing through the pores of the skin every vestige of water in the human system, and no drinking water at hand to answer the cry of the flesh for water; water; thus to restore the balance of nature. Oh! For shade and water! Water and shade!

With what feelings of joy they at last reached Daylight Springs! All their fortitude was necessary to exercise the restraint with which a thirsty man must take in water, following a sojourn under the summer sun, in desert air, which combine in an effort to dry him up completely.

When they had rested as long as they dared, considering the depletion of their commissary, and had judiciously satisfied their thirst, they struck out across Death Valley. By way of Folly's Pass, they crossed the mountains on the confines of Death Valley and reached Panamint Valley.

Farley, Towne and Cadwallader, one and all, had had experience in prospecting for gold and silver. As they struggled along in this strange country, they were often desirous of stopping to examine the rock formation of the land. But with their minds bent upon the search for water; with their strength waning; with the urgent necessity for making progress out of the inferno of the red-hot desert, and with their craving for food hourly becoming more insistent, they dared not pause. Their lives were at stake and the search for gold could wait.

They did, however, from time to time, pick up a piece of rock that they thought might be valuable ore, and put it into their pockets. In one place, thought to be in the Panamint Mountains, they found what they afterwards described as a silver ledge so extraordinarily full of free silver that one of them said:

"The virgin silver glittered in the sun."

They gazed in amazement at the brilliant sparkle of the shining silver, fixed in a ledge of exquisite pink quartz. But their condition of weariness and exhaustion forbade them to

24

halt longer than was necessary to break off a few pieces of the ore and to stake their claim.

They threw out all other pieces of rock from their pockets, and replaced them with pieces of this wonderful ledge of strawberry quartz so overfull of the precious white metal. The ledge stood out boldly, clean and clear, and exposed a vein four or five feet in thickness, so full of silver that the metal, free and white, could be seen all over it.

It might be remarked here, parenthetically, that if, as tradition says, they found this wonderful ledge in the Panamint Mountains, then it follows that they found it in the vicinity of Folly's Pass, through which they had come on their way out of Death Valley into Panamint Valley.

With reluctance they struggled on their way, stayed by their resolve to return on a more asupicious day and work the ledge, with a good outfit that would insure their comfort while doing so. In due course, they arrived at the "Last Chance" spring, where they found water. Here they camped for several days, recuperating their strength.

While relaxing at the "Last Chance," the two wagons that had straggled away from the caravan of nine, came to the spring for water. The party was amazed to find the three men parked there by the spring. The caravaneers had a tale to tell of hardships which rivaled that of the three companions.

The caravan was made up mostly of men and women who knew nothing of desert and mountain; their leaders being of the stubborn type who could not profit by the experience of others and were impervious to advice. They had suffered incredibly from heat and thirst; their water supply had given out shortly before; their food was almost gone, and they were compelled to ration the remainder of their supply in order to exist at all. They had lost their way many times, and had had to back-track, when they needed all their strength to go forward. Their horses and mules were very nearly starved, and practically broken down for want of rest and water.

What the little band craved then was to get on to some

beaten track that they could trust to bring them at last into California. They were willing to forego any further experiments of their own.

One of the wagons was occupied by a man named King, and his wife. Mr. King was a Methodist minister from the East. He and Mrs. King were on their way to California where they were to join relatives and make their home.

Farley, Towne, and Cadwallader took a liking to the Kings, and as they sat around the campfire, they told them of their remarkable discovery and showed them the pieces of ore they had in their pockets.

Mr. King did not know anything about minerals and mining, for metallurgy is not a part of the course in theology. But he was a bright man, interested in his fellow man, and he had no disposition to doubt what his camp-mates told him about the kind and quality of the beautiful ore which they showed him.

The three men wanted to take King back and show him the ledge, but a discussion of the matter indicated it to be not practicable at that time. They were all worn out from hardship, weakened from the wear and tear of their sufferings, from shortage of water and rations, and there was a long trip ahead of them yet. No; it would not be possible; they might perish in the attempt.

The three men joined the wagoners, and, this time, determined to stay all together, they started out in a southwesterly direction; ere long they found the wagon trail into San Bernardino and their troubles were over.

Mr. and Mrs. King went on from San Bernardino to the Santa Clara Valley and joined their relatives, who listened with sympathy to their tale of hardship and adventure. Mr. King's account of the great silver ledge was received with much interest, though at that time, California was so enthusiastic about the great gold discoveries that silver was of secondary importance.

When Farley, Towne, and Cadwallader arrived at San Bernardino, they separated without making any plan for returning to develop their precious silver ledge.

Cadwallader joined some kindred spirits and went on a protracted prospecting tour down into Sonora, Mexico. Farley and Towne, having a taste for city life, settled finally in Los Angeles, but not until they had made a number of trips about Southern California, meanwhile making very big talk about their wonderfully rich silver mine near Death Valley, and showing the specimens of ore to all and sundry.

Finally Farley and Towne fell into the hands of some promoters in Los Angeles who were attracted by the pieces of ore which the two men displayed with so much braggadocio. These promoters made an agreement with Farley and Towne to organize a company and develop the mine.

Thereupon, they gathered in the money to make the necessary assay and equip an expedition to go to the ledge and make a start on operating the mine. The ore was sent to San Francisco and assayed, the test showing eighty-five per cent silver. Nothing less than a bonanza, and there was no lack of confidence that all members of the company were to become millionaires in very short order.

Mining equipment was purchased; provisions were acquired; a party of workmen fitted out, and with Farley as their guide, they started on their way.

When they had almost reached Folly's Pass, Farley, somewhat heady with importance, and no doubt with redeye also, became involved in a violent quarrel with another member of the party, a man named Wilson. Mr. Wilson, quicker on the draw, shot Farley through the heart and he fell dead.

The wonderful silver ledge that was to make them all millionaires may have been but a mile away, but with Farley dead, there was nothing to do but retusn to Los Angeles and find another of the three original discoverers to guide them.

In Los Angeles they located Towne and informed him of Farley's death. Mr. Towne was engaged in the fascinating enterprise of courting the lady who was pledged to become his wife, and made serious objection to leaving the city at that time.

27

Eventually, he consented, and the expedition started out again. The party reached Owen's Lake, on the eastern side of the Sierra Nevada Mountains. There Towne was taken sick at night and when morning came, he was dead.

This second catastrophe was a very severe shock to the members of the party, but in the West in those days, people soon became reconciled to the fact that the dead remain dead and only the living live.

Once more they made the weary trip back to Los Angeles, but there was no intent in the minds of the leaders of the expedition to give up the project. They had one more card up the sleeve. They knew that no guide, no mine; no mine, no millions. So Cadwallader must be found; not only found, but induced to accompany them and point out the way.

A trustworthy scout was found, who, for a price and a share in the proceeds, consented to go down into Mexico and hunt Cadwallader, and bring him back to Los Angeles where they could negotiate with him. The scout had instructions to bring him back at any cost; to make him any proposition that would prove acceptable to him. For the farther the lost ledge receded into the remote reaches of improbability, the more valuable and the more desirable it became.

Cadwallader was found, not without considerable expenditure of time and money. But he had been on a drunken spree of such intensity and long duration that he was in no condition to talk business, or even to understand any proposition laid before him. When finally he was sobered enough to listen intelligently, outraged nature failed him, and he died.

With Farley, Towne, and Cadwallader all dead, the members of the company kissed their hopes good-bye, and gave up the Lost Ledge forever.

Three years later, the illusive treasure came into prominence again. A young man known as Lieutenant Bailey let it be understood that he had rediscovered the now famed Lost Ledge. Bailey said he had explored Death Valley and the Panamint, was thoroughly familiar with the country, and was prepared personally to head an expedition to the locale of the ledge, provided he could raise the necessary capital and organize a company to exploit it.

Bailey appeared in San Francisco with some specimens of very rich ore, which he represented as having come from the ledge. He possessed an engaging personality, and had no difficulty in obtaining a large amount of capital for the purposes of the new company. It is told to this day that he gathered in about $75,000.

His scheme is described as rather ingenious: He made no attempt to sell any part of the great quartz ledge, but merely sold subscriptions on a prospective continuation of the ledge, which would, according to his so-called geological prognostications, show a large quantity of very high grade ore. In those days no scheme was too fantastic to attract capital, if only it promised riches.

With plenty of money, Bailey returned to Los Angeles and fitted out his expedition. A reasonable amount was spent for wagons, mules, provisions, implements, and personnel, and the start was made.

The program was for the expedition to proceed without Bailey. He would set out later and would overtake them near Owen's Lake, at which point they were to wait for him. From there he would fall into his role as guide, counsellor, and friend, and lead them to that wonderful deposit of precious metal which was to make them all millionaires.

The party reached Owen's Lake and camped. They continued to camp. In fact, they camped and camped. They camped for days, weeks, months. They may be camping there yet, but not with Bailey, for he never showed up.

Shortly after the failure of the Bailey expedition, David Buel concluded to try his hand at finding the Lost Ledge — for by this time the ledge had reached the dignity of capital letters. Buel was a hardy and fearless prospector and explorer, well seasoned as a mountaineer and desert rat. In 1855, he made an extensive and hazardous tour into unknown country to find a new route to the Colorado River.

Buel had come into contact with several persons who

were in the wagon train in 1852, and who had been in that small band which included Farley, Towne, and Cadwallader from the "Last Chance" spring to San Bernardino. From the descriptions which these persons gave, Buel believed he could go to the very place where the ore was found. He set forth alone.

With two mules, one of which he rode, the other packed with provisions and water, he disappeared. After an absence of two months, he appeared in Austin, Nevada, on foot. He had renounced the search for the Lost Ledge, and had a hard story to tell — a story of the usual sort: agony from thirst and excessive heat; battles with hostile Indians; starvation. His mules had died; his clothes were in rags. He figured that the Lost Ledge could stay lost for all of him; he was through.

Then came Breyfogle.

Sometime between 1865 and 1867, another company was organized to hunt the Lost Ledge. Breyfogle was one of the leading spirits in this band. Those who knew him say he was a county official of Alameda County, California, well known and well liked, and not at all the sort of man who would be likely to go chasing some will-o'-the-wisp.

At the time he joined the expedition to prospect for the Lost Ledge, he was burdened by some heavy debts, and he saw, in finding some rich lost treasure, a quick way out of financial stringency. He announced his intention to "find the Lost Ledge or die in the attempt."

"I shall come back a rich man," said Breyfogle, "or leave my bones in Death Valley."

With six other men, he started. They went south, along the Toyabe range of mountains, striking off into the desert heat of Death Valley. Along the foothills of the Panamint Mountains, they examined the slopes and rocks in as thorough a manner as their conditions would permit. Time after time, they found the trail Buel had followed.

They spent a night at Poisoned Spring, amid the bones of dead men and wild animals. They went on to Folly's Pass, and examined much geological formation there. Up and down, over and across, they studied the Panamint Valley. Their supply of water gave out, their food ran short, their animals wore out. The six men were for giving up.

"No, boys; tomorrow we may find it; let's not give up today. Just one more day, and we'll find it yet," was the continual argument of Breyfogle.

By that time, they were a hundred miles from the nearest camp. Their food was almost gone. Their lives were in the balance. Back to some civilized center, or starvation would be their fate. Breyfogle's six companions were determined to make a quick dash for San Antonio, California, a hundred miles away.

Breyfogle meantime was in a queer state of absent-mindedness and nervous excitement. He was determined not to give up. He begged his companions to stay by the search for two days more.

No; they were adamant. They had no food. They knew the relentless cruelty of the desert. They were short of water. They were weak and getting weaker. No aid could possibly come to them. Only one thing could be done and that was to get away before they became so weak they could not travel. Otherwise, death was certain. All this they tried to impress upon Breyfogle.

His gaunt, thin face was set. His bloodshot eyes glowed with an unwonted fire. He never batted an eyelash nor moved a muscle of his face when his companions stated their decision to give up and try to get to San Antonio.

"All right, boys," he said; "I've sworn to find the Lost Ledge or leave my bones here, and I'll do it."

He resisted the pressure they put upon him to go with them. Had they been stronger, they probably would have carried him bodily away. With the greatest reluctance, they said good-bye and left him. And with continued hardship through one hundred miles, they reached San Antonio.

Breyfogle kept up the search, over mountain and in desert, alone. His clothes were in rags and his food was gone. He was living on frogs and lizards, which were neither filling nor sustaining. He was very weak and his mind had begun to play tricks on him. But he must have been sufficiently in his right mind to appear perfectly sane to a small party of Indians who were watching him.

Indians will go to great lengths to avoid a crazy person, for they believe the devil has taken possession of him. They evidently had no notion that the devil had taken possession of Breyfogle, for in a moment when they saw that he was practically helpless from weakness, they sprang upon him, beat him into insensibility with their clubs, robbed him of his poor rags of clothes, and as a crowning infamy, they scalped him, leaving him for dead.

Nevertheless, Breyfogle survived.

When he recovered his senses, he found that the wound upon his scalp seemed to restore his faculties; his head was clear and he marveled that he had for so long forsaken his usually sound judgment.

Two days later, a wagon train passed by his camp, on its way from Los Angeles to Salt Lake City. Breyfogle immediately remembered an unfilled engagement he had in the Utah city, and joined the party.

Many times he regaled his companions with the story of his efforts to find the Lost Ledge. In his subsequent travels throughout the West, he told his adventures so often that the wonderful deposit of white, heavy silver in the beautiful pink quartz gradually lost its name of Lost Ledge and became known as the Lost Breyfogle Mine.

As stones that never roll gather moss with the passing of the years, so lost treasures become festooned with various versions of adventure as time crawls on. Of the several accounts of the Breyfogle mine, two have in recent years been published.

John D. Mitchell, in his *Lost Mines of the Great Southwest*, published privately in 1933, tells of hunting the mine in 1912. He describes the ore: ". . . a pale yellow carbonet full of black silver sulphides, horn silver and rich in gold."

J. Frank Dobie, in his *Coronado's Children*, published in 1930, gives a history of a Breyfogle mine as told to him by Donald F. McCarthy, who hunted the mine in 1899. Weighing the various accounts of the mine, Professor Dobie gives preferred status to McCarthy's, for McCarthy had it firsthand from Jake Gooding who had at one time employed a prospector named Breyfogle. Gooding had received the tale from this Breyfogle himself.

McCarthy's description of the Breyfogle ore is: "float rock of a soft grayish-white cast with free gold showing plainly all through it."

It was well established that the Lost Ledge which Farley, Towne, and Cadwallader discovered was free silver in strawberry quartz.

The adventure herein related was given soon after Breyfogle had his "hair lifted" by the Indians. This version may be regarded as authentic, as it is told by a friend of Breyfogle's, who went to Salt Lake City to see him upon his arrival in the wagon train, but found that he had left that city for Montana. That friend was J. Ross Browne, who caught up with Breyfogle soon thereafter, and published his interview with him in the late 1860's.

Chronologically nearer to Breyfogle's experience, Browne's report can be accepted — because of that fact, if for no other reason — as more truly historical. It seems to indicate clearly that the mine described by Mitchell, which he says was also known as the Lost Mormon mine, carrying gold, was another mine. It also seems to show, by algebraic process, that the man described by McCarthy was another Breyfogle. It all adds up to this, as this writer believes, that these three stories point to three lost mines, rather than the same one.

Some day the lost Breyfogle mine will be found. There can be no doubt that there was such a ledge as Farley, Towne, and Cadwallader described: many persons saw the specimens of ore, and heard the accounts of such disinterested persons as Mr. and Mrs. King and others in the small party that met at the Last Chance spring.

It should be remembered that the ledge was in timbered country, not far from Folly's Pass, in the Panamint range. And it should be borne in mind that, with the years, new growth has come over the land, and that the ledge by this time must be covered with brush, leaves, dirt, and wind-blown soil.

But the wind, through the years, covers and uncovers, and may yet again uncover the Lost Breyfogle Ledge.

4

The Missing Judge and
The "Lost Pegleg"

IN 1930 the public mind was shocked and mystified by the
sudden and inexplicable disappearance of Judge Joseph
F. Crater, a prominent justice in the New York State Su-
preme Court. On August 6, without any discernible reason
or conjectural motive for withdrawing from his home and his
conspicuous public position, the judge simply vanished.

For several years, both public and private investigating
services were vainly engaged in trying to solve the mystery
of Judge Crater. Authorities were eventually convinced that
he had vanished of his own free will and not by an act of
crime.

The story of the search for the missing judge is fascinating for itself, but it is no more engaging than the mystery
which we believe the learned judge set out to solve when he
so suddenly, and with no announcement of his intentions,
withdrew from the background and routine of his well-
appointed life.

LOST MINES and HIDDEN TREASURE

What motive was of such compelling power that it could move Judge Crater to leave his position, his prestige, his home, his wife, his round of whist playing, theatre going, and other activities of New York society? Granted that he was bored and wanted to get away from it all, where did he desire to go and what did he desire to do in some distant place, by himself alone?

If you know the character of a man, you do not need a crystal ball to tell you what he will do in a given set of circumstances. If you had the All-Seeing Eye, and could look into the heart of every man, woman, and child, you would travel far and look long without finding even one who had no yearning for romance and adventure, no love for mystery.

"Nothing is real but adventure," writes Eric Muspratt, British hobo, author of *Fire of Youth*. And nothing is so thrilling as the adventure of discovery. And again what if that discovery is long-lost or hidden treasure — thus solving a long-continued mystery? How many of us, age eight to eighty, have gone into the cave with Tom Sawyer and Huckleberry Finn and found the cache of gold there! How many of us have sailed the sea to Treasure Island with wicked Long John Silver, and had the time of our lives, though we brought no treasure home, save in our hearts!

And should Judge Crater be an exception and have none of that universal passion for such adventures? Did the judge, when a boy, ever find adventure in a junkyard, retrieve some trifle from a city dump, or search for gold coins on the seashore? Did any childish episode ever thrill him with the wild joy of discovery? The answer to that we can never know. There is reason, however, to believe Judge Crater had what it takes to evaluate the joy of life in adventurous freedom, and to seize it before it was too late.

In 1930, the year Judge Crater disappeared, the story of the famous Lost Dutchman mine, which for some years had faded out of the press, once more came to public attention. Many feature stories from the typewriters of Arizona's best known authors appeared in various magazines and Sunday newspapers, setting forth with great dramatic effect much his-

36

tory and more fiction about the old "Dutchman" and his fabulous hidden gold mine. This long-celebrated lost treasure is in the Superstition range in central Arizona.

World-wide publicity has been given the Superstition range in Arizona, not only because it is the locale of the famous lost mine, but also because of the many tragedies which have occurred there. Not so many persons know there is also a Superstition range in Southern California. It may seem an improbable coincidence that the Superstitions in California have even a greater number of romantic tales of lost treasure than the better publicized range in Arizona. And what is more, among the many tales of buried treasures and lost gold and silver mines in the California range, there are factual accounts of the rediscovery of some of these values, proof they are no myths.

The revival of public interest in the search for the Lost Dutchman mine also renewed the same interest in the half-forgotten story of the Lost Pegleg mine and several other once famous legendary lost treasures in Southern California.

The years passed. Five years. Six years. One more year and Judge Crater could be declared legally dead. The judge remained lost, and the public went on reading about the Lost Pegleg mine, the Lost Dutchman mine, and the Superstition Mountains.

Suddenly there flashed into the news the startling statement that Judge Carter had been seen alive and well: he had become a prospector, so the story went, and in the mineralized region north and west of the California Superstition mountain country, he was searching for the hidden deposits of gold and silver. Outfitted with pack and burros, dressed like all traditional prospectors, but well shaved like a city man, he made no secret of his name, nor of his purpose: gold in the ground.

One hot day in mid-August, 1936, a man walked ponderously into the sheriff's office in San Diego, California. Not tall, but weighing about 300 pounds, he sported a pair of huge mutton-chop whiskers. His bright shoe-button eyes, in retreat under heavy brows, showed alertness, both physical and mental, despite his 65 years. His ten-gallon hat on the back of his head offered no concealment to his weathered face, and his occupation was further proclaimed — as he evidently intended it to be — by his high boots, characteristic of prospectors. In his belt he carried a six-gun.

"Hello, sheriff," he said, fixing his piercing eyes on the man at the desk. "You fellows still looking for that New York guy, Judge Crater?"

"Hello, Blackie," responded the sheriff, heartily. "Yeah, we're still looking for him. Good-bye, Blackie."

"Good-bye, sheriff, if that's the way you feel, but I'm telling you Judge Crater is a prospector now, same as me. Good-bye, sheriff."

And "Lucky Blackie" Blackiet went out, the tread of his heavy boots beating a dull accompaniment to his mumbling as he walked down the hall. On his face was a sneer for the sheriff whose previous experience with Blackie had all been cut from one piece, and who now had not the slightest reason to guess that today Blackie had a more exciting bill of goods for him than he had ever had before.

A few days later — August 26, to be exact — "Lucky Blackie" Blackiet walked into the Bureau of Missing Persons, in the Los Angeles police department, and met Walter C. Allen, captain of detectives.

"Hello, captain," said Blackie. "Are you still looking for Joseph F. Crater, that New York judge?"

"Yes, Blackie, we're still looking," said Captain Allen. "What do you know?"

"Well, captain, Judge Crater is a prospector now, just like me."

Captain Allen looked up with interest. He had heard of stranger things, and he knew from experience that many a Very Important Person had gone into the desert for diversion, when on vacation, hunting the mysterious Lost Pegleg mine.

"How do you know he's Crater?" asked the captain. "Sit down here and tell me all you know about it."

Blackie sat, and in a few words told his story:

"I met this fellow in a lonely spot in the Cuyamaca Mountains where I was following up a clue. It was near Santa Ysabel, in San Diego County.

"One night, about a month ago, I had made camp, and after my supper, I sat by my campfire before turning in. I thought I heard the tread of burros, and in a moment a man showed.

"He was a big fellow, six feet tall, and must have weighed at least 200. I could see he was a city man, though a prospector. I asked him to stop and have some grub. I gave him some beans, bacon, and coffee, and we sat for some hours talking.

"He told me his name was Joseph F. Crater; and said he was from New York. But he didn't tell me why he left New York, nor how he happened to come to California, nor why he decided to become a prospector.

"But there he was, with a burro and a pack, roaming around the mountains. And he told me, looking kinda funny when he said it: 'If I can stick it out another year, I'll be legally dead.' "

"You say this happened a month ago? That would be late in July. Why didn't you tell me sooner, Blackie?"

"Well, captain, I'm a man that minds my own business. So I went my way and he went his. But I decided the next time I came into town, I'd let you fellows know about it. You can take it or leave it."

Captain Allen decided to take it. He discussed Blackie's story with chief of detectives, Harold Seager.

"There's only one chance in a thousand that the man is Crater," said Chief Seager, "but we'll make every effort to see it through, for it's too big a story to ignore."

Consulting with the sheriff's office, Seager learned from deputy sheriff, August Grand, that Mike Morani, a 51-year-old prospector in the desert mountains, had reported he had met a mysterious stranger, looking for gold in the desert two years before, and had spent two months with him in a prospecting venture.

"If we add what Blackie knows and what Morani has to tell, maybe we'll have something to start with," said Chief

Seager. "First, I'll get a description of Crater from the New York police."

With full approbation of the New York officers, who confirmed Blackie's description as applying to the missing jurist, Chief Seager despatched Captain Allen and lieutenant of detectives Chester Lloyd, to the Cuyamaca Mountain region to follow up the clue to the elusive stranger. Relying upon Blackie's promise to act as their guide, the detectives, with Deputy Sheriff Grand, headed for Santa Ysabel, four miles from Warner Hot Springs, where Blackie had a homestead.

Before they left Los Angeles, the news had leaked to the press. Captain Allen held nothing back:

"We are convinced," he said, "that a man who fits the description of Judge Crater has been seen in this part of the country within the last two months."

Accompanied by a party of reporters, news photographers, and newsreel trucks completely staffed, the police car moved on to Santa Ysabel, where they were to pick up their outsized guide.

On his home grounds Blackie's spirit of cooperation had congealed. Money, not adventure, had risen uppermost in his mind.

"Pay me 50 bucks or no guide," he announced, standing beside the police car, his feet wide apart, his hands nervously pawing in his whiskers.

"You think I've got nothing else to do but play nursemaid to a bunch of city coppers?"

The twenty newsmen in the party climbed out of their five cars to add their persuasion to that of the three officers. Blackie remained imperturbable as the rocks. The hat was passed, but the Fourth Estate could dig up only a measly $25. Convinced that this was all the traffic was going to bear, Blackie relented. He took the $25, entered the police car, and the caravan moved on, amid the stinging sandfleas, under the sizzling August sun.

The road to the beyond was a rocky trail through rugged mountains along the edge of the bone-dry desert, over a portion of the old Butterfield trail, the route by which the mail was carried from St. Louis to San Francisco in the stage-coach days of '49. Six miles distant, said Blackie, was the spot where he met the judge. Fearing lest the burning heat would discourage the men of the press — for misery loves company — Captain Allen reassured them:

"It's tough, but we can't afford to pass up this tip; it's too big to take lightly. It might end this six-year mystery. Blackie's story fits too well with other evidence."

Where Blackie expected to find a clue to Judge Crater, there was no sign of him. The posse proceeded to Warner Hot Springs, where they met Mike Morani. Under Sheriff Grand's questioning, Mike repeated his former testimony. When shown a photograph of the judge he said:

"Yes, that's the man. Him and me were out on a gold hunting trip for two months, two years ago; that was 1934. He told me his name was Crater, and I think he said he was from New Jersey. He had plenty of money and paid for everything; he bought the burros. He told me he had drawn out $7,500 from his bank. He was well educated and knew about rocks, but he couldn't get used to the rugged work of prospecting."

"You say he prospected with you for two months?" asked Sheriff Grand for the benefit of the newsmen.

"Yes, and then we went to Julian, 20 miles from here, on a spree. It was then he told me to keep it dark that his name was Crater."

About twelve miles farther on, they came to a trading post kept by Mrs. Marie Eisenmenger, who had sold supplies to the mystery man on two occasions.

"Yes," said Mrs. Eisenmenger, "a man who resembles that picture of Judge Crater bought supplies here twice, and each time he went away toward the desert. He came once last May and again in early July."

Yet another witness was discovered. A few miles down the hillside from Morani's cabin, they came upon the little home of Mrs. Grace Bahr, who was known to Deputy Sheriff Grand. Mrs. Bahr unhesitatingly related:

"I remember well that Mike Morani had a friend named Crater staying with him about two years ago."

Four credible witnesses, with nothing to gain by misrepresentation!

After another fruitless day in the burning August heat, the search was abandoned. The whereabouts of the New York justice remained cloaked in mystery, but not his purpose: Free as a bird; divested of all care; the learned judge — if it be he — was living in the land of his dreams, seeking adventure, guided by the gossamer hope of rich discoveries.

If the mysterious prospecting stranger was indeed the missing New York justice hunting gold in the desert, natural inference is he sought the well known, historic Lost Pegleg mine, or the Lost Treasure of Pedro Pedrillo, or the Lost Dutch Oven mine. Tradition places all these and many others in the general region of the stranger's deviating journeyings.

To sense the lure that could draw a man of Judge Crater's character, induce him to forsake his conventional way of life, to follow a dream promising great wealth and complete freedom in the wide open spaces, let us glance briefly at the traditions of treasure that lay at hand if his eye could but discern it:

There were two Pegleg Smiths, both prospectors over the same region; both discoverers and both losers of fabulous gold deposits in an area known to be gold-bearing at every turn. Both Peglegs have given rise to a vast amount of prospecting history and tradition. In searching for the Lost Pegleg gold, it is engaging but not necessary to know which of the two Peglegs found and lost the special deposit you are searching for. Just go right ahead with your search, for gold is gold, wherever you find it.

Thomas L. Smith, the first Pegleg Smith, started out as a trapper. But it seems nothing could stop him from an unhappy connection, direct or indirect, with gold discoveries, even after he lost his leg and wore a wooden leg on the left side. Lady Luck kept right on offering him opportunities for fabulous wealth, time after time, which he was destined forever to miss.

He muffed it first when trapping with a party in the region where the Virgin River joins the Colorado River in Nevada near the Arizona line. A companion brought to him some very heavy gold-bearing rock, extremely rich. Pegleg declared the metal element was copper, and the piece of rock was laid by and temporarily forgotten. Later, when it was found to be pure gold, Smith could never find the canyon adjacent to their Virgin River camp where his fellow trapper had found the ore.

Smith continued as a trapper, and later turned up in what is now Yuma. He had accumulated a quantity of furs and determined to sell them in Los Angeles. Accordingly he set out across the desert with a man whose name has been forgotten. This trip was distinguished for the numerous and terrible hardships they encountered.

When their canteens were empty, Pegleg mounted a small butte to get a view of the surrounding country, hoping to see verdure that would indicate a spring. On top of the butte he saw innumerable small black stones. Indeed, the butte seemed to be made up of them; they were everywhere, on all sides. Not seeing any green that would indicate water anywhere in the distance, he sat down and picking up some of the black stones, he threw them aimlessly about. Noting how heavy they were, he broke one, pounding it upon another. The rock was full of gold! He thereupon broke several more; each one was the same.

Water being then a more pressing necessity than a gold mine, Pegleg put several of the black rocks into his pocket, joined his companion, and went on. The following day they found water, and in due course arrived safely in Los Angeles, where they sold the furs without any loss of time. Then for a round of the saloons.

In the city Pegleg became involved in several escapades, took up horse-trading, grew tired of the West and went back east to Missouri, and then returned to California to find his long neglected gold discovery on the butte. In telling of his hidden gold mine to his companions he had so many times given false clues to its location, that after so many bouts with his close and constant friend, Al Cohol, he could not remember the true from the false. Year after year, he kept on searching, but he never could find the little butte. In 1866, he died in the county hospital, in San Francisco, strangely enough, of alcoholism.

In this volume, on page 192, item No. 17, title, Black Gold in Fumes of Death, will be found an account of the other Pegleg Smith, whose true name is said to have been James Smith, and his discovery of danger in gold, under Indian guidance.

Many men have made a lifetime career of hunting Pegleg's lost gold, and the countless yarns incident to this three-quarter century search would make a vast literature, if published. The search has been mostly made in the general area where the stranger identified as Judge Crater was known to be prospecting. For examining and testing, he had a wide choice of specific locations: from the Chocolate Mountains, the Superstitions, and Fish Mountain; to the Borego Badlands, the Santa Rosas, and all the desert south and east of the Cuyamacas and Warner Hot Springs where, according to Blackie Blackiet, he was last seen.

Those who have consistently sought the lost treasure of Pedro Pedrillo, in the California Superstitions, which this writer believes might have been the real objective of Judge Crater, make up a smaller company. Since the details of this treasure were disclosed in a suit-at-law, it would be most likely to come to the notice of the New York jurist.

In 1874 a strange lawsuit came into the court in San Diego, California. The members of a company designated in the legal papers as "The Treasure Trove Company" were bringing suit to determine questions involving rights of members.

The treasure claimed by the company was an ancient cache of gold dust buried in 1682 by Spanish explorers. The company organized to retrieve the treasure was formed in 1873 by a Mexican prospector, Pedro Pedrillo, in San Diego. The members prospected for the buried gold for a year with no result, and then Pedro Pedrillo died. The lawsuit followed

44

and much information was disclosed which Pedro might have preferred to keep secret.

Pedro, when prospecting in the mountains of Southern California, had found an ancient cross which had fallen upon its side, resting upon one arm. The end of the cross-arm was well down in the sand. In his attempt to raise it, he disturbed much of the soil at the base, and as he pulled it up, he noticed in the hole a curious object of dull metal. It proved to be an antique lead container. He broke it open and found inside it a scroll, with writing in archaic Spanish, most of which he was able to read. Translated, it said:

> I, Captain Jesus Arroa . . . brig *Isabella Catolica* . . .
>
> wrecked in great storm on coast . . . 29 March 1682 . . . went inland to high mountain . . . found placer gold and mined a great quantity . . . Indians . . . killing and wounding our men . . . We retreated, they follow . . . I fear death to us all tomorrow . . . I write where we have hidden our gold . . . If find, buy golden candlesticks for altar of San Diego in Sevilla and masses for the repose of my soul.

In the court proceedings it was shown that the weight of the treasure would make it worth $800,000 at the then prevailing price of gold.

The members of the company, impelled to disclose the location of the treasure, said it was buried in the Arizona desert, south of the Gila River. If this be true, the treasure would be in the general region of the Superstition range in Arizona, which, however, lies just north of the Gila. Other prospectors say the truth of the matter is the treasure is concealed in the California Superstition range, on the eastern slope. They say the key to the waybill is a certain rock formation when shining in the sun.

Another treasure which Judge Crater may have been seeking was the Lost Dutch Oven gold mine. This rich deposit of lost gold was found again in 1941 and is no longer available for prospecting, though as late as the summer of

1948 two old prospectors lost their lives in the heat of Mojave Desert while searching for it, unaware that it had already been rediscovered and claimed in another area.

The New Yorker may have been encouraged in his search for gold by the knowledge of the Dorfmeyer discovery in Eagle Mountain, lying in the general location of his searches. In 1899 two brothers named Dorfmeyer, when prospecting in Eagle Mountain, found, at an altitude of 1658 feet, a rich deposit of gold. To work this gold mine, they would first have to remove a heavy overburden of iron ore. So they abandoned the project and it was forgotten.

Recently a persistent prospector rediscovered this gold and iron, and it is now the personal property of Henry J. Kaiser. Now Henry is mining the iron for his steel plant at Fontana. For transporting the ore, he has built a railroad, called "The Flying Eagle," with its lower terminal at Ferrum on the Salton Sea. And the gold is his.

What would probably have meant little to Judge Crater in 1930 or 1936, is the recent discovery of uranium right there in his old stamping ground. Near the jagged rim of the Borego Badlands, north of the California Superstitions and some little distance south of the Santa Rosa Mountains, "hot zones" for the Lost Pegleg, Fred Hinds, a well-known local rockhound, made a discovery of strange yellow rock, responding to the Geiger counter with all the force of uranium. He made this known in Borego Springs, October 28, 1948, while waiting for the government men to announce whether he was due the government bonus for his claim.

There's gold in them thar hills in California, from the Colorado River to the Pacific, and if the mysterious stranger was Judge Crater, he was having more fun than he could have had on Fifth avenue or the Bowery.

The Lost Pegleg: Follow the level desert west out of Yuma toward Los Angeles until you come to a group of three little buttes, the third one separated a little from the other two. Examine all three, for black gold-bearing stones may be found on each. Some of the old-timers say these buttes are on the edge of the Cocopah Mountains; some say on the north side of the Chocolate Mountains; while others say the Superstitions, and still others say the west side of Fish Mountain. Old prospectors have claimed that rich placer gold has been found in the old stream bed at the south end of Fish Mountain and between Seventeen Palms and the Superstitions, and that following this placer would lead to the Lost Pegleg as the mother lode. Other old prospectors say the Pegleg gold is in the south side of the Santa Rosas; near an extinct volcano. Others hunt in the Borego Badlands.

The Pedro Pedrillo lost gold: The clue to this cache of gold dust, old-timers say, is a beam of light. Tradition says that Pedro determined the place for concealment by sitting where he could see rays of the setting sun strike upon a certain rock, reflecting in the form of an arrow. The point of the arrow indicates the spot where the gold is buried. Reflected light is more easily discerned upon a steep mountainside than upon a level desert. So, when the December rays of the setting sun form an arrow when shining on a rock on the steep side of Superstition Mountain, sloping to the desert on the east, it may point to the long lost treasure. Don't forget, if you find it, to say masses for Pedro's soul, as well as for the long-gone Jesus Arroa. And what about those candlesticks for the shrine of San Diego in Seville?

5

The Lost Treasure Vaults
of the Lemurians

A T THE MEREST MENTION of hunting for the
lost treasures of the ancient Lemurians — a lost race
once inhabiting a continent which completely disappeared
12,500 years before Christ — one would be prone to say:

"Oh, shucks! That's so far back, it's ridiculous! And
anyhow, it's incredible! Hunting Captain Kidd's treasure
would be different."

But wait a minute. Don't be so sure. At any rate, it
isn't so ridiculous but that an expedition was planned, the
approximate location indicated, and a goodly company of
explorers — mostly sensible and substantial men and women
— signed up to undertake the search, no further back than
1934. And no farther away than California, where more
things than the weather are truly unusual.

For human interest, strangeness, and singular combination of apparent fantasy and proved reality, the record is
not surpassed by any story of historic adventure in America.
The factual character of the episode would be seriously

open to suspicion, were it not authenticated by the United Press and certain eminent California scientists whose reputations and positions place them beyond question.

The story of the lost gold and of the modern scheme to search for it is no more fascinating than the story of the lost continent and the people who are said to have lived upon it. Do not make the mistake of thinking to pursue the story in a straight line, for the researcher will find it to take an arc curving to the point where infinity merges with zero. Yet its fascination and lure never diminish and its practical aspects remain as mathematical as any modern problem in metallurgical discovery.

In 1904, the Lord Cowdray Mining Company, of London, England, engaged a man to do prospecting for some gold properties for them, in the gold-bearing region of California. He called himself J. C. Brown, though that may not have been his name. Brown was then 49 years of age, and anxious to make a good gold strike for his corporation that would enable him to retire.

Ranging north from the gold country lying northeast of Sacramento, he struck into the Cascade Mountains. In a mountainside, he accidentally discovered signs of a landslide, not of recent origin, and as he sat down upon a rock and gave his attention to studying the geological formation of the mountain, he discovered faint indications of the mouth of a tunnel.

He picked away the soil and growth with difficulty. With no visible signs that human beings had been around that area, it was hard to believe that human hands had made a tunnel in the mountainside. But there is often an equal interest in noting the queer things that nature sometimes does, and to satisfy his curiosity, he persisted in moving the rock, soil, and vegetation. At last he stood convinced that man had, at some time remote in the past, been operating in that locale.

In time he had the mouth of the tunnel clear and clean. Cut in solid rock, it opened into a long and narrow room. The walls were lined with *tempered* copper, and hung with

49

shields and wall-pieces made of gold. At the back, this room opened into other rooms filled with countless objects of gold and copper. The floors were strewn with human bones — the bones of a race of giants.

On some of the gold and copper plates and wall-pieces were certain drawings and hieroglyphics, repeated many times. Inferring that the designs so frequently recurring had some historic or religious significance, or formed some record, Brown fixed them in his mind, with the intention of putting them on paper when once he should be out of the wilderness.

It is not clear why Brown left this scene and took no definite action that can be traced. It may be that he wanted this mysterious treasure for himself, without reporting it to the Lord Cowdray Mining Company. Or he may have had other reasons. Possibly he found hardheaded mining men sceptical of what he had to report.

The career of Brown, for the next three decades, is shrouded in mystery, but it is known that he spent a great part of that time studying the lore of prehistoric races, touching upon those known to the Indians of the United States and Mexico as *los gigantes,* the giants, about whom little has been written. His investigating led him to the literature and philosophy pertaining to the lost continent of Mu, and "the lost race of Lemuria."

Years of study and comparison of the hieroglyphics and pictographs found in the tunnel convinced him, by their agreement with similar antiquities found in many diverse places in the world, that these records had been written by descendants of the ancient people whose land, now known as the lost continent of Mu, inhabited by the lost race of Lemurians, had been destroyed by fire and water.

In 1934, after a long wait of thirty years, Brown was again in California. In April of that year, when he was 79, he appeared in Stockton, and was quartered in a government shelter. He was apparently in funds, for he asked no favors, accepted nothing, and maintained his independence.

His first move was to make contact with the editor of

a Stockton daily, to whom he told his story. His account of his adventure and discovery and of his historic and scientific investigations was so circumstantial and consistent, that he could not be lightly dismissed.

The editor introduced Brown to the curator of a local museum, a man of mathematical, scientific, factual mind, whom it would be difficult to hoodwink. Together they questioned Brown in every conceivable detail. At every angle his story stood up. His character, his demeanor, his extensive information on his subject inspired respect, and both editor and curator, being human, sensed the spell of the adventure, the romance, and the mystery.

Before one begins to grin in derision at belief in the lost continent of Mu, it is well to invoke the American custom, popularized by politicians, of looking at the record. Boiled down to a few words, the record is from these: Manuscripts and tablets discovered in Egypt, India, Burma, Japan, China, Greece, the South Sea Islands, and Central, South, and North America.

Some of the most tangible records best known to savants and antiquarians are: the Lhasa records; the Easter Island tablets; certain Greek records; the Troano manuscript in the British museum, of indeterminate age, estimates of which range from 1500 to 5000 years; the Codex Cortesianus, a Maya book about the same age as the Troano manuscript; and certain petroglyphs in Arizona and Nevada.

The story these records tell is, briefly: The land of Mu was a huge continent lying in the Pacific between Asia and the middle part of the American continent. Mu was the motherland of the human race — the land where man was created. The people of Mu had a highly developed civilization and all other countries were her colonies. Proof is accepted that the civilization of Mu preceded that of the early Greeks, the Chaldeans, the Babylonians, the Persians, the Egyptians, and the Hindus.

The Lemurians, as Mu inhabitants are now called, were in ten groups, or tribes, but living under one government. They were much larger than present-day man, and if the skeletons of *los gigantes,* found in many places in America, are truly remains of the Lemurian race, they had a much more substantial bony structure, and a correspondingly greater strength — the strength that would be required for the mysterious, inexplicable engineering feats necessary for making, moving, and setting up the giant stone figures on Easter Island, believed to be the only remaining portion of the land of Mu.

Their population of 64,000,000 was divided into three classes: the leisure class, the middle class, and the laboring or lower class. The leisure class, cultured, and accustomed to luxury, developed many sciences. The Lemurians had trained navigators, built seaworthy ships, and carried their civilization to other lands which they attached to their government and administered much as Great Britain administers her colonies.

They had the same uses for gold and jewels that we have today, and their gems were the same elements and compounds of nature that are ours.

The ships of Mu sailed to eastern Asia and to North America and there the Lemurians made permanent and extensive settlements. It follows then that a colony of Lemurians was living upon the American continent at the time of the catastrophe which destroyed the motherland, and that their descendants persisted for some centuries before succumbing to whatever forces eliminated them from the American scene.

For Mu was wiped out, with the single tiny exception previously mentioned, Easter Island, by a calamity scarcely conceivable by the modern mind: The immense continent *of Mu "sank in a watery abyss and was envelope in flames as she went down."* The motherland of the race *"vanished in a vortex of fire and water."* In words of one syllable, an earthquake rent the land so deep that the internal fires of the earth burst forth, the water rushed in and turned to steam, creating a mist which cut off the light of the sun.

The date of this disaster has been fixed at somewhat less than 15,000 years ago, or circa 12,500 B. C. One can only take it or leave it, unless one has the time to cover the ground which has been already examined in a lifetime of research by certain well-known savants.

And parenthetically, with this date in mind, it may be passed on as *lagniappe* to those who feared Adolph Hitler and all his works, that the swastika has been found among other symbols used by the Lemurians at this date. To the Lemurians the swastika was the symbol of *"the Four Sacred Commands,"* an important feature of their ethical system.

When Mu went down, in a cataclysm so severe, other continents were shaken. Some portions went down, some were raised; water rushed out at some points, and into others. The contour and altitude of continental mountains were also changed, and it is conceivable that the Cascade Mountains were raised and their inhabitants were thus saved. Some of Mu's colonists were no doubt submerged as by a flood, reducing the number of Lemurians left to carry on the race.

In Havasupai Canyon, Coconino County, Arizona, a petroglyph of extreme antiquity has been found, accurately picturing a mastodon. This is taken as proof that the ancients were living in Arizona at the same time as the mastodon, which as a species became extinct 12,000 years ago. It cannot be shown who these ancients were or where they came from, but it is certain they must have come from beyond the sea. The sceptic cannot do more than say, "You're another," to him who believes they were Lemurians.

There is no way to show that the North American Indians are not descended from the Lemurians. The Hopis and the Zuñis use sacred symbols, *"virtually those of Mu,"* including the swastika. The Nootka Indians of Vancouver use symbol-writing identical with Mexican, Egyptian, and Oriental forms used in describing the destruction of Mu.

In Nevada, writings on rocks not only describe the destruction of the lost continent, but are in other forms which have not been deciphered. In Grapevine Canyon, Nevada, a prehistoric petroglyph has been photographed which is claimed to be a ground plan for a temple. A part of the plan is read to mean that the temple is to be dedicated to the land of Mu, and that *"she is no longer living; she is dead."*

In Gould Gulch, Beatty, Nevada, is a rock covered with symbol writing, some of which, in translation, is said to mean:

"Mu, with myriads of souls, has been submerged. The sun shines no more upon her. She is in darkness; she is dead."

Two other symbols on this rock are said to mean:

"A mouth opened, fires came forth with vapors, the land gave way and went down."

The bones of a giant race of men have been found, some very recently, in California, Colorado, Nevada, Arizona, Sonora, and Chihuahua. These bones indicate the stature to have been from seven to nine feet. So many giant skeletons were found in Chihuahua south of the Big Bend, Texas, that a vast plain in north Chihuahua is known as *Llano de los Gigantes,* Plain of the Giants. Sealed in caves away from the air, or buried deep in the earth, they have remained intact for countless years.

Brown was not the only one to discover remains of the civilization of the vanished race in that western region. A few years ago, two prospectors, combing the southwest mountains of Nevada for signs of gold, came upon some deep caves, each one opening into another. In the far reaches of the caves, they found furniture of vast size, as if built for giants.

Also they found dishes of gold and of other bright, shining metals which they could not name, but which they surmised to be of some imperishable alloy, able to withstand the years. They described an immense table which seemed to have been set for dining.

The caves had many evidences, they said, of extreme age and of having been undisturbed for centuries. But there is no legend telling who the vanished ones were, where they came from, or for what reason they disappeared. It is permissible to believe they were a remnant of the giant race of Lemurians, but we shall probably never know with certainty. But whoever they were, if they left gold and other treasure behind, it will eventually be known and searched for.

All of which brings us back to J. C. Brown and his reappearance in Stockton, in April, 1934. Brown told the editor and the curator his object in returning to California was to organize a group of responsible people who would accompany him, at his expense, to relocate and reopen the tunnel in the mountainside which he had discovered thirty years before. He would have plenty of funds, he said, at the right time, to provide a yacht to take the party up the river to the Cascade Mountains.

The curator introduced Brown to John C. Root, a retired printer then living in Stockton, known to be a deep student of the occult. In a very short time a group of 80 was formed, to go ahead with the explorations, and the Root home became headquarters for the proposed expedition, with nightly meetings, for "listening to Brown's intriguing tales."

For six weeks the meetings continued and the enthusiasm grew. Some gave up their jobs to join the company of treasure seekers. Others sold various items of their personal property with a view to rearranging their personal lives after the success of the venture should have been demonstrated, so certain were they of the outcome.

The date was set for the expedition to start, June 19, 1934. Upon that day, Brown's yacht was to call in Stockton harbor and pick up his disciples to take them north.

On the evening of June 18, Brown left the meeting of his followers, promising to meet them on the morrow with a surprise. The morrow came, and the group waited for him. They waited in vain. Brown disappeared that night, and so far as can be learned, was never seen again.

When the members had waited for Brown for twelve hours, overwhelmed with anxiety, they called in the police. Relating to them Brown's tales of a prehistoric giant race and its store of treasure in the Cascade Mountains, Brown's followers asked the police to hunt for him.

The officers, however, not versed in the lore of antiquity, were mystified by what seemed to them a lack of motive for Brown's "tall stories" and for foul play. Brown had collected no money, asked for no contributions, sold no shares, promoted no stock, and had convinced all his followers of his open-hearted sincerity in desiring merely to explore and rediscover the lost treasure vaults of the ancients.

One prominent man in Stockton, of those best acquainted with Brown, whose character and position give his opinions weight, asking not to be quoted, said:

"So far as I know, Brown did not profit in any way. He collected no money. He appeared to be a gentle, almost timid old man, in very poor health. I would say he was perfectly sane. His stories 'tied in' with all that has been written on Lemuria, and sounded perfectly logical and possible, once one admits the existence of the lost continent and its marvelous civilization in ages past.

"I enjoyed Brown. I'd like to listen in again on his thrilling tales!"

Brown is gone, but there are many people who know his story. Many believe he was telling the truth. They know the Cascade Mountains, and they know the many devices which science can bring to bear for the discovery of metals in the earth. And it will not be at all amazing if the morning paper sometime reports the rediscovery of the hidden treasures of the lost race of Lemurians.

Indeed, since the above was written, the morning paper has come up with impressive spot news giving astounding and startling reality to the whole speculative subject of the lost continent of Mu.

An article in the Los Angeles *Times,* signed by William S. Barton, tells that an expedition of the University of California and the United States Navy returned to San Diego, on November 4, 1950, with a report that they had discovered a 1000-mile-long mountain range, with peaks rising 14,000 feet, but hidden a mile beneath the waters of the

Pacific between Hawaii and Wake Island. Barton compared the submerged range to the Sierra Nevada system, and said the discovery may rank as one of 1950's outstanding scientific achievements. The expedition included two laboratory ships, 30 scientists, and a crew of 85. Barton wrote:

> Huge stores of almost pure manganese were found, and indirect proof that the earth's core contains enormous amounts of uranium and radium . . Intriguing as it is speculative is the suggestion that the tremendous range once formed the ceiling of the legendary lost continent of the Pacific.

Northeast of Sacramento is a well known gold region. Look north of this gold country, in the Cascade Mountains, where the slopes are steep, rocky, and covered with thick verdure; where the tree growth is extremely old and terrain undisturbed for a very long time. Age is a significant element here.

AUTHOR'S NOTE: In "The Lost Treasure Vaults of the Lemurians," the quoted sentences and the phrases italicized have been taken from *The Lost Continent of Mu*, by Colonel James Churchward, published by Ives Washburn, Inc., New York City. Also the descriptions and other material pertaining to the lost continent, though not quoted verbatim, were gleaned from the same source. Mr. Washburn has generously granted permission to use this material. Since it would scarcely be possible to present the story of J. C. Brown and his adventure in California, without this lore from Colonel Churchward, the author feels confident that the reader, as well as the writer, will be grateful to Mr. Washburn for this courtesy.

6

The Lost Mine of Doctor Thorne

AMONG THE OLD-TIMERS and prospectors in Arizona, next in interest after the celebrated Lost Dutchman comes the Lost Doctor Thorne mine. For three-quarters of a century, men have been going into the hills, hunting it.

At this date, one dares assume that no man now living remembers just how it happened that Doctor Thorne was captured by the Apaches. Both history and legend are very vague as to how and when it occurred, and these data are not material to the story.

The band of Apaches who captured him were living in a camp more or less permanent, in the flats which lie about the foot of Four Peaks, of the Mazatzal Range. Old Four Peaks stands about 80 miles northeast of Phoenix, and is not far from Roosevelt Dam.

In these flats the Apaches had set up their wikiups at the base of the mountain where they had easy access to the water then called Rio Salada, but now known as the Salt River. In these wikiups they were accustomed to leave their squaws, the papooses, the old men and the sick, while they went forth on their tours of pillage, rapine, and murder.

This camp was fairly well concealed, by reason of being so difficult of access in those days. It was reached by a rough and rocky trail over red and brown volcanic rock, upon which the tread of man and horse left no trace. Those who have made the thrilling trip along the scenic Apache Trail, a modern highway leading from Apache Junction to the Roosevelt Dam; or over the scenic Miami Superior Highway, in central Arizona, will be better able to understand the sort of country Doctor Thorne was immured in. And they will also get a glimmer of the difficulties that lay in the way of his escape and return to the white settlements.

The Apaches, assured that the white doctor was a docile captive, took him to their ranchería and permitted him to move freely about among the members of their families, though always under the watchful eye of a guard. He had no idea how far the Apache camp was from any avenue to civilization, and considering the rugged, rock wasteland surrounding him on all sides, he could not devise any way of escape. He decided to be patient and await what might turn up.

Meanwhile the months passed into years. During this time many occasions arose in which he was able to minister to various tribesmen and their women and children in sickness. His "medicine" proved so effective in relieving distress that the Apaches considered him a miracle-man. This service, combined with his gentle manner and his complacent acceptance of his environment, endeared him to the savages and won their confidence.

The time came when homesickness and a craving for contact with his own race so overcame Doctor Thorne that he determined to ask the subchiefs then governing the camp for their permission to return to the white settlement.

The Apaches were not incapable of a feeling of gratitude. They had ceased to look upon him as an enemy; their trust in him had been well established. After all, he was only one, not a multitude. The subchiefs expressed themselves desirous of having a pow-wow to deliberate upon his request.

The pow-wow was held immediately, lasting several hours. Many grunts, a few words, and much tobacco smoke issued from the lips of the deliberating Indians. When finally the sense of the meeting was sifted down, it was to the effect that since the doctor had always been docile, friendly, and trustworthy during the long term of his captivity, there was no good ground for believing he would ever be otherwise. They must be grateful for what he had done for them. However, they might need his "good medicine" at some future time, and this consideration made them hesitate to decide whether they should let him go or retain him as their vassal.

They concluded they would ask their big chief, Red Sleeves, for permission to release Doctor Thorne, but they would impose such conditions that the doctor would not leave them.

The result of the conference was conveyed by messenger to Chief Red Sleeves without delay. The chief's command was:

"Let the paleface medicine man go."

When the report was brought to the Apaches that Chief Red Sleeves desired them to set Doctor Thorne free, they said in effect:

"We want this man to stay with us for a while longer. We will set him free, but we will give him no horse and no weapons. He will hesitate to set out to return to his people, alone and unarmed, with no food, through this wild and perilous country, with danger lurking at every turn. He will stay with us, and when we need his miracle-working power, he will be here."

Their logic was correct. Doctor Thorne made no immediate move to leave the tribe. He remained peacefully and helpfully in camp, making no sign of a desire to return to his own people. He completely won the confidence of those murderous, thieving, treacherous savages.

During his sojourn among them, Doctor Thorne had often heard from both the squaws and the braves, about the

60

rich yellow treasure in the ground — the hope and desire of the white man, the one metal for which any white man was always ready to do and dare, to shed his blood if need be; to undergo every hardship and to commit every crime in the calendar.

But the old doctor also knew that this same yellow metal was of little use to the red man. He knew the Indians were aware that traffic in this metal, between the red and the white races, always led to trouble, in which the red man was likely to come off second best. He knew the Indians would never mine for gold on their own account.

The Apaches had no use for gold in the sense of its being wealth. They had no need of money. Whatever they wanted they won either in combat or by stealth. They made little use of gold for ornaments, as they were not a metal-working tribe. Sometimes they used gold for bullets, and now and then they made a gold-tipped arrow. One of their time-honored traditions forbade their showing a source of gold to a white man.

One day, as proof of their faith in him and of their love for him as a member of their tribe, the Apaches told the doctor they would show him their rich secret gold mine. Though he had often seen fine specimens of their pure gold in quartz, he had never been able to discern its source.

The Indians were shrewd. They were often able to pre-judge the motives of the white man, even through a figurative stone wall. But just what they expected Doctor Thorne's reaction to be upon beholding their wonderful secret treasure, is not easy to conjecture. The doctor was never able to convince himself that making him a party to their secret was meant to be a reward. On the contrary, he later had cause to suspect it was an example of their tantalizing cruelty and love of torture.

When, therefore, the Apaches told Doctor Thorne that they were going to show him their secret gold mine, he became inwardly excited. Though he understood their words and half believed their expressions of brotherly regard, he could not fathom their true motives. Distrust kept pace with his curiosity. He therefore concealed his interest and maintained a face as stony and stoical as their own.

On a clear, bright day, resplendent with Arizona sunshine, the Apaches mounted the doctor on a sturdy pony. They blindfolded him, impressing upon him the necessity of secrecy. His pony was then turned around several times, to the left and to the right, and led backward and forward; every device conceivable by the Apache mind was used to confuse the doctor with regard to direction.

After a hard ride over a long and rocky trail, which took him both up and down, the pony was halted and the blindfold removed from the doctor's eyes.

"I expected to see something astounding," said Doctor Thorne, when describing his adventure, after his return from the Apaches, "but my wildest imaginings had pictured nothing so clear, rich, and simple as what was before me.

"I was standing in a narrow canyon. At my feet there was a vein of quartz at least eighteen inches wide, cutting across the canyon and running up the other side. The sun was shining on the vein and it was almost half, pure, shining, naked gold.

"As I looked, my thoughts, in my utter amazement, almost stood still. But in a glimmer of rationality, it flashed through my mind that sometime I should want to come back to this canyon alone.

"I dared not glance about for landmarks, but stealthily my eyes made a quick search for some feature by which I should know this terrain if once I saw it again.

"From where we stood, down deep in the canyon, I looked up for the skyline. I could see the serrated profile of old Four Peaks plainly outlined against the deep blue sky. But in my excitement and confusion, I did not know on which side of the mountain I was then standing.

"I was not allowed to look long. Just long enough to assure me that the secret gold mine of the Apaches, of which I had heard such frequent mention, was no fraud."

The blindfold was replaced, and after more maneuvering

62

to confuse him, he was returned to the Apache camp, free to go or to stay.

He did not stay with the Apaches long thereafter. A restlessness of spirit seized him, and he was animated by an intense desire for freedom. Dreams of the great treasure hidden in the canyon of the Four Peaks country were disturbing his peace of mind.

With great difficulty and many hardships of which he seldom thereafter spoke, the doctor returned to the white settlements in Arizona. His thoughts and his dreams never for long left the theme which became the driving passion of his life — the search for the canyon of the gold.

For years after this, the Apaches were on the warpath. When finally they were subdued and placed on government reservations, Doctor Thorne returned to the Four Peaks, trying to locate the wonderful vein of gold. For the remainder of his life, this was his vocation and avocation. He made trip after trip, with as many different approaches as the topography would allow.

"No matter how many trips I made," he said, "nor from what angle I approached, it never looked the same to me."

He kept up the search, year after year, until he became too old to go into the mountains alone. When at last infirmity compelled him to desist, the motive power was gone: the search for the gold had become his life, and when that search ended, he died.

One old account says that in 1852 Dr. Thorne and a party of seven men were traveling east from California, and arrived at Maricopa Wells, an Arizona stage station, just in time to participate in a battle with Apaches. The only white survivors of the battle were Dr. Thorne and a man named Brown. Both were captured by the red men. Later, Brown made his escape, leaving Dr. Thorne as the sole living trophy of the fight.

In *The Fish Manuscript,* a history of Arizona written many years ago by Joseph Fish, an early Arizona pioneer, the historian says:

"On July 12, 1869, C. E. Cooley, A. F. Banta, and Henry

W. Dodd left the Zuñi village, with a small party of Indians, to hunt a gold mine known as 'The Doc Thorne Story.' "

One school of prospectors makes the claim the Doctor Thorne mine lies in the White Mountains, in an arroyo not far from the Black River. Another group believes it to be a day's ride on horseback from the confluence of the Salt and Verde Rivers, in the eastern angle between the two. Still another group says that the old Lost Adams Diggings and the Lost Doctor Thorne mine are one and the same. A fourth group maintains that Doctor Thorne himself described it as being "somewhere in a triangle formed by Four Peaks, Weaver's Needle, and Red Mountain." Considerable territory, yet with very definite limits.

One recorded account says that Doctor Thorne's rich mine lies somewhere along Salt River beside two little red hills. And one of the earliest accounts of it to find its way into print says the mine is in the Mazatzal range, below the junction of the White and Black rivers.

But since the doctor in his later expeditions often set out from the villages of Mesa and Tempe, it is safe to assume he himself believed the lost treasure to be in Superstition foothills — in the heart of Apachería — and somewhere in the direction of the scenic highway now known as the Apache Trail. This is in accord with those who say Doctor Thorne was right in ascribing the magic spot to be in the triangle whose points are the Four Peaks, Weaver's Needle, and Red Mountain.

Doctor Thorne has gone the appointed path. The Apaches no longer spread terror over the land. Smiling peace walks serenely over mountain and desert. Four Peaks stands there eternally. Populous cities are near at hand. The radio, radar, and the airplane have become important aids to the prospector, and the burro is ever ready to offer his companionship for the trail. The narrow canyon with its great mass of virgin gold awaits him who can find it.

The prospector is given above plenty of material from

which he can make his own waybill. But remember, the vein of quartz, full of pure gold, was lying on the floor of the canyon, according to the statement of Doctor Thorne.

7

Squawman's Fateful Gold

"SEARCH FOR THE LOST DUTCHMAN, for the Lost Tayopa, or the Lost Dr. Thorne mine, if you will," said a lost treasure hobbyist in Tucson, "but when I go on my next treasure hunt, it will be for Yuma's Lost Gold."

Perhaps, after all, Yuma's is the most promising of the old lost mines, and has been hunted for by but few. While it has not been forgotten, during the past sixty years, no organized effort has been made to find it.

The eagle eye of the hostile Indian is now removed, and the red man no longer stalks the canyons and mesas in its vicinity. The old-timers who shared the excitement of the great discovery are now gone, and to their posterity it is only a legend. Its vast riches still await the adventurer who, with or without modern scientific aids, has faith in its reality.

Whatever Yuma's real name was, let that pass. But be assured he was an aristocrat from Kentucky, whose kith and kin wore the most prominent names in that proud state. In his boyhood, one of his closest companions was a young Crittenden, a name synonymous with honor, character, and integrity, everywhere in America.

It may be kindness to Yuma's kinsmen to permit his identity to remain hidden; disclosure of names and vital statistics will not help to recover the long lost gold. Let the evil of which he was guilty, if any, be blown away in the Papago desert with his dust.

Following a traditional family pattern, it is said, Yuma undertook a military career, and was graduated from West Point. After a few years of service, he was assigned for duty with a regiment stationed in Arizona. Quartered in Arizona City — renamed Yuma in 1873 — he was placed in control of army supplies. Through some manipulations on the part of dishonest government agents, with which Arizona was overrun in those days, he was blamed for some irregularity with money and commodities. Not able to clear himself of the charge, he was severed from army service in disgrace.

Proud and sensitive, unable to vindicate himself, Yuma decided to leave the world of white men. He joined the tribe of Yuma Indians, married a beautiful young Yuma squaw, and covered his identity by adopting the name of his wife's tribe. From then on, those with whom he came into contact knew him simply as Yuma.

Apaches, Yumas, and Papagoes had the utmost trust in him and he became a trader among them. Historians have never accounted for the fact that the Apaches were willing to engage in trade with him, for they were the implacable hereditary enemies of the Yumas and the Papagoes. Upon this alone may have rested the ultimate destiny of Yuma and his wife.

His lane of travel extended from the Colorado River, east, across the Papago Indian Reservation, northeast to the mesas south of the Gila, near Aravaipa Creek and the San Pedro River, where the Pinal Apaches had a ranchería. His wife traveled with him when, with a packtrain loaded with goods for his Indian customers, he set out on a business trip.

These trips were exceedingly profitable. He acquired a

nice judgment as to what commodities would specially appeal to the primitive minds of the tribesmen, and in exchange for his goods, he was given the purest gold. The Papagoes, Apaches, and Yumas all had access to authentic gold mines, being acquainted with gold only in its purest form.

During the years in which Yuma was engaged in this way of life, he must have received and have cached a vast amount of nuggets, ore, and gold dust, for it is certain his life as an Indian did not call for much expenditure of money beyond the invoices for his goods.

In the months from 1869 to 1871, the Aravaipa Apaches, that is, the Pinal Apaches living on Aravaipa Creek, had been especially deadly and pestiferous, straining themselves in their efforts to make life difficult all up and down the San Pedro and Santa Cruz valleys, killing white ranchers and miners, and repeatedly attacking Tubac and Tucson. The white men were becoming desperate, and Apaches were shot upon sight. Both sides seemed to be at their wits' end, neither making any headway in exterminating the other; but if there was advantage on either side, it lay with the Indians.

Yuma had established friendly relations with the Aravaipa Apaches, since through him they were able to get guns and ammunition which otherwise they could have acquired only by stealing them from the ranches in the valleys, or by inveigling them away from the soldiers at Camp Grant.

The Apaches paid Yuma for these weapons with extremely rich gold ore in pink quartz. So Yuma knew they had access to a highly desirable gold deposit; and he surmised that this deposit lay somewhere near to Camp Grant, for their chief ranchería was not more than five miles from this military post.

Although knowing how devastating to the white settlers was the continual warfare of the Indians, Yuma persisted in selling them guns and ammunition. His actions seemed, however, to indicate that he wavered between a desire to furnish the Apaches with the means to destroy the white men, and a desire to induce the Indians to be friendly and permit the settlers to live in peace.

Finally, though his contact with the white world was very slight, even he heard the rumors which began to drift about, that the Americans were enlisting Papago allies, intending to make an expedition against the Aravaipa Apaches and exterminate them, root and branch.

He prepared for an expedition to the Aravaipas, to see if he could persuade them, through their chief, Es-kim-en-zin, Big Mouth, to "lay off," and be satisfied to live more quietly with the white men.

Leaving his wife behind, and desiring to avoid contact with the military lest some soldier or officer recognize him and recall his disgrace, he passed without notice around Camp Grant, and reached the mesa on the north side of Aravaipa Canyon, where the Apaches had their home.

In this ranchería were then encamped about 210 of the Aravaipa subtribe. In the talk that ensued, Yuma was not able to get any promise that the Apaches would moderate their behavior toward the white men, and he knew enough of Indian psychology to perceive that argument was useless.

But he also knew that if the Apaches kept up their program of murder and pillage, they must eventually lose, and he desired to learn, before that might happen, the location of their marvelous vein of free gold in pink quartz which they had in such seemingly inexhaustible quantities.

He casually brought up the subject with Es-kim-en-zin in this wise:

"I will give you almost anything you would like to have, if you will show me the place where you get this pink quartz ore. Two of my horses, a bright new gun, and plenty of ammunition."

A study of Es-kim-en-zin's career shows him to have been superlative among a group of vicious and murderous savages. Though an unmitigated coward at heart, he was bloodthirsty, ruthless, crafty, and traitorous above all the others of his tribe; accepting subsistence and ammunition

69

from the government through the officers at **Camp Grant,** in return for his promise to maintain peace, while he was at the same time leading his braves upon frequent raids against the white settlers, stealing their stock and murdering them and their families.

At the time of Yuma's offer, Big Mouth was badly in need of horses. Also he had other needs, for he had his eye upon a certain young squaw — whom he afterwards married — whom he preferred to win by favor rather than by force, and for his courtship purposes he required some bright red cloth, a handsome new blanket, and some small mirrors.

Keeping Yuma in suspense by the traditional Indian pause, he finally enumerated these special needs; his answer was to this effect:

"We will go, tomorrow morning. But we must go out as if hunting for turkeys, for the soldiers at Camp Grant take all the turkeys I can shoot. If my braves even suspect that I would show you the gold, or that you might be looking for it, they would kill you."

Yuma knew he was taking a terrible chance. But he was willing to risk it. When the sun rose the next morning, he took his rifle and joined Es-kim-en-zin in going afoot to the west and slightly to the north of the ranchería, as if hunting game. Once away from sight and sound of the Apache camp, the wily old chief led Yuma along the west bank of the San Pedro, cut by many ridges, canyons, and ravines, into very rugged country, such as was always the preferred terrain of the relentless Apache.

In a northwesterly direction from the Apache camp, they ascended a long ridge, very rough and rocky. They followed the top of the ridge for about three miles, reaching the crest of a low and winding range, "overlooking the San Pedro Valley to the east."

Still with a general northward trend, they kept on for about six miles. Traveling along the side of a gulch, Es-kim-en-zin halted. He was standing beside a sort of saucer-like formation on the slope, round in shape, from six to eight feet in diameter at the bottom, shallow, and with the rim formed of rock.

"Right here," he said, waving his arm in a circle and looking far off into the sky.

Yuma knew the traditional manner of Indians when acting not in accordance with their conscience, or when in the grip of fear of acting contrary to their tribal teachings. He realized that the treasure he was seeking lay at the Indian's feet and not off in the ethereal blue. He knew in a flash that the "saucer" was the secret repository of the gold the Apaches were known to have in such vast abundance and such remarkable purity.

The chief moved away as if to continue his hunting, but more likely for the purpose of not seeing the white man take the gold, lest some member of the tribe, lurking in ambush, discover Es-kim-en-zin's betrayal of the tribal tradition.

Yuma dug down into the "saucer" with his hunting knife. Through a few inches of soft dirt and desert debris on the top, he struck hard rock — so hard he found his knife useless. He picked up a heavy, sharp-edged stone from the rim, with which to work, more by shoving the edge into crevices in the rock than by pounding, for the reverberation of the noise might be his death knell.

At last he broke off some pieces and saw that the rock was a pink quartz full of pure, free gold!

He scraped away more of the dirt to look at the vein from which he had broken the ore, and the amount of free gold he saw in the hard, pink quartz was a realization of that well-known dream of avarice.

Discerning that he now had a secret which would fill the rest of his days with interest and occupation, he hastily put the ore samples into his pocket and again covered the vein carefully, trying to make it appear undisturbed and stale.

Making full use of his army training in observation, as well as following the custom of the Indians, he studied the "lay of the land," noting it for approach on all sides, look-

71

ing for landmarks in rocks and shrubs, observing that the small ravine below him came to an end not many rods farther on. The extreme ruggedness of the country and the dangers from roving Apaches made discovery of the treasure very difficult and therefore very unlikely.

As he quickly moved away, the chief rejoined him and together they made their way in a direction to resume hunting — to divert suspicion if observed by any straying Indian likewise in search of game.

Yuma knew he could expect to be killed without mercy if the Apaches ever found him in that region, for they would assume at once that he had found their secret gold, or was, at least, looking for it.

When he rode away from the ranchería, he headed straight for Tucson. In that town he had a friend, a member of the Crittenden family from Kentucky, who, like himself, had been an army officer, and who was at that time engaged in freighting between Tucson and Arizona City. Yuma had made up his mind to show young Crittenden the gold ore and invite him to become his partner in the perilous business of working the mine.

This hazardous undertaking made ready appeal to the adventurous spirit of Crittenden, who was utterly without fear. The first step in carrying out the plan was, of course, for the two partners to make a trip to the mine and put up their "monument," preparatory to legalizing their claim. Arranging his affairs so that he could be absent for a few days, and giving out the statement that he would be gone for a short hunting trip, Crittenden met Yuma outside the town and together they went to Camp Grant. Though stopping at the military post was a great concession on Yuma's part, it was necessary for resting and feeding their horses.

Upon one of the horses they had packed a pick and shovel and a couple of rawhide bags, but before going into the military camp, they carefully hid these articles in the brush. After they had refreshed themselves in camp, and the horses were also in condition, the two men proceeded on their mysterious way, back-tracking a short distance to retrieve their hidden belongings, without which their purpose could not be so readily accomplished.

For five miles they traveled northward from Camp Grant, west of the Apache rancheria; skirting that mesa on the southwest side, they continued generally northward for five miles more. Then Yuma said:

"Across the San Pedro from here, and up this west ridge."

After considerable climbing on foot, leading their horses, they came to the western ridge, where about half way down the sloping side, and where the ravine at the bottom came to an end only a few rods farther on — there was the saucer-shaped repository of the gold.

They tethered their horses, and Yuma started at once to clear away the debris from the floor of the depression on the side of the slope, and in a few minutes Crittenden was as convinced as Yuma that they had a bonanza.

Under the necessity of working as silently as possible, in order not to call the attention of any lurking Indians, they broke away considerable rock, and picking out about fifty pounds of the best, they filled the two rawhide bags, and covering the rest with rock, brush, and sand, they left the scene with all the haste they could make. In their excitement they neglected to set up their monuments.

They returned to Tucson, traveling by the west side of the San Pedro, in order to avoid Camp Grant, and after covering the 65 miles from the scene of their bonanza to Tucson, they arrived, too elated to note their fatigue.

Assays of the ore were promptly made, the returns showing more than $40 to the pound. And when they had their fifty pounds milled, the secret could be kept no longer. A gold stampede resulted; but to their satisfaction and amusement, the gold-seekers, for the most part, expended their efforts to the southeast, in the general direction of Tumacacori. It was this brief gold excitement which dated and fixed Yuma's discovery in the minds of the old-timers.

Yuma and Crittenden saw, however, that the public interest in their discovery made it undesirable to make any further moves to recover their treasure until the gold fever in the old pueblo had abated. Accordingly they resumed from where they had left off with their regular business. Once more Yuma and his wife went into the desert on a trading trip. Their history ended there, for they were never seen again.

It seems probable that after Crittenden and Yuma visited the deposit of gold, the Indians discovered that someone had been robbing their "bank." For soon thereafter they began a most desperate and vicious campaign of pillage, murder, and destruction — as though for revenge — all through the southern part of the state, and the white settlers regarded their lives and property as utterly foredoomed.

After waiting a reasonable time for Yuma to return to Tucson and join him for a return trip to the gold mine, Crittenden concluded that both Yuma and his wife had been killed while on their trip among the Papagoes. Though he knew the Aravaipa Indians were on the warpath and had been for some time, he could not relinquish the idea of going back to the mine. He thought he could outwit them in making a trip there and back.

He set out alone. Arriving without mishap at Camp Grant, he stayed with the soldiers for two or three days, showed them samples of his ore, told them where he was going, and how he had been there once before with Yuma, and how they had got away without detection. The soldiers were amazed. They advised him against going into that Apache country at that time, especially alone, and more especially to take away any Apache treasure.

But Crittenden thought he knew what he was about; he had confidence he could find the gold and get away safely. He went his way, in the early morning, saying:

"I'll be back to the camp tonight."

And that was the end of Crittenden. He was never seen again, dead or alive.

Some days later, his horse was found, hobbled, and almost dead from thirst, on the west side of the San Pedro River bed and about ten miles north of the old Camp Grant.

Traces of Crittenden's travels on foot were also found, but no gun, no garments, nothing to show his fate.

It is almost certain that the Aravaipa Apaches discovered who was robbing their bank, and taking him completely unaware, they killed him, and then — which was very unusual for them — they buried him. Maybe; but why did they not take his horse? A horse represents wealth, to an Indian, far more than gold.

Is it not conceivable that some soldier from Camp Grant, knowing the purpose of Crittenden's one-man expedition, and having seen the free gold in the pink quartz, followed him, waited until he had reached the mine, and when assured that Crittenden was at the right place beyond all doubt, shot Crittenden and buried him, intending to claim the gold deposit for his own? Indian or white man, it will never be known.

Soon after the disappearance of Crittenden, the Aravaipa Apaches made a death-dealing raid up the Santa Cruz River. They went as far as the San Xavier settlements, driving off stock from the ranches, and farther on, near Tubac, they killed L. B. Wooster and his wife, and Trinidad Aguirre. Immediately the rumored organizations of Americans, with Papago and Mexican assistance, for the protection of the settlers, began to take concrete form, and the climax was reached on Sunday morning, April 30, 1871.

Though nearly one hundred Americans in the vicinity of Tucson had pledged themselves to join the reprisal raid, only six of them kept their word. These heroic and determined six were aided by 92 Papagoes and 48 Mexicans. On Friday, April 28, they swept down the valley of the San Pedro; delayed en route, they reached Camp Grant on Saturday, and on Sunday at daybreak they swooped upon the ranchería of the Aravaipas and massacred every person then in camp, with the exception of 29 young children whom the Papagoes took captive, to be sold as slaves, in accordance with their custom.

Chief Es-kim-en-zin and a party of his braves were away from their families, hunting in the surrounding mountains.

75

Returning while the fight was still in progress, and observing from a distance the terrible slaughter of their tribe, they saved themselves by fleeing into the brush and the foothills. Big Mouth was able to save only one member of his family, a little girl, two and a half years old. In that fight, six of his family perished. But if the members of his family were of the same stamp as he, it was fortunate for the white settlers in the country that they took leave of life when they did.

The whereabouts of Yuma's gold in strawberry quartz passed into complete limbo after the Camp Grant massacre, when the Aravaipa Apaches were almost entirely wiped out, and peace settled over the region which had been so repeatedly subjected to their devastations. Those of the sub-tribe who survived were dispersed, allied with other scattering Apache tribes, and their knowledge of the marvelous gold deposit never again emerged.

With his tribe finally reduced to submission, and his glory as a chief departed, Es-kim-en-zin was given a reservation which embraced the very area where the lost gold mine lies. About ten miles northeast of the junction of the San Pedro River and Aravaipa Creek, east of the town of Winkelman, is Es-kim-en-zin's Spring. There can be no doubt that as long as that old scoundrel lived, he kept a sentinel eye upon the gold which cost Crittenden his life, and which has perpetuated in Arizona legend a brave man whose greatest desire was that the world might forget him and his name forever.

"I think there is a better chance to find Yuma's lost lode than there is to find any of the other famous lost gold mines," said Henry Aden, once an active gold-hunter, of Tucson. "I'm not going to hunt for it, however, until some inventor comes along with a device that I can take up in an airplane, get a wide range, and tell by color, vibration, radiation, or magnetism, where gold is likely to be. Then I'll fly over that ridge south of the Gila, west of the San Pedro, and I'll find it.

"And don't you doubt there'll be such an instrument invented. There's a gadget now that aviators take up with them, which, by timing the vibrations, tells the aviator how far the plane is from the ground. I don't see why a further development of the same principle couldn't be used to determine the location of minerals and other material in the ground.

"Seems to me if they can tell by vibrations how far away the ground is, they could carry the idea a little farther and tell what kind of ground, that is, how far they are from what. When that happens, I'm going after Yuma's lost mine."

As I write, a beginning has been made along this line, and a device now exists, known as the "scintillometer." In November, 1950, it was used in Montana by Kent Howard and Dick Peterson, of Price, Utah, for hunting uranium by airplane. It is claimed the invention picks up ground radiations from 1500 feet and lower.

Persons who can speak with authority about Yuma's gold are agreed that it will be found to be of the formation known in mining parlance as a "chimney." A chimney is not a common formation. The most famous Arizona mine of the chimney variety is said to have been the well known silver bonanza, the Silver King, discovered in the Pinal range, not many miles northwest of the ridge where Yuma's gold must be.

"A 'chimney' is a deposit, or lode, which goes far down below the surface, sometimes in the form of a spiral, but always without a great deal of spread," says an old pioneer prospector who is still prospecting. "It gives up a lot of riches in small area and permits it to be taken quickly. The description of Yuma's mine certainly sounds like a chimney."

It is of first importance not to mistake the site of the later Camp Grant, now Fort Grant, for the old Camp (Fort) Grant. The old Camp Grant referred to in this account was directly above the junction of Camp Grant Wash with the San Pedro River, about two miles from the present town of Feldman, and 55 miles north of Tucson. The San Pedro

River runs north — when it has water — into the Gila, and it is of consequence to observe that, in this case, "above" means "south of."

One seriously contemplating an expedition to find this lost gold mine will do himself a favor to request from the United States Geological Survey, Washington, D.C., a topographic map, entitled the Winkelman Quadrangle of Arizona. If you can get one dated 1924, so much the better; but a later one will do. Drawn to a scale of five miles to three inches, the map shows the ridges, the washes, the mesas, and the gradual rise in elevation. For this invaluable aid to your researches, the government requires the payment of a few cents in cash money.

When you have this map, trace on it the moves of Yuma and Crittenden as described in this story, and you will have as accurate a waybill as can be devised. And be warned in advance that in this region there is stupendous natural scenery, with extraordinary mineral possibilities never yet touched.

8

Lost Treasure in Nevada

IF I HAD NINE LIVES to live I would like to live at
least two of them in Nevada. This sparsely settled state is
a vast reservoir of values not yet realized. If I ever meet you
in Reno I will lay you 16 to 1 that if I could go over the
state from end to end with the most modern, most sensitive
mineral locator, I would find not only every one of the precious metals, the rare metals, and the useful metals, but also
many other elements of interest — archaeological and an-
thropological, as well.

Nevada offers not only many mysteries in lost treasures,
but also in lost peoples, lost towns, and the appurtenances of
a lost civilization.

A few years ago, my good friend, Henry Aden, of Tucson,
Arizona, with a companion, went up into Nevada on a prospecting tour for a vacation. When he returned, he gave me
an account of their adventures. In southern Nevada, he and
his "podner" had met two professional prospectors who related some rare tales of what had happened to them several

years previously when they had been combing the southwest mountains of Nevada for gold.

They came upon some deep caves, the two strangers told Aden, one cave opening into another. In the far reaches of the caves, they found furniture of immense size, as if built for giants. Also they found dishes of gold, and of other bright shining metals, which, because of their apparent great age, they surmised to be of some imperishable alloy. They described a huge table which seemed to have been, at some time, set for dining. The caves had many evidences of extreme age, they related, and of having been undisturbed for centuries.

For reasons not too difficult to guess, the two prospectors did not give Aden a waybill to the caves, nor did they tell what they had done about claiming the treasure therein, so the mystery of the caves has not been solved — at least, for the general public.

Some months later, I was visiting the prehistoric village, Pueblo Grande, which the city of Phoenix maintains as a municipal archaeological project. There I fell into conversation with a stranger, a woman tourist from Nevada. To my amazement, she told me the same story of the mysterious cave, with much the same detail: the cave within a cave; the outsized furniture; the golden dishes, the strange alloy.

But there is no legend to tell who the vanished ones were; where they came from; where they went; or for what reason they disappeared. Were they a remnant of the giant race of Lemurians? No one knows; and shall we ever know? But whoever they were, if they left gold behind, there is always the possibility of finding it.

Nevada abounds in tales of adventure and discovery — and of lost values awaiting the determined spirits of modern De Sotos, La Salles, and Coronados. We have space here to give you four of these tales. The third among them, "The Prison Window Cache of Gold," is included by kind permission of the editors of *Ghost Town News,* in which magazine it made its first appearance.

1. The Lost Cabin Mine.

When hunting lost gold mines, it is usually necessary to look down — down into the ground, or into a tunnel in a hillside. But on the contrary when hunting for the Lost Cabin mine; for this lost gold the searchers must look up, not down, straight up toward the sky! Straight up, 2,500 feet!

The Lost Cabin mine has been the object of search by the mining men of Nevada, and by straggling tenderfeet for sixty years, and though the search, up to now, has been fruitless, it is still going on.

Discovered in 1890, and receding at intervals from public notice, the Lost Cabin mine became spot news again during the memorable depression which began early in the 1930's. Countless men out of work with nothing but time at their disposal, renewed their hope of fame and fortune, or at least of bean money, by following the lure of adventure in hunting lost treasures. A new search was made then for the Lost Cabin gold, but like its predecessors, the enterprise ended in disaster.

Near Tonopah, Nevada, is a rugged precipitous mountain with a sheer bluff on one side, rising more than 3,000 feet straight up from the foot of the mountain. In the late autumn of 1890, two prospectors met in a saloon in Tonopah, and striking up an acquaintance over their drinks, decided to throw in together for a spot of prospecting.

As the two were leaning against the bar, one of them, more observant than the other, and better acquainted with the region, mentioned the tall mountain nearby, and the bartender overheard the following conversation:

"I would like to examine that mountain inch by inch. I believe it is full of mineral; probably many other things besides gold and silver."

"No doubt you're right," said his companion. "If we could thoroughly examine that bluff side, we could just about tell what the whole mountain's made of. What say we have a go at it?"

And so it was agreed. Whether they really made a com-

81

petent geologic and metallurgical survey of the sheer side is not known. More likely they brought to bear merely the general knowledge of the average prospector trained only by experience. But the entire population of Tonopah learned in due time that, by a more circuitous route, the two men succeeded in reaching the top.

From the top, they looked down the steep side, and seeing an area about 500 feet below which gave promise of some special mineralization, they determined to find a way down to it to examine it. Risking their lives in a hazardous descent, they safely reached the spot and found a narrow overhang affording enough space for a good foothold, with enough to spare so they could look around a little.

In the rock a few yards above this overhang, they found a rich vein of pure gold!

They decided to stay right with it until they had taken out the values. By carefully maneuvering one piece of timber at a time down the narrow dangerous trail, they built a rough but substantial little cabin hanging to the rock on the face of the bluff. Inside it they built a rock fireplace. Then they put in a generous supply of foodstuffs from Tonopah, and started work without delay.

Winter came on apace. One cold night, the two were sitting snug in their cabin by their fireside, though the wind was roaring and a blizzard raging outside. They heard a terrifying sound, as though a part of the mountain was being ripped away.

Hurriedly stepping out the door to see what was going on, they were caught in a gigantic snowslide and dashed to death at the foot of the bluff, 2,500 feet below.

Of course, they left no record of what happened. But local residents of Tonopah, who have given much thought to these events, have concluded this is the only possible explanation.

It was months before their fate was discovered. The townspeople remembered the date of the snowslide, and the disappearance of the two prospectors. They reconstructed the tragedy as told above. By the time they became concerned as to the fate of the missing men, time, sun, and wind had destroyed all sign of their trail to the cabin. That trail has never been retraced.

Many men have tried to reach the cabin site, but all have failed. The usual method has been to attempt to scale the face of the bluff. One man making the same attempt, in 1934, by going up the sheer side of the mountain, reached within 100 feet of his goal. He slipped and fell and was dead when he reached the ground, hurtling through 2,500 feet of empty air.

The cabin is the only clue to the gold, untouched throughout the years. There is not only the rich vein, but also the gold which the two prospectors had already mined and stored within the cabin.

Whatever else you may do, do not be persuaded to try to reach the cabin site by scaling the sheer bluff side, as so many have stubbornly tried to do, in spite of all warnings. Remember the two prospectors apparently circled the mountain and chose another route to the summit. They had a safe trail downward for the few hundred feet from the top, where they were secure until the snowslide caught them.

These two prospectors were probably as right as rain when they suspected there were many values in the mountain besides gold and silver. Of all the states in the Union, Nevada offers the best chance of finding many precious and strategic elements concealed in the ground. If prospectors who search for the Lost Cabin mine will but bring a little science to bear, and provide themselves with some labor-saving modern equipment, they cannot fail to discover some mineral values of importance.

To get to the mountaintop, by all means ignore the bluff side. But as you face this side, look to the right and the left to determine at which side you will be likely to find the easiest slope for safe foothold. From the top, look down the sheer side for an angular trail leading to a narrow ledge, a few hundred feet below. The cabin may have fallen from its base to the foot of the bluff, but the narrow ledge upon

which the cabin rested will still be there, and the timbers
upon which the floor was laid may still be in place.

2.   Twice-Lost Gold-Lined Cave.

In days gone by, the pioneers knew, if by no other means than intuition, that the deserts and mountains of Nevada were richly mineralized, and that the day would come when vast fortunes would be taken out of the ground. In this they were right, though many missed their hopes of sharing in the riches so grudgingly released by Mother Earth.

In 1880, Henry Knight was among those who knew there was gold in the Nevada hills, and he made it his business to find it. Knight, commonly called Hank, in accordance with an old Nevada custom, was out one day "looking for sign" in the Painted Hills. Close-mouthed, lone wolf, long-time prospector that he was, he little dreamed that the most enduring result of his trip would be the placing of his name in Nevada tradition forever.

The Painted Hills are a small range of mountains in Churchill County. On one side of the range was a small town known as Painted Hills; on the other, a town not quite so small named Sand Spring.

In the hills between these two towns, Knight discovered a small but promising vein of gold. Tracing this vein to a volcanic vent, he there sunk a shaft of fifty feet. At the shaft's end, he broke into a cave.

The cave had been made by natural forces, and its interior was almost completely lined with free gold. Knight knew at once that his prospecting days were over; he had only to break away the ore from the hanging walls and his fortune was made.

He immediately set to work to prepare the rock for shipping by taking it off the walls and piling it on the floor. The more rock he broke away, the more gold he found. There seemed to be no end to it.

While he was at work, he began to feel ill. He went out of the cave into the air, thinking the sickness would pass.

As he then felt worse instead of better, he decided to go at once into the town to see a doctor. It would never do to die now, with the promise of such great riches within his grasp.

Knight told the doctor all about his good fortune. All except the location of the gold-lined cave. Fate was kind neither to the doctor nor to Hank Knight, for the patient died, leaving no waybill to the treasure. In time, the lost cave of Hank Knight became a Nevada tradition.

In 1933, George Forbes, another prospector of the same independent type, was wandering, with his burro, through the alkali desert near Sand Mountain. He camped, one night, on the mountain where, looking to the northwest, he could see the Painted Hills. When the moon came up, the outlines of the hills reminded him of a similar range where he had once made a gold strike. Taking this for a sign of luck, he decided that, come daylight, he would explore those hills for gold.

Forbes rediscovered Hank Knight's gold-lined cave. He rushed in to town, and told all and sundry, enjoying the excitement the news created, talking freely to news reporters. One important little item he held in reserve; he did not tell where the cave was.

"The floor of the cave," he said, "is quartz. My assays show a value of $1,160 to the ton. Tons of the ore are piled on the floor and the walls shine with free gold."

"How large is the cave?" a reporter asked him.

"It extends farther than I could throw the light with my carbide lamp," he replied.

Forbes set about acquiring the means to make a quick clean-up of the cave. The depression was in full swing; cash and credit were tight. Before he could arrange for the desired capital and equipment, President Franklin D. Roosevelt placed a ban upon gold in the hands of the people, and Forbes was confronted with a new problem. One day, while cogitating upon the ethics of the gold situation, Forbes disappeared, and today no one knows where the gold-lined cave is, in the Painted Hills of Nevada.

Many of the up-to-date maps do not show Painted Hills; call it a ghost town if you will. But in recent Nevada maps, such as are available at gas stations, Sand Spring is clearly placed on interstate highway No. 50. Remember that Painted Hills is over the mountain from Sand Spring. Look for a volcanic vent, with piles of small rock nearby, in the hills northwest of Sand Mountain.

3. Prison Window Cache of Gold.

In the pioneer years, when the hills of Nevada resounded to the pick of the independent, free-lance prospector, that state added a great amount of gold to our national resources. The metal was reduced to bullion in local smelters and sent to the San Francisco mint. At least a part of the journey to the mint was made by stage, a method of transportation always hazardous and thrilling.

One day a stage well laden with gold bars was leaving Empire, a mining town just northeast of Carson City. It was taking also a sizable group of passengers. An extra detail of guards had been assigned. Driver, guards, and passengers had all been forewarned that an attack by bandits could be expected, and it would naturally be thought that all in the stage would be on the alert.

The driver and the guards, as well as most of the male passengers, were, of course, adequately armed. By reason of the liquid refreshments deemed necessary for supplying them with the requisite courage, considerable jollity prevailed, and they set off in a state of relaxed vigilance.

The stage had not proceeded far out of Empire when it was held up by three bandits, bare-faced, hatless, and easily identifiable. The onset was very sudden and entirely contrary to the established bandit custom of not attacking when close to a town. Without threatening or molesting the passengers, the bandits seized the gold and were on their way. The ladies aboard promptly went into hysterics, which, by disconcerting the gentlemen, operated in favor of the outlaws.

The guards meanwhile collected their wits, gave chase, and shot two of the highwaymen dead. The third, notwithstanding the difficulty of managing three horses, got safely away with the gold. He made his way to the hills surrounding Carson City, and there he buried the bullion, intending to retrieve it when the excitement of the manhunt had blown over. Looking townward from the spot where he had concealed the loot, he could see the dark walls of the Nevada State Prison.

His time of freedom was short. All too soon he showed up in a Carson City saloon. He was recognized and captured. Almost before he could say knife, he was convicted and imprisoned. When about to be committed to a cell in the State Prison, he made the request that he be assigned to that side of the prison where he could look out into the hills. Since there seemed no reason for denying such a simple human request, it was granted.

Eventually his fellow convicts, as well as the warden came to know that from his prison window the bandit could look out into the nearby hills and see the spot where he had buried the stolen bullion.

He patiently awaited the expiration of his sentence, when with time off for good behavior, he expected to reclaim his treasure. Before he had earned his release, however, he was taken sick and died. He had never told anything which could be definitely considered a waybill to the loot, and the mystery was the only legacy he left to his friends.

Many a convict has studied the hills from the same window; but forgers, highwaymen, and larcenists are not as skillful in reading "sign" as a prospector would be, and prospectors usually manage to keep out of jail. The bullion is still there.

In 1935, Matt Penrose, then warden of the prison, seeking some profitable occupation for the then idle prisoners, considered the proposition of using convict labor to develop a gold and copper deposit near Carson City. Discussing this proposal at a conference with the state authorities,

the story of the bandit's buried treasure was revived, and
the suggestion that the convicts be allowed to hunt for the
bullion was considered. No action was taken, probably because no solution was then available to the problem of a
convict with illegal gold in his hands.

*To find this treasure, first take up your residence in the
Nevada State Prison. Wangle an assignment to a cell from
which you can look out on the hills toward Empire. Study
the landscape of the hills, and try to figure out where the
ground would likely be soft enough for you to bury quickly
a bunch of gold bars, if the law were close on your trail,
and you were hampered by three horses. Then when out
on parole, go there and dig.*

4. The Lost Mormon Mine.

In 1863, when the town of Las Vegas, Nevada, was only
a valley ranch, a German prospector named Mashbird came
that way from Utah, where he had been living with a
Mormon colony, as he was an adherent of that religion.
From the ranch he went into the mountains, south, hunting gold. He was accompanied by another man, whose name
is not known.

After an absence of about a month, Mashbird reappeared
at the ranch, alone, out of his mind, muttering incoherently.
It was soon discovered his skull was broken. He was given
food, shelter, and good care. After the pattern of old-
fashioned western hospitality, he was asked no questions.

In a week or two, he was more like himself again, and
gave an account of his adventures.

Up in the mountain, he said, he and his companion had
made camp beside a small spring, and as there was plenty
of game to supplement their provisions, they were very
comfortable while prospecting for gold. They therefore pro-
longed their stay.

One day an Indian came into their camp, and seeming
friendly, they asked him to rest, to share their dinner, and
to drink from the cool spring water. After he was refreshed,

he asked them if they were looking for gold. If so, he said, he would show them a vein of "the pretty yellow stone," only a short distance away, farther up the mountainside.

Not suspecting treachery, Mashbird left his companion by the spring, and went with the Indian to a slight rise in elevation to see what the Indian had to show. On the trail, the tribesman stepped aside to let Mashbird pass. Suddenly from behind he struck Mashbird a terrific blow on the head with a rock, stunning him; then turning his victim over with his foot, he left him for dead.

Mashbird recovered consciousness, though his skull was fractured. He seemed, however, to remember clearly all that had happened. Though doubting the Indian knew of any mine, yet to prove to himself whether or no, he got to his feet, determined to go on and test the Indian's story. After all, his objective was gold, and he knew he would never come this way again.

Not realizing how bad his condition was, he staggered on. About two miles farther, on and upward, traced by a dim trail, he found a rich deposit of black silver, and horn silver with free gold.

Returning at once to camp, his pockets filled with specimens of the ore, he found his partner killed, their food gone, and the camp in chaos. He stopped long enough to bury his partner; then his head began to pain him unbearably. He felt dazed; his memory began to grow dim, and he slowly struggled back to the Las Vegas ranch.

Though he never thereafter fully recovered his mind, he often hunted again for his lost mine of horn silver and gold. He never could find it.

Samples of the ore were frequently given to other prospectors who stopped at the Las Vegas ranch, and the lost strike became well known throughout the West. Many have hunted for the fateful mine, but it has never been located since the day Mashbird walked away from it, his skull broken and his pockets full of ore.

This lost mine is sometimes referred to as the Lost Breyfogle mine, for Mashbird is often confused with Breyfogle;

but the strange deposit of gold has passed into Nevada tradition as the Lost Mormon mine. The Breyfogle is in California, a deposit of silver in pink quartz.

In the McCullough Mountains, south of Las Vegas, and about fifteen miles northwest of Searchlight, Nevada, up a considerable elevation from the mountain's fold, but where the line of least resistance winds in a gently spiraling trail. This, while elevated, is not up a steep ascent.

9

The Seven Golden Cities
of the Humpbacked Bull

IN 1940, the southwest United States celebrated the 400th anniversary of Coronado's first footfalls within this country's boundaries; his expedition having been a follow-through of the initial move made by Fra Marcos de Niza in 1539, in the search for the Seven Cities of Cíbola — the seven golden cities of the humpbacked bull.

The commemoration in 1940 was not to celebrate the mysterious seven cities, which Fra Marcos and Coronado were never able to find; it celebrated merely their explorations into an unknown territory and the new knowledge gained, which gave to the world a treasure far more precious than all the wealth of the Incas:

Millions of acres of growing grain; vast herds of sheep and cattle; countless rich mines; cities crowded with manufacturing plants; fertile farms producing food for populations comparable to the sands of the sea, and a culture which today inspires the envy of the world.

LOST MINES and HIDDEN TREASURE

Though a complete survey of the outcome of Coronado's explorations would stagger the mind, the romance of the glittering adventure — its objective the long-famed cities of fabulous riches — still makes the stronger appeal to every passionate heart. The history of the expedition is known to every schoolboy, but to Americans the mystery of the Seven Cities of Cíbola is as deep as in 1540.

Many a scholastic mind has concerned itself with a solution of this mystery. But the location of the seven golden cities of the humpbacked bull is no mystery in Mexico, where the simple natives know nothing of written Mexican or American history, but are familiar by oral tradition with the ancient historical romance of their country. It is one of the commonly known traditions of their land: told by father to son, from generation to generation. The Mexicans in the river valleys in Sonora know exactly where the seven cities are, and where the vast amount of treasure is buried.

Seven cities, rich in gold, silver, and precious gems!

The story of the Spanish attempts to find in reality their dreams of the golden cities, is so replete in romance, adventure, and hardship, that it has obscured the story of the cities themselves; and among the white people of the north there are few who know the fate of the seven cities and of the treasure that lies yet therein.

Their hope becoming a firm belief that they were at last upon the trail to the towns where all common things were made of gold and the lintels of the doors inlaid with gems, the *conquistadores,* with undue haste, plunged on into the north country as far as Colorado and Kansas, after exploring Arizona and New Mexico. Failing to find the objects of their search, they returned to Mexico, frustrated and defeated, with no conception of the importance of their reports of the new land — sensible not of what they had gained but only of their failure to find the seven cities of their dreams.

The story of the seven cities so fabulously rich was brought to the new world in the caravels of Columbus, in 1492, along with the tale of the Amazons. Gold and women

— the two tangibles dearest to the heart of man; dearest in 1492 even as in 1940.

The Spaniards had the tale from the Portuguese for seven hundred years before the sailors who had ventured with Columbus mentioned it among themselves in those anxious hours while looking over the endless waters for they-knew-not-what. It needs no proof to know that, speculating upon what might be before them, they turned their thoughts to treasure — and to love. Gold and women: the seven golden cities and the amorous Amazons.

In Columbus' day, it was folklore in Portugal and Spain that about the year 750 A.D., a bishop of Lisbon, driven to desperation by the ruthlessness of the Arabs, set out to sea with some of his followers; determined, in his extremity, to get away from a land where any of that hated race might be found. Not knowing of any land beyond the sea, he was literally sailing to nowhere.

His boat landed on a certain island, one of a group; perhaps one of the Azores. On these islands, so tradition has it, seven towns were found, well ordered and very rich in gold and goods.

This tradition is substantiated by Gregorio Garcia, in his *Origen de los Indios,* in which he says the Seven Cities were found by the Portuguese, on an island, in 1448.

When Columbus and his crew finally found themselves in a strange land, of which they had never heard and could not even have imagined, they no doubt searched their minds for recollection of the past by which to interpret the inexplicable foreign world into which they had come.

At least two of the age-old legends of the Iberian Peninsula burst from them as soon as they found a way to communicate, even sketchily, with the bronzed inhabitants of the strange country: the legend of the Amazons and the legend of the Seven Cities.

They knew they were on an island, and the traditions of both the Amazons and the Seven Cities demanded an island west of Spain. Here might either or both the *tradiciones antiguas* be verified.

93

Before long the Spaniards had made the natives understand their meaning. And as Spanish enterprise was extended and the European appetite for gold and other treasure was better understood, the ancient grapevine system of communication carried the news to the other islands, thence to the mainland, and finally into Mexico.

When the Indians heard the newcomers were looking for the Seven Cities, they made their first error with regard to Spanish mind and character.

The Aztecs themselves had a tradition of the Seven Caves, involved in their account of the creation of the world and the birth of the first man and woman. This was, of course, in connection with their religion.

They, therefore, believed the Seven Cities were a feature of the religion of the Spaniards; but later, when they observed that, notwithstanding all the labors of the devout and zealous Blackgowns, the Spaniards really adored only gold, they knew that the foreigner sought the unknown cities solely for the treasure in them. This knowledge was later an indirect cause of much exploration, travel, teaching, learning, trade, trickery, and treachery, on the part of both Spaniards and Indians.

The Indians found it expedient, if not indeed necessary, to resort to subterfuge and misrepresentation in order to move the invaders onward, divert their minds, and keep them busy in the direction of their objectives, and so defer, if possible, the enslavement and extermination of their people, upon which they could see the Spaniards were, incidentally, bent.

It therefore happened that the Europeans heard the story of the Seven Golden Cities from the Indians themselves.

In a manuscript written by Pedro de Castañeda, a soldier in Coronado's expedition, he tells that in 1530, Nuño de Guzman, then president of New Spain, owned an Indian slave named Tejo.

"When I was a little boy," Tejo told Guzman, "my father was a trader, and he traveled over the interior of the

94

country, selling the feathers which Indians use for head-dresses. He sold them for gold and silver, which were very plentiful in that region.

"I went with my father once or twice, and I saw towns as large as Mexico City and its suburbs. There were seven of them and there were rows and rows of streets inhabited by workers in gold and silver. To reach these towns we crossed a desert for forty days. There was no vegetation except very short grass, and it was north between two oceans."

This story was widely circulated among the Spaniards; it confirmed their belief in the Seven Cities, so full of riches, for which they were willing to undergo any hardship, even to risk their lives.

It seems not to have occurred to the Spaniards that to "cross a desert for forty days," would take them away from those Indians among whom they were then living, upon whom they were practicing their arts of Spanish cruelty, enslaving them, making demands upon them almost impossible to fulfill. It seems not to have entered the Spanish mind that their departure to some far point was the event most devoutly wished by the Indians.

Castañeda, who describes himself as a poor, uneducated, private soldier, was naively free from suspicion that Tejo had been instructed to recollect and describe so nicely his experience when traveling with his father. Castañeda seems merely to have accepted the statement of the Indian slave at its face value. In any event, he passed the information on, apparently in good faith.

President Guzman was so much impressed by Tejo's narrative, he announced his intention of sending an expedition to find those mysterious seven towns. He enlisted about 400 Spaniards and several thousand friendly Indians.

They went from the city of Mexico, west, through the province, Michoacán, toward the place which Tejo indicated as the point of departure for the journey of forty days. Guzman estimated the "forty days" would mean about 200 leagues — approximately 680 miles — and that their progress across the country would be plain and easy.

95

But he was mistaken. The written word of Castañeda says when the party reached the province of Culiacán, they found the difficulties of travel increasing at every step. Between them and the deserts they wished to reach were mountains extremely steep and rugged, known to them only by rumor.

The party camped in Culiacán, for a while, planning the most favorable route northward. While they waited, news was brought to Guzman that Don Hernando Cortez had returned from Spain, loaded with new titles and estates from the crown, and heavy with power newly bestowed. Guzman had had acquaintance with Cortez of a character which caused him to deem it best to return *pronto* to the city of Mexico and look after his affairs before Cortez had time to take over all the detail of the government in New Spain.

So, in the greatest haste, he made the necessary moves for his campsite to become the permanent town of Culiacán, and then hurried back to Mexico City. Not long after that, Tejo died. "And thus," says Castañeda, writing in 1596, "the name of these Seven Cities and the search for them remain until now, since they have not been discovered." And indeed they remain even until now.

Six years after Guzman's fruitless expedition, Mendoza being then in office, there arrived in Culiacán four survivors of the unfortunate Narvaez expedition to Florida: Cabeza de Vaca and his three companions, equals in courage as in misery, Andrés Dorantes, with his slave Estevan, a young Arabian Negro, and Castillo Maldonado. Lost on the coast of Florida by shipwreck, in 1528, they wandered across the continent on foot, through a period of eight years, reaching Culiacán in 1536.

Cabeza de Vaca and his companions told many strange things, among the most striking and significant being their descriptions of what they termed "the humpbacked cows." These they called *"vacas de cíbola,"* their name for the buffalo, or bison. Immediately the region described became known as the country of the cíbola.

SEVEN GOLDEN CITIES of the HUMPBACKED BULL

It became current in Mexico that Cabeza de Vaca and his companions had reported that in the country of the cíbola they had seen and heard much about seven large, rich, and powerful towns, four and five stories high. There and then the cities took the name by which they have since been known: The Seven Cities of Cíbola.

It is doubtful that the shipwrecked Spaniards gave any such accounts, for in the official reports made by the three, and in the book later written by Cabeza de Vaca, no mention of any such towns, cities, or pueblos is found. But by Spanish writers who immediately followed them, they are charged with telling of "powerful villages, four and five stories high, of which they had heard a great deal in the countries they had crossed, and other things very different from what turned out to be the truth."

One difficulty was that the Indians understood Spanish very imperfectly, and the Spaniards were in even worse case, for their explorations and operations brought them into contact with various tribes whose languages differed each from each, and the system of communications, that is, by copious signs and meagre words, left much to the imagination.

The difficulties of keeping separate two such important items of news arising simultaneously can be imagined better than described. The inevitability of the two stories meeting and merging is seen at a glance. A few dramatics, a noun and a verb here and there from the Indians, and the complete story is put into Spanish, meeting a wish fulfilment.

It was consistently overlooked that what represented vast wealth to an Indian was but squalor and dirt to a cosmopolitan European, and no allowance was made for the fact that Indian words translated in good faith into Spanish would present totally different pictures to the sophisticates.

The story of the Seven Cities as related by Tejo, and the rumors that Cabeza de Vaca had seen seven similar rich cities in the country of the humpbacked bull, reached the ears of Fra Marcos de Niza, a Franciscan padre, lately come to Mexico from Peru, where he had gone with Pizarro, and where he had become familiar with the commonplace use of gold and silver by the Incas for every purpose.

With the cooperation of Mendoza, "the good viceroy," who had succeeded the hard-boiled Guzman, Fra Marcos organized a party in Culiacán to go north into the unknown, to seek the seven elusive towns. To serve as guide, Mendoza sent the black-skinned Estevan, because of his having once been through some of the north country with Cabeza de Vaca.

The party, made up mostly of Christianized Pima Indians, set out on the morning of March 7, 1539. As they went along, a great many natives, though indifferent to the definite objective of the expedition, attached themselves to the party, like small boys following a circus. They were acceptable to the leaders for they made themselves useful by acting as interpreters and by supplying edible game.

On the way northward, Fra Marcos halted his caravan at a place in central Sonora, the exact location of which is now in dispute because of lack of agreement in the ancient manuscripts, and of the vague and confused statements of distance and direction, and the lack of place names. But since the exact place is not now of grave consequence, let us accept the word of Fra Marcos that it was at Vacapa he first saw seven cities of "sizable populations," and was told they were well supplied with gold and other valuables.

What Fra Marcos later reported verbally of this journey, one of his chroniclers has set down thus:

"In a valley stretching eastward below Vacapa, he saw far off seven *'poblaciones razonables,'* and heard gold was plentiful there, but deemed it best to postpone a closer examination."

Vacapa, or Bacapa, now called Metapa, shown on Father Kino's map, 1699, and called by the early padres San Luis, was an ancient Indian pueblo considerable distance southward from Sonoita. Fra Marcos and his party remained there nine days. He was visited by Indians who lived to the northwest, and who, because of their custom of painting their faces and bodies, were called by the Spaniards, *"los pinta-dos"*: the painted ones.

The mine from which these Indians derived the paint is near the shore of St. George's Bay, an arm of the Gulf of California. Nearby is an ancient village named Zuñi, and the region east, north, and south was then and still is extremely rich in gold.

A placer strike of surprising richness was made in this region in June, 1939; and before a month had passed, a hamlet of twenty inhabitants grew to a town of 3,000 families. Not only was gold as easily to be had in 1539, but not far to the northeast were notable mines of turquoise, which are still operated.

From Vacapa, Fra Marcos sent Estevan ahead, commanding him to send back a cross if all was favorable for the party to proceed, the size of the cross to be determined by the conditions as he found them. After four days, the fra received by messenger a cross as large as a man, and glowing reports of seven great towns with big buildings, the lintels of whose doors were studded with turquoise, and with gold plentiful everywhere. This meant that Estevan was but two days — not four — distant.

Could Estevan have traveled from Vacapa, in central Sonora, to the Zuñi villages in New Mexico in two days? No. Not even with an automobile; he could not have traveled the trackless desert and have negotiated those uncharted mountains in two days or four — feeling his way through the unknown.

The cross brought by the messenger lured the fra still farther north. It cannot be shown exactly how far Fra Marcos continued on his northward way before turning back to Culiacán; but there is proof he went as far as the Salt River Valley, for he left an inscription of his name and the date, 1539, upon a rock south of Phoenix, an inscription which, perfectly legible today, is being preserved for posterity. He could not, however, have tarried long in this region for his return to Culiacán is dated May 30, of that year.

99

The expedition of Francisco Vasquez de Coronado followed in the next year; another quest for the lost Seven Cities of the Humpbacked Bull, and another failure in finding them. Notwithstanding these failures, historians keep right on insisting that the seven squalid little Zuñi villages in northwest New Mexico were the rich and comfortable Seven Cities of Cíbola.

H. H. Bancroft, historian, says: "The identity of Cíbola and the pueblo towns of Zuñi is so clearly established by all the evidence and has been so generally confirmed by such investigators as Simpson, Davis, Prince, Bandelier, and others, that I do not deem it necessary even to fully recapitulate the proofs."

But where are the proofs? Each of these writers seems to have accepted the conclusions of the one who preceded him. If Cabeza de Vaca and his companions had seen the Zuñi villages and had known them as the Seven Cities, Estevan would also have seen them. Whereas every description of Estevan's behaviour when he reached a small village — now assumed to have been Zuñi — as the courier of Marcos de Niza, indicates it was as strange to him as he was to the natives, who had never seen a Negro before, nor such animals as the huge dogs accompanying him.

Fra Marcos may have seen the Casa Grande on the Gila River, six or seven stories high; or the cliff-dwellers, living in apartments hundreds of feet above the base of the rock; or the Casas Grandes in Chihuahua, equally high. What the facts were, cannot now be known, but it is conclusive that somebody lied.

"We crossed a desert for forty days," said Tejo. It can be assumed that Tejo and his father were rapid runners, like all Indians of that day, and forty days traveling in level desert would represent considerable distance.

"There was no vegetation except short grass," he explained. But the desert country in Mexico and southwest United States has always been covered with bush growth: mesquite, ironwood, greasewood, creosote, sage, catclaw, and many conspicuous varieties of cactus. It would be practically impossible to find forty days' desert travel with no vegetation but short grass.

"And it was north between two oceans," he said. This would point to the desert area of Lower California. If Tejo was not telling something made up out of whole cloth, he was trying to say he and his father had traveled north to the head of the gulf and there had turned to the peninsula of Lower California, lying "between two oceans."

The "rows and rows of streets inhabited by workers in gold and silver," might have been either the product of Spanish imagination and lack of ability to translate Tejo's language, or Tejo's confused recollection of the Aztec gold and silver workers in Mexico City, with which he was familiar.

Are the Zuñi villages of New Mexico in a goldbearing region? Not noticeably.

Where, then, are the Seven Cities of Cíbola, richer than the palaces of Montezuma?

In recent years, several savants have attempted to answer this question by following the route as understood from the manuscripts of Marcos de Niza, Coronado, and Castañeda, but the data so arrived at are open to question. The locations, distances, and directions as set down in writing by the *antiguos,* years afterward, detailing from memory their experiences in a country uncharted and without place names, are, at this date, as has been said, if not entirely without meaning, at least utterly confusing.

The missing data, however, are not important, except to those who joy in historical research. The answer is with the Mexicans, who, though aware of the location of the treasures of the Seven Cities of Cíbola, are content to "leave her lay," because "God does not will it."

The old Spaniards, much given to hyperbole, do not seem to have had a good sense of distance, especially when harking back through thirty or more years of memory, for their *relaciones.* In the clear, dry, light air of the Southwest, 't is impossible to judge distance by vision or by time.

Fra Marcos specifically says the Seven Cities were south

of Vacapa. With Vacapa fifty leagues — not miles — south from Sonoita; with Sonoita south of the boundary which separates Sonora from Arizona, it is plain that the location of the seven towns as described by the fra more nearly agrees with the location of the cities referred to in the oral traditions of the Mexicans, and that they are nowhere near the Zuñi villages of New Mexico.

If the researcher should confuse the Sonoita in Arizona, slightly north of the international line, with Sonoita in Sonora, it would not be the first time those who write as they run deceived themselves.

In 1911, John Donald Mitchell, mining engineer, descendant of Kentucky pioneers, was engaged in business in Navajoa, southern Sonora. He spent his leisure time in traveling about the country, visiting the mines and cattle ranches, feasting his eyes upon the magnificent scenery.

Fluent in the local Spanish patois, Mitchell cultivated the acquaintance of the natives, some of whom were pure Indian; some an admixture of Spanish and Indian; some an olio of Spanish, Indian, and Negro. From them he gathered a vast store of ancient history, tradition, and legend: historical material which hitherto has eluded writers and researchers. Among the most engaging are the oral accounts of the Seven Cities of Cíbola, and the fate of Estevan, the black-skinned courier of Fra Marcos.

The Seven Cities, so the Mexicans told Mitchell, were in Mexico, slightly south of Sonora, practically on the boundary between Sinaloa and Chihuahua. They lay at the foot of a high cliff, upon the top of which there is a mesa, known as the Mesa del Toro. The mesa is so named because at the edge of the cliff, conspicuous from the valley below, is a colossal rock whose contour is the form of a buffalo bull, the cíbola.

The cities at the base of the cliff — lively communities for centuries before ever a Spaniard set foot in the new world — also took their name from the rock above.

Mitchell determined to go to the Mesa del Toro to see for himself the location of the mysterious cities which have

102

baffled historians and treasure seekers for 400 years.

Proceeding by the Orient Railway to Fuerte, on the river of the same name in Sinaloa, he continued by burro to Choix, a distance of about 80 miles, and on, another thirty miles, to the mesa. On its top, standing near the bull of rock, he saw below, in "a continuous valley six leagues long," the site of the seven cities, now in complete ruin, worn down by centuries of wind and rain, almost beyond recognition.

"Enough remains to show they were once well-populated and prosperous communities," said Mitchell. "In each there was the large central community house, surrounded by smaller houses. The streets were laid out fairly straight, though some were curved, taking the direction of the Arroyo del Toro, which can be seen a few miles away.

"On the ground round about, both above and below the cliff, are innumerable arrowheads and battle-axes, significant of much fighting in heavy battles," he continued. "Antique gold trinkets are almost daily picked up from the sand. From time to time, especially after the severe storms which are common to that country in summer, gold and silver objects of many sorts are uncovered by the wind and water. Some of them are richly set with turquoise.

"Not only do the Mexicans living around Fuerte and Choix have their history of the Seven Cities direct by word of mouth from their forefathers," Mitchell stated, "but there are records extant which confirm these traditions and also explain the ultimate fate of black Estevan."

Shortly after Estevan sent back word to Fra Marcos that he had found the cities, news was brought to the fra that at the village just ahead of where Fra Marcos was then halted, Estevan and his companion scouts had been set upon by the natives, and Estevan among others had been slain. None among them, however, could bear witness to his death.

Mexican oral tradition says Estevan was not killed; he was wounded and thrown down with a number of dead and wounded piled upon him. He lay still until darkness came; then he crept out from under and fled unnoticed in the night. Bancroft relates that Estevan was later in a convent in Mexico.

Again he was captured by the Indians. Since he was an adept in the art of escape, they cut off his legs to assure his abstinence from travel. Given a pair of women for his wives, he reared a family of four children, tradition tells.

Old Mexican records show, according to Mitchell, the bloody battles which raged through successive generations between the Spaniards and the Indians for control of the west coast of Mexico, reached a climax in 1611, in the region of the Seven Cities.

In that year, the chief of the Indians, realizing that a fight was imminent, commanded the inhabitants of the cities and the environs, to collect all their goods: their gold, silver, and jewels, and to store them in a cave prepared for the purpose, in the bank of the arroyo opposite to the cíbola on the cliff.

The commands were obeyed. The treasure was collected and stored. The cave was sealed and placed under custodians whose orders were never on any account to cease guarding it. The battle was fought; the chief was slain; the Indians were killed or put to flight.

Only the guards of the treasure, not participating, remained unscathed. Their descendants are still on guard, maintaining their secret. The Indians are not greedy for possessions, and as they say, "God does not will it," that the gold, silver, and gems should be taken away by alien hands. If the white man discovers them, it will be by his own wit, for the lips of the Indians, sealed through three centuries, will ever remain silent.

Treasure hunters who seek the Seven Golden Cities of the Humpbacked Bull, are assured a most engaging adventure if they go to Sinaloa, Mexico, and follow the route described herein by John D. Mitchell. His statements are sustained by the late Harry Carr, author of Mother Mexico, *though neither Mitchell nor Carr made any impression* on "historians," who do their researching in the ivory towers of far-off libraries, absorbing whatever errors, if any, may have been made by their predecessors.

10

Lost Treasure in Arizona

MANY PERSONS, alert to adventure and romance, who keep an eye open to opportunities, believe that Arizona tops the list of states offering a chance of finding a lost mine or a buried treasure. This may or may not be true.

However, the unique attraction in mountain and desert, in climate and scenery, and in the wide variation in topography and seasonal weather as distinguished from climate, draws visitors from all corners of the world. With the dry, light air, they breathe in the history, legend, and tradition which hang over the state like a golden haze. Being human, their eyes glisten and their ears prick up at the mention of the lost treasures, which naturally suggest adventure. If they return whence they came, thinking Arizona abounds in such alluring elements — well, maybe I agree with them.

Even a brief stay in Arizona will convince the most indifferent and skeptical that underneath the surface of the earth, within the limits of Arizona, lie many great values in metals and gems. How inevitable, then, that many treasures would be discovered, by intentional search or by accident, only to be later ignored, forgotten, or lost.

So it is not difficult to recognize that Arizona is a province of lost mines and buried treasures, dating on down from the Conquest by Cortez to the present time, and will be so on into the future until they are rediscovered.

If the adventurous and romantic souls to whom this book is addressed feel inclined to charge that many of these stories are merely campfire tales and old legends, I can assure them that no narrations of this kind ever grow up and live without a firm basis in fact.

There is well-established, indisputable history for every one of the accounts which follow in this chapter, as can be readily inferred from the names, dates, and places. In fact, the state was settled and developed as a white man's country because of the search for gold; gold first rumored, then authenticated, and the claims recorded. The tales given here are but a small part of those that can be told.

1.   The Mine of Golden Bullets.

"Felix" Aubrey is remembered as the little French Canadian who established the speed record for the pony express between Independence, Missouri, and Santa Fé, New Mexico, in 1846.

After the discovery of gold in California, he made many trips across the Southwest for the purpose of reporting on railroad and trade routes, and for other purposes.

He had many skirmishes with Indians of various tribes; and all during his brief life, he passed from one exciting adventure into another. He was killed in Santa Fé in 1854, before he was quite thirty years old.

In August, 1853, Aubrey, with a party of eighteen white Americans, was passing through the country of the Coyotero-Apaches (wolf-men), the most bloodthirsty, cruel, and treacherous of the Apache subtribes. These tribesmen at this time made their headquarters in the Tonto Basin, under the Mogollon Rim, a country bleak, forbidding, not easy of access, and not much traveled by white men.

The Aubrey party felt secure, for they mistakenly regarded these Indians as friendly. When entirely unsuspecting of Indian treachery, they were suddenly attacked by the
Coyoteros close at hand. It was only by the quickest action
with their Colts, then a new invention, that they saved their
lives.

As they continued through the country of the hostiles,
they established trading relations with a few straggling
Coyoteros, who appeared in the Aubrey camp by ones and
twos. The white men traded some old clothes for $1500
worth of gold nuggets, which the Indians had in great number. In fact, the supply of gold which the Coyoteros had
was so bountiful, so pure, and so little valued by them that
they made bullets of it for shooting rabbits and other game.

It is a matter of record that one old Coyotero loaded his
gun with three bullets of purest gold to kill a small jack-
rabbit which he offered to the Aubrey party. Returning
gift for gift, they accepted the animal, extracted the bullets,
and ate the rabbit.

The white men could not wait long enough to learn the
source of the hostiles' gold, having important business elsewhere. But in any event, the Indians of that day and of
that tribe were too ferocious for any peaceful relations. The
Coyotero gold mine which must have been full of free gold
easily worked — for the Indians did not know gold in any
other form — has never been discovered by white men.

As one studies the locale and examines into the traditional and historic statements of other gold mysteries in
Arizona, it appears more and more likely that the source of
the golden bullets used by the Apache Wolf-men was the
deposit of gold which was later sought in the mistaken belief that it was the Lost Adams Diggings. This mysterious
gold source was once known as the Lost Yavapai Ledge, for
in Aubrey's day this region was a part of Yavapai, "mother
of counties."

*This gold is surely going to be found some day, though
it will probably need some scientific instrument to detect*

gold from a distance, or from the air. Search under the Mogollon Rim, in the Tonto Basin, below Promontory Butte, where the East Tonto Creek arises.

This area was a runway for Coyoteros, and south of here, it was said by the old-timers, they had their chief rancheria. The Mogollon Rim is an almost perpendicular cliff, of rich color, extending for many miles, and I have always believed it to be highly mineralized. Look for the gold to be near a small stream, such as East Tonto Creek; for the gold will be found in the form of pure nuggets in coarse gravel.

2. White Strangers and Papago Gold

"The route from Tucson passes through a country abounding in exceedingly rich gold mines," wrote Major P. St. George Cooke, commanding the United States Second Dragoons, in his report to Colonel J. J. Abert, of the United States Topographical Engineers, December 6, 1847.

Major Cooke and his company of dragoons were blazing a trail across the Arizona wilderness to California. It is not clear how he got his information about the "exceedingly rich gold mines," though he certainly was correct. He did not, however, know the ancient tradition of the Papago tribe through whose territory, south and west of Tucson, he traveled in safety: the tradition about the strangers with the milk-white skin, who came among them mysteriously, and were cruelly slain by the enemies of the Papagoes before the tribesmen had learned the strangers' history.

Had the soldiers known of the vast cache of treasure in the vicinity of their route across the territory, Major Cooke might have had non-military adventures to report. For what soldier or civilian can resist the lure of lost or hidden treasure?

The prehistoric Papagoes who claimed the region from northern Sonora to the Gila River, lived in a country rich in gold and silver. Finding the precious metal in such profusion in its native form, they used it freely for ornaments and utensils, regarding it wholly for beauty or for common use, since they had no conception of money. They gave it

109

away freely, never knowing any reason for hoarding it, on the principle that, no matter into whose hand it came, it would eventually serve the purposes of Montezuma. This was their attitude until they learned that gold was the cause of all their trouble with the white men, when the white men came to settle among them.

In a time so long ago that the Papagoes cannot date it, some gentle-mannered, peaceful white foreigners came among them, lived with them for a little while, and did so many kind things to earn their affection and respect that the Papagoes looked upon them as demi-gods.

These strange men wandered about Papaguería collecting all the gold and silver they could find, and in various honorable ways, acquiring it from the natives. Thus they secured a great mass of it.

The foreigners made their headquarters in a ranchería thirty-three miles northwest of the more recent city of Tucson, near the present little village of Redrock, in Pinal County. Somewhere along the road out of Redrock to Silverbell, in a southwesterly direction, they concealed the masses of gold and silver that fell into their hands. In a few years they had a fabulous amount collected and stored. But bear in mind, at this time there was no Redrock, no Silverbell.

What the strangers intended to do with all this treasure is not accounted for in the Papago tradition, though they tell its destiny. They say that one day a tribe of the Papagoes' enemies from the north — perhaps the forerunners of the Apaches — fell upon the ranchería and killed everyone there. Not a Papago nor a white stranger was spared.

When the tribesmen from farther south visited the ranchería soon thereafter, they found it in unwonted silence, leveled with the ground, with not a living thing on two legs or four. They knew at once what had happened.

About twenty-five or thirty years ago, some spears, swords, and other objects, marked with archaic Latin inscriptions, were unearthed in this region, and gave rise to considerable speculation and controversy among archaeologists. By some it was claimed the objects were faked; others believed in their authenticity. If authentic, then one thing is certain: they had at one time been the possessions of inhabitants of Europe, persons above the common class, who had been educated in the language then current for writing. This would apply to almost any country of Europe where the people were literate in the Middle Ages.

Did these objects once belong to the men of the milk-white skin who so long ago came among the Papagoes? And were they the Norsemen of the upper class, educated, literate, skilled navigators and geographers? No one can now say.

The objects described above were found at what was perhaps the campsite of the long-gone foreigners; their treasure cache was no doubt a little distance away. But neither Indian nor white men has ever discovered the huge treasure buried by the strange men from overseas in the prehistoric days. Where they buried it, there it remains.

From Tucson, take the Southern Pacific Railroad to Redrock. Out from Redrock, take the road to Silverbell, now a ghost town. Imagine yourself in the skin of the prehistoric foreigner in deciding the best place to camp. Assuming the possibility that the spot you select may have been the campsite of the white-skinned strangers, apply your witching wand roundabout. Or, ask to see the archaeological objects mentioned, at the museum of the University of Arizona, in Tucson, and ascertain from the university archaeologists exactly where they were found. That will give the point of departure.

3. Captain Espejo's Lost Silver.

Word had been received by the archbishop in Mexico City, that three Franciscan padres, who had been sent to propagate the Holy Faith in New Mexico, had disappeared, and all efforts of the local Christian Indians had failed to find them. It was feared the padres had been killed by hostile natives.

As the rumor circulated, it reached the ears of Antonio Espejo, a mining engineer from Cordova, Spain, who had

111

made a large fortune by the discovery of precious metals in the New World. From Santa Barbara, Mexico, where he was then sojourning, he sent word to the archbishop that he would "at his own expense," organize a party to go to New Mexico, and learn, at first hand, if possible, the fate of the three missing padres.

Accordingly in the fall of 1580, Captain Espejo, with fourteen men, set out for the north. He was eager to do this service for the church, as that gave an official aspect to his expedition. But he had also another object in view.

He had heard reports of immense deposits of gold and silver in that northern country, notwithstanding Coronado had failed in his attempts to find them. Encouraged by his own previous success in locating treasure, he longed to examine with his expert eyes the mineral possibilities in that far northern region.

It was 1581 before he reached the Zuñi and Moqui villages, known to him through the records left by Coronado, whose journey to these parts won him eternal fame. In Zuñi, Captain Espejo found three aged Christianized Indians who remembered Coronado and received the Espejo party with friendliness.

The Indians at Zuñi told him that 60 days' travel from their villages there was a big lake, and upon its shores there were many fine towns; that the inhabitants had much gold they wore as bracelets and earrings. They told Espejo that Coronado had started for the villages, but failing to find water after twelve days, he returned to the Zuñi.

The Indians did not tell the Cordovan captain they had, from sad experiences, learned to tell the white men there was much gold and silver to be found far off after many days of travel. For they had discovered early in the great game of the foreigners' explorations that the Spaniards would travel from hell to breakfast for the promise of gold, and it was good strategy to describe rich deposits of the yellow metal as lying a long journey distant.

Espejo and his companions departed, to find the rich country the Zuñi described. After traveling "28 leagues west," he came to a settlement of about 5,000 Indians. Through an error in spelling in the archaic Spanish used in the manuscript from which this account is taken, this number appears as 50,000.

These Indians received Espejo kindly, giving him extravagant gifts. According to the Spaniards' report, so great was the natives' joy at beholding the white men, the Indians "poured maize upon the ground for the horses to walk upon, and they presented Captain Espejo with mantles of cotton, white and colored, and many towels with tassels at the four corners, and rich metals which seemed to contain much silver."

Traveling due west from there, which brought them well into the Arizona region, he and his party found the silver mines, and "with their own hands," they took out a large quantity of native silver. The silver was in a broad vein, "in a mountain easily ascended by an open way to the same." Several Indian pueblos were round about. Nearby they found two streams on whose banks were groves of walnut, grapevines, and "flax like that in Castile."

They returned to Mexico without finding the lost padres, and apparently forgot all about their silver strike, for it is not again mentioned in their records. Captain Espejo returned to his native Spain in 1583 and never again visited the New World.

Some historians believe the "two streams" were the Verde and the Little Colorado. Some believe the silver was near the base of Arizona's San Francisco Mountains, about fifty miles from Prescott. The historian, Bancroft, thought it to be near Bill Williams Mountain. Others think it was in the Santa Maria Mountains where Walnut Creek flows northwest into Chino Creek. Along Walnut Creek seems the most logical location.

On the banks of Walnut Creek, the pioneer Mormons found many fine old walnut trees, some of which bore evidence they were at least a century old. They also found the ruins of many pre-historic dwellings of such extreme antiquity they could not venture to date them. But with all

their engaging archaeological discoveries, they never discovered the lost Espejo silver.

*The ancient records say Espejo's party went 28 leagues
west from Zuñi, or Cíbola, to a town called Zaguato; from
Zaguato, 45 leagues due west. The league in Espejo's day
was approximately 3.45 miles. Therefore, when you have located Zaguato, go due west a little more than 155 miles.
You will then certainly be within the State of Arizona, and
probably near Bill Williams Mountain. Today a good point
of departure for the search would be the town of Williams.*

*But remember also the Bradshaw Mountains not far
away, were once known as Silver Mountains, because of the
heavy deposits of silver known to be there. The Darell
Duppa lost silver strike in the Bradshaws, may be identical
with Espejo's lost silver.*

4. Lord Duppa's Lost Silver Strike.

Among the oldest of the old-timers in the Salt River Valley there are some who still remember Darell Duppa, the
wealthy Englishman who gave the name to the town of
Tempe, Arizona, naming it for "the beautiful vale" in
Greece, where he visited when on his grand tour with his
tutor to mark the completion of his formal education.

It was Darell Duppa who named Phoenix also, suggested
by his vision of the magnificent city which he prophesied
would arise upon the ashes of a civilization known to have
once existed in the valleys of the Salt and Gila Rivers. Duppa, who had been educated in France and England, was
learned in various languages and in much classical lore. To
his friends, who were many, he was a beloved vagabond; to
others, he was a no-account remittance man, known as
"Lord" Duppa.

It was not generally known among Duppa's associates
in Phoenix that he had a valuable silver mine, north of the
city. But in his letters to his home folks in England he often
wrote of his mine as in a place much beset by Apaches.

Years after Duppa's death, his nephew, in Maidstone, England, gave to Leland Lovelace certain definite information from Darell Duppa's letters which started research into the history and location of the lost Duppa silver.

When Jacob Walzer, known in Arizona history and legend as Jake Waltz, or "Old Dutch Jake," first settled on a ranch near the Salt River, 1868, he shared his lot (no pun) with two other old Germans, Jacob and Andrew Starar.

Darell (one r) Duppa settled on a ranch adjoining, to the north, and became a daily visitor to the Germans' ranch. With the two Starar brothers he was especially congenial, and when the Duppa quarterly remittance of $1,000 a month came in, the three always celebrated its arrival by going on a spree until the money was gone.

Walzer was of temperate and cleanly habits, instilled into him by years of military training in his early life in Wurttemburg. He found the dissolute behavior of the Starars repugnant to him. He turned over to them the ranch which he had started on its way to development, and moved away somewhat nearer to the river, where he re-established himself alone within smaller limits.

About six years after Jake came into the valley, he discovered the gold mine in the Superstition Mountains, the story of which has become the favorite tradition of the Southwest. He tried to keep his mine a closely-guarded secret, but as the years passed and his circle of acquaintance widened, it began to be whispered about that Old Dutch Jake had a valuable gold mine, "somewhere in Superstition Mountain."

Darell Duppa remained even more secretive about his silver mine, and with the exception of Jake Starar, not even Duppa's closest friends knew anything of it. His possession of the secret silver was practically contemporaneous with Jake Walzer's holding of his secret gold mine.

A curious angle of Duppa's discovery of the silver was that he stumbled upon it by chance when trying to "put something over on Old Dutch Jake."

The Starar brothers had told Duppa that Jake Walzer

115

had a secret source of pure gold ore. They knew, so they said, he brought his gold from "somewhere out behind" Superstition Mountain. They wouldn't be so unsportsman-like as to follow Jake into the mountain, but, they reasoned, if Jake could find gold in the Superstitions, they could also.

Therefore upon several occasions when they knew Jake to be engaged with the work upon his ranch, Duppa and Jake Starar— then aged but still hardy — went prospecting into the Superstitions along Salt River.

They found it more convenient to prospect upon the north side of the river than on the south. For on the north they could wander far afield from Phoenix without getting too far away from a source of supply of whiskey, without which both would have found life insupportable. Their wanderings led them too far out of bounds for Old Dutch Jake's treasure, and having circled around to the northwest, they found themselves on the fringe of the Bradshaw Moun-tains, with access to both Wickenburg and Prescott.

A flipped coin turned them toward Wickenburg. While on their way out of the Bradshaws, they made a fine silver strike — a heavy vein of silver! A strike so replete with values, Duppa found it well worth writing home about, with an outline of his plans for developing it — apparently a device for making his kinfolk believe he was busily en-gaged in something productive.

Duppa and Starar did not tarry long in the vicinity of the precious vein, for their need of good liquor was insis-tent. As they proceeded, an agreement was arrived at be-tween them that the mine was to belong exclusively to Duppa, and he laid vague tentative plans for developing it. They further agreed to say nothing of it upon their return to Phoenix.

As time went on, Duppa, to whom money meant nothing, became indifferent to his opportunity, and forgot all about his intention of silver mining. His lips remained sealed, though in his letters to his kinfolk he continued to refer to his silver mine, and to describe its location as perilous because of Apaches, by whose arrows he had several times been badly wounded.

Jake Starar also remembered his promise to keep mum about the silver, though he spoke of it several times without disclosing its location or confessing he had agreed to lay no claim to it.

When Duppa died, in January, 1893, nearly two years after the death of Jake Walzer, he had so little interest in the silver deposit, he neglected to mention it. And later, when Jake Starar died, he, too, had forgotten he had an important secret for the traditional deathbed disclosure.

South of Prescott; north of Phoenix, Duppa's find was on the southeast edge of the Bradshaw range, not far from the point where State Highway 69 crosses the Agua Fria River. The Bradshaws are known to contain much silver, though little has been mined in that region. If you don't discover Duppa's lost vein, do not despair; for in that same locality, you may find some other hitherto undiscovered deposit.

5. Lost Gold at the Camel's Tinaja.

On the north side of the Gila River, not many miles east of the Colorado, a region once celebrated for its gold, John Gordon, a Scotsman, and Juan Perez, a Mexican, were prospecting together at the foot of the desert mountains. It was in a summer which set a record for heat — the summer of 1871. The gold placers of Arizona were still in bonanza, and new discoveries were being made with considerable frequency.

Before Gordon and Perez had found any ores worth claiming, their water supply ran short. They realized they would be in serious difficulty if they did not soon find a way to refill their canteens. The two rivers were too far away for a man on foot to reach either of them in time for relief in the intense heat.

Perez, a Sonoran, familiar with the desert, suggested looking for a *tinaja*. A *tinaja*, he told Gordon, is a natural declivity in the rock, which forms a tank for rainwater, and

117

in seasons when the interval between rains is not too long, the *tinaja* acts as a reservoir, storing water for the birds and wild animals, and sometimes for man.

For some time they looked in vain, becoming more exhausted hour by hour. Finally, where a large rock cast a small strip of shade, they sat down to figure out a way of finding water, and in which direction it would be found the most quickly.

Suddenly a strange shape appeared in the desert below them, moving toward them from the south. At first they thought it was a heat mirage. As it continued to move slowly and rhythmically toward the mountain, they saw it was a camel. Of course, they had no way of knowing it was a remnant of the camel herd brought to the United States in 1856 for the American government.

The two prospectors sat watching in breathless amazement. The camel seemed to know exactly where he was going, as if on familiar ground. They saw him amble around the rocks at the foot of the mountain, not far from where they were sitting, and disappear from view. They followed him silently at a distance, until they again spied him. Wondering if their eyes deceived them, they saw the camel approach a rock and drink. The exotic beast had led them to a *tinaja* with water!

After drinking, the camel moved on, never noticing the men, there being no wind to carry the scent. When the animal was out of sight, they hastened to the *tinaja* and found the water — not very clean but acceptable in their extremity.

Several times they drank, then filled their canteens as best they could. As they loitered about, loath to leave the water while it was yet daylight, they were startled to find that at the base of the rock the ground fairly groaned with gold nuggets; nuggets of all sizes and shapes, too coarse to be placer, too plentiful to be float.

Tense with excitement, they gathered up as much as they could before nightfall. That night they slept a short distance from the rock, to avoid frightening away any ani-

118

mals coming to drink. In the morning they set out for Yuma, where they reported their find, showed the gold, outfitted themselves for a stay at the camel's *tinaja,* and started on the return.

Through the trackless and unmarked desert, they could never find their way back. Time after time, they tried to retrace their steps exactly, but it was futile. The gold at the camel's *tinaja* was not for them.

This story I caught on the fly, one night, around the campfire, and wrote it for the editor of *Ghost Town News.* Through his courtesy I am permitted to include it in this collection. It will answer several questions for amateur archaeologists who sometimes find camel bones in the Arizona desert and are at a loss as to whence they came.

Not much help is available for finding this deposit of native gold. Look, however, in the Tank (Tinaja) Mountains, southeast of the S.H. Mountains, northeast of Yuma, on the north side of the Gila.

And lest you have as much trouble finding the S. H. Mountains as you may have finding the gold, take note that these mountains are easily found on many Arizona maps. They are so named because their outline, against the sky, seen from a certain approach, resembles the outline of a small edifice commonly found behind country houses, made conspicuous in modern literature by Chic Sale.

In the Tank Mountains are several tinajas of varying sizes, well known to the early Mexican prospectors, who regarded them as life-savers. Look for one of a suitable height for a camel; at the base you may find the gold nuggets.

6.   Gold Pockets of Laguna.

In the days when Yuma was known as Arizona City, lying on both sides of the Colorado River, a big Chemehuevi Indian chief came into town and showed to the astonished inhabitants a mass of pure solid gold as large as a child's fist. It gave rise to emotions of greed in many a breast, for in those days it was the hope of everyone to find himself a gold mine; and nuggets of clean virgin gold of such magnitude were rare.

The chief took the gold to the general store and promptly traded it in for colored beads and rotgut whiskey; meanwhile proclaiming loudly to all within hearing that he had plenty of the "pretty yellow stone" and would bring some more.

While the big fellow was going through the process of becoming completely drunk, several white men offered him various rewards if he would tell them where he had found the gold, or if he had received it from another Indian. Soldiers from the fort even attempted to frighten him into telling. But no; nothing they offered could persuade him to disclose the source of the nugget.

When he became dead drunk and lay down on the edge of the street, two white men sat beside him all through the night, hoping that when he sobered up, they could dragoon him into talking, in return for a "hair of the dog to cure the bite," the usual medicine after a binge.

During the night they took several deep swigs of whiskey to keep away the cold, and went to sleep. When they awoke, shortly after dawn, the Indian was gone.

Several times he came into town with similar nuggets and traded them for whiskey and trifles worth only a few cents. Each time, he got drunk, sobered up, and went his way, stolidly resisting all efforts to force or entice his secret from him.

He came for the last time early in 1863. When he returned no more, it was told about the town that he had been killed in a fight. No white man ever solved the riddle of his big gold nuggets. The mysterious source of his treasure became known in southwest tradition as the Lone Indian's Lost Mine.

In tracing the story it is well to remember there is gold on both sides of the Colorado River, both above and below Yuma. The Chemehuevi may have had the gold from any of these points, but as his people had their hogans mostly

120

*above Yuma on the Arizona side of the river, it is safe to
assume he found no occasion for crossing the river.*

*South of Laguna dam, on the Arizona side, is an old-
time placer area. This is a short distance north of Yuma.
Mexican prospectors who followed close on the heels of
the Spanish missionaries found many large pockets of gold
in this place. And in the Laguna Mountains nearby, gold
was discovered in May, 1854.*

*The form of the big chief's gold gives the clue. The In-
dians did no smelting, and the big, round nugget of clean
pure gold silently pointed to the pockets of Laguna.*

*If there are pockets of gold on the east bank of the
Colorado (Arizona), it is more than likely there are similar
pockets on the west bank also (California). And there is
nothing to show all the gold has been taken away that was
placed by Mother Nature under the surface in the Laguna
Mountains.*

7. Estrella Mountains Hide Gold Bars.

Many years before the United States concluded the
Gadsden Purchase treaty, the Mexicans and Spaniards knew
that the region contiguous to the Gila River, on both the
north and south sides, was good hunting ground for gold
and silver.

A big fat Spaniard named Ortega, living in Guadalajara,
having made a sizable fortune in silver, south of the Mayo
country, decided to try his luck farther north, in the Gila
River Valley, prospecting for gold. He organized his party
of peons and Indians and set out to reach the river through
Papaguería.

He was of a mind to stop in the land of the Papagoes,
for it was well known they had plenty of gold which they
obtained from their own mines near their villages. But the
Papagoes were unfriendly and bellicose to his party, and as
Ortega was bent on prospecting and not especially on fighting, he hurried through Papaguería to the Pima villages
farther north. The Pimas were friendly and gentle until
they had reason to be otherwise.

121

The Pima villages were on both sides of the river, with small ranges of mountains on the south, west, and north. The Pimas knew of many gold desposits in these mountains, but for several centuries they had kept secret all their knowledge of the yellow metal because of certain religious teachings connected with their ancestors. The Pimas for the last century have had no gold, as their forebears had in Montezuma's time, and they do no mining.

Señor Ortega and his band proceeded north of the river to the Estrella Mountains, and there, after a few days of prospecting, they discovered, high in the ridge, a heavy vein of gold, and considerable placer in the canyon below.

His men were put to work taking out the ore from the vein above and panning the dust from the canyon floors. An arrastre (a device for concentrating) was made so the gold could be reduced and cast into bars. Pelts from the game which supplied them with fresh meat were made into leather bags to hold the gold dust, preparatory to their return to Mexico.

Word came that a regiment of American soldiers was on its way west, and would pass through the desert at the foot of the Estrella Mountains. The American soldiers, at this time, bore a fearful reputation among the Mexicans, and Ortega believed that the invaders would naturally appropriate any available gold, silver, and gems, in the same manner any Spaniard would.

He decided to close his mines, hide his gold, send his men away, and make himself scarce until the Americans had either gone their way farther west, or had returned whence they came.

He instructed his workmen to make ready his fifty bars of gold and his thirty leather bags of gold dust, for packing onto his string of burros, and then to go on ahead around the southernmost point of the mountains, past Montezuma's Head. There they were to make camp and wait for him.

One lone peon he retained back at the mine, to help him with the burros. And one Pima boy he sent in the lead to watch the burros as they went down the trail.

122

He planned to hide his treasure in a cave farther down the mountain, and later, when the time was right, he would return and retrieve it.

As soon as the workmen were out of sight, Ortega and his trusted peon loaded the bars and bags of gold onto the pack animals and drove them down the mountain, the boy ahead being instructed to hurry back if a burro slipped from the trail, or if any stranger came into sight.

The sun was about one hour from setting, and the workmen were already making camp on the plain below Montezuma's Head, when Ortega and the peon entered a short deep canyon, with a cave in the wall. In the back of the cave they dug a hole into which they placed the bars and bags of gold. Then with a hard quick blow upon the peon's head, Ortega killed him.

Shoving the body into the hole with the gold, he covered it carefully and completely. Then he looked around for the young Pima, but the boy could not be found. Hastening on to join his waiting party, Ortega reached their camp at nightfall.

Perhaps the exertion overtaxed his greedy heart; perhaps his fear of the American soldiery did its deadly work, for during that night, Ortega died in his sleep, believing none knew the secret of his buried gold. No one knew — except one small Pima boy, who, unknown to Ortega, had seen him enter the cave with the peon, heard the peon's cry of pain when stricken down, and saw Ortega emerge alone from the cave.

Through the boy the adventure became known to others of his tribe; they, having no interest in the gold, have never spread abroad any word that would lead to its recovery.

On the east side of the Estrellas, south of Butterfly Peak, in a short, deep box canyon, running west, probably about half the distance from the Peak to Montezuma's Head, is the place to look for the cache. The vein is farther north and up the mountainside.

8. The Lost Shoemaker Placer.

A little old cobbler sitting at his bench, toiling over his task of making stout leather into shoes, is as much entitled to his dreams as any fairy princess. The fairy princess, as is natural, may dream of love, but the little old cobbler is more likely to dream of treasure. Not only to dream of treasure, but to do something about it to make his dream come true.

In the early pioneer days of the Salt River Valley, those who needed to have their shoes repaired or new ones made, went into the then little hamlet of Phoenix and applied to Charles A. Rodig, who at that time was the only shoemaker available.

Charlie was a Prussian, who came to Phoenix in 1876. Renting a little store from Alex Steinegger, he soon had all the business he could take care of. Charlie was perfectly at home in the valley, for there was a fair-sized group of Germans there, and he found as much or more occasion to speak in his native tongue as he did in English or Spanish. The little English at his command was spoken haltingly and with a very heavy accent.

But everyone liked little, short, stubby Charlie, for he was a hard and systematic worker, with an acute sense of time, which, in a timeless country like frontier Arizona, made him outstanding. And he had that old-fashioned virtue of attending strictly to his own business.

One of Charlie's customers, and his close friend, was Jake Walzer, known to pioneer Phoenix as Jake Waltz, and now of world-wide fame as Old Dutch Jake. Jake wore out many shoes and had frequent recourse to Charlie for making new ones and mending the old. For such service, through several years, Jake paid him with pieces of ore heavy with gold.

So Charlie knew beyond all doubt that Jake had an unfailing supply of gold, freshly mined and never minted. Of course, Charlie wanted to know all about it. By hints and even by direct questions, he did his best to find out the secret of the source of Jake's gold ore. But all he found out

124

he learned from others, for Jake told him absolutely nothing. All Charlie learned was the mine was "somewhere in Superstition Mountain."

Following the terrific flood which overtook the towns of Phoenix and Tempe in February, 1891, Jake Walzer died. Some say — though this is not true — that Jake died in Charlie's house. Though Jake was gone, he was not forgotten, and many men who knew of his close association with Rodig, questioned Rodig about the mysterious mine.

The little old shoemaker invariably said that Jake never had a mine, and he always followed up the assertion with stern advice to stay away from the Superstition Mountains, predicting a dire fate at the hands of the Apaches.

Nevertheless Jake had not been buried very long when Charlie began to lay plans to go into the mountain to ferret out Jake's secret mine.

When the warm weather came on and people left the valley for the summer, Charlie's business fell off, and he decided then was the time to shut up shop and go into Superstition, with a proper outfit, prospecting, an occupation he knew nothing about.

His first expedition into the mountains was of two months' duration, in 1892. Unaccustomed to the wild life of mountaineer and miner, he met many dangers and endured many hardships. He must have been a glutton for punishment, for he withstood them all, and returned to his shoemaking business in Phoenix, not much the worse for wear. But he found no traces of gold.

From then on, however, his mind was constantly dwelling upon the farther reaches of the mountain where he believed the fabulous gold vein was concealed. During the winter months, while making shoes, he thought out every small detail for making a comfortable, simple, and systematic expedition into the mountain in search of the treasure.

Thereafter for fifteen years, every summer, taking with him a cook and all the essentials for maintaining health and strength while in the wilderness, Charlie hunted the

125

Lost Dutchman mine, though he did not know it by that name. On the south side of the Salt River, and on the north side, every place except where it is, he searched.

And every summer he met with some catastrophe: lost his equipment; was attacked by Apaches; lost his burros by drowning; nearly perished from thirst; was overcome by the heat, and suffered other mishaps. Nothing could discourage him from his quest. And every summer his adventures furnished diverting material for the columns of the Phoenix newspapers.

In the summer of 1895, Rodig, accompanied by his cook, went into the mountains for his annual hunt for the Lost Dutchman. He extended his prospecting on the north side of the Salt River, near the foot of Four Peaks.

They found a spring of good water near a deep canyon, and made camp nearby. While the cook was cooking, the prospector was prospecting on the floor of the canyon, where there was a large deposit of black sand. As Rodig dug into the sand, he suddenly realized that it was full of gold. He called the cook to come quickly with the gold pan, and they started panning. From a shovelful of sand, they panned out in a few minutes $75.00 worth of gold!

With their attention concentrated upon the business in hand, they were somewhat dazed when, at the sound of a war-whoop, they realized they were attacked by Apaches. They barely saved their scalps, and in their hasty retreat, they reached the bank of the Salt River without noting landmarks sufficiently definite for a return to the canyon of the black sand.

Many times Rodig returned to the north side of the river, in the vicinity of Four Peaks, seeking his lost placer, but could never find it. Not until he became too old and infirm to go into the wilderness under his own steam, did Charlie Rodig give over the struggle to find the two now famous lost treasures, the Lost Dutchman and his own lost placer.

In 1912, after a long career divided between mending shoes and hunting Nature's cache of gold, Rodig entered the Arizona's Pioneers' Home, at Prescott, and there he died, in 1920, at the age of 84.

Let us not say that he died without profit, for he had, at least, the huge pleasure of the pursuit. His lost placer in black sand is known, in the roster of Arizona's lost mines, as the Lost Shoemaker Placer.

Many an old prospector in Arizona thinks this black sand was the placer mine discovered by Old Dutch Jake and his partner just before they learned of the gold-in-quartz in the canyon, which became famous as the Lost Dutchman. If so, he who rediscovers the black sand placer will have the key to the most celebrated lost treasure in the West. Remember: in a canyon on the north side of Salt River, at the foot of Four Peaks, high mountain in the Mazatzal range, in central Arizona. The canyon runs southwest to the river.

9. The Squaw's Lost Gold Strike.

No list of Arizona pioneers is complete without the name of Ed Schieffelin, discoverer of the famed Tombstone silver mines, and founder of Tombstone, "the town too tough to die."

After Schieffelin relinquished his hold upon the Tombstone mines, he spent many years running hither and yon, from Mexico to Alaska, wherever he heard a rumor of a gold or silver strike. Because of his aggressiveness in tracing down many stories of gold discoveries, his name is associated with a number of them; one of these is the Arizona classic known as the Squaw's Lost Mine. A more appropriate name would be The Gold Ed Schieffelin Never Found.

One day when in Yuma, Schieffelin was told that an old squaw of the Yuma tribe had found a very rich deposit of gold, and, as is usual with Indians and some others, she had refused to point out the place where the vein was located. Schieffelin pricked up his ears. Perhaps he could induce this tribeswoman to talk, though all others had failed.

He sought out the old woman in her desert hogan north of Yuma, and with much quizzing, with Job-like patience,

127

he prevailed upon her to tell her story. Digging for gold was as nothing compared to digging for data from the taciturn woman. Her scraps of information, pieced together, gave a perfectly logical account of her adventure. Now well crystallized in Arizona tradition, it ran as follows:

The squaw had reasons of her own, which she did not disclose, for accompanying two braves of the Yuma tribe on a journey along the trail between Yuma and Wickenburg.

As they passed along, their faces northward, a bright stone, lying by the wayside, caught the old squaw's eye. She picked it up, examined it, and passed it on to the two braves. They took a lively interest in the rock, and concluded it might be a pretty stone of concern to white men, and it might, therefore, be exchangeable for firewater. So they carried the stone along with them. When they returned to their Yuma home, they still had it.

One day soon thereafter, some Mexican miners, prospecting along the Colorado River, detoured to the Indians' lodge, and were shown the piece of rock. The Mexicans became highly excited. They said the rock was a piece of rich gold, and demanded that the Indians lead them to the spot where it had been found.

The Indians knew nothing of its origin beyond their having seen the woman pick it up. When the Mexicans talked about the vein or the *madre* of the small piece of ore, they had no idea what the Mexicans were talking about. And the prospectors had no Yuman vocabulary to explain what they meant by "mother lode." The Indians had nothing to tell the Mexicans except the simple fact that the old woman had picked it up as they walked along the trail when going from Yuma to Wickenburg.

The old squaw could not remember the exact place where she had found the ore, but the Mexicans were so insistent and displayed such an ugly temper, the Indians thought it best to humor them.

The squaw therefore led the prospectors along the trail, and when she was duly tired out, she indicated the spot where she was standing as the place where she had picked

128

up the rock. But, she said, they would have to find the rest themselves.

Leaving them then, she returned to her lodge, and the Mexicans began a thorough search for the vein of gold. They, of course, failed to find anything of value, and returned to the hogan where the old woman lived, to make sure she was not holding out on them. She did her best to convince them that she had told them all she knew, but they would not believe her.

They gave her a severe beating, and carried her off with them, to compel her to show them the right place. While they held her captive, they repeatedly beat her, and threatened to kill her if she did not take them to the gold.

Escaping one night, she returned to her lodge, only to find the two Yuma braves who had accompanied her on the trail, had been killed in a fight. She alone remained of the trio who had witnessed the finding of the ore.

But the news had leaked out through the Mexicans that the squaw had found a wonderfully rich gold mine. In order to lure the old woman into a disclosure of the exact location of such great wealth, many persons sought to make her intimate acquaintance. It was through some of these that the rumor had reached the ears of Ed Schieffelin.

This was her story as he understood it.

But although he had succeeded in inducing her to talk, he was never able to persuade her to lead him to the place where she had picked up the ore. And what he apparently never found out was that the old woman probably had not taken special notice of the exact place where she made the find, and could never identify the spot again. She had merely snatched up the stone as she walked along, busy with her thoughts of where the next meal was coming from, and she naturally never expected to be called upon to show the place.

And even if so, as Ed Schieffelin very well knew, the Indians of every tribe have a centuries-old tradition, a stern tribal teaching, that they must never, never lead white men or Mexicans to the pretty yellow stone. Never! The gold belongs to the gods, they say.

129

*John J. Fraser, aged Arizona pioneer, was an old ac-
quaintance of Ed Schieffelin, from whom he had heard this
tale. Fraser told this writer that many people of Schieffelin's
time believed the squaw's little rock was a piece of float
from the gold deposit which was later discovered and developed as the Harquahala bonanza.*

*But if you want to make a stab at finding it, follow the
old trail from Yuma to Wickenburg, skirting the Harquahala Mountains. As you go northward, along the talus of
this small range, look on the right side of the trail for dark
rock in which the gold glistens free and pure in bright sunlight.*

*It is not likely that all the rich values have been dis-
covered in this area, and who knows when and if the gold
in the vein of the Squaw's Lost Mine will come to light and
be carefully laid away at Fort Knox.*

10. Gold in a Rincon Cave.

In the Rincon Moutnains of Arizona, near the Buckhorn
Ranch, about 60 miles from the Mexican border, is a treasure
cave, extending into the mountainside like a mining shaft.
High enough and deep enough to hide a string of horses
and a small herd of cattle, the cave is the hiding place of
considerable gold bullion and gold dust.

Through a misadventure of several Mexican padres,
the treasure was lost 150 years ago and never recovered.
The padres' *conducta*, returning to Mexico, was attacked
by Apaches who were after the horses. The Indians captured
the animals upon which the gold was packed, but events
proved they were to benefit by neither horses nor gold.

A few years ago, two Mexican cowboys, on one of the
most inaccessible ranches northeast of the Rincons, happened upon the cave when rounding up cattle. One of the
cowboys was chasing a large unruly cow with a calf. Suddenly
she seemed to disappear into the mountainside as if vanish-
ing into thin air.

He called to his companion and together they investi-
gated. They found the cow and her calf had simply stepped

behind an outsized manzanita bush into a large cave. Following the animals, they found the floor of the cave covered with the skeletons of horses and cattle, and the skulls and other bones of several human beings, though they could not say whether Indians or white men. The two men knew at once they had found a treasure cache. Leaving everything just as they found it, they reported the cave to their employer.

Mexicans are strongly influenced by an old tradition among them, centuries old, that, when by chance they come upon money or other treasure buried by someone unknown, or by someone they know to be dead, if they attempt to take or to disturb the cache, the treasure will turn to ashes; as they say, to *carbón*.

This tradition has a substantial base. Many a time, a Mexican, digging for some purpose of his own, came unexpectedly upon a mass of ashes or an olla of charred wood. Thereupon he ceased to dig, and went no further in that particular spot.

In those days and those places, there were no banks and no private safes. It became the general custom to bury money, gold, and other valuables to safeguard them from theft. Even when buried, they needed protection. Playing upon Mexican susceptibility to superstition, a mass of ashes or an olla of *carbón* was placed above the cache. Any Mexican then digging down to the valuables would know for a certainty that the treasure of another, not meant for him, had turned at *carbón* at his approach.

Skeletons of men, and sometimes of horses, they believe, bespeak the nearby presence of buried treasure, and they "leave her lay." For the spot is *embrujada*, bewitched, and sure to be haunted by a *chiso*, a phantom.

The Mexican cowboys thought they had found the cave from which a band of Indians had stood off a small group of Spanish padres, after the redmen had stolen their cattle and packhorses loaded with gold.

When the Mexicans told the story of their discovery to the rancher, a number of his men attempted to find the cave, to examine it for signs of the bullion and gold dust. But none of them to this day, has ever been able to find it. All that is assured now is: it is somewhere in the Rincon Mountains on the Buckhorn Ranch.

This is the tradition as handed down to the Sonorans: Sometime between 1780 and 1810, at one of the Mexican missions not far below the present border of Arizona, plans had been made for extending the labors of the padres into the north, in the country of the Apaches who roamed north and northeast of Tumacacori mission, in the mountains along both sides of the San Pedro River.

Three padres, with a number of Christianized Pimas, set forth to explore that region. They took with them a goodly number of horses and cattle and other equipment for stocking a ranchería, should they find a suitable location where the Indians were friendly.

They were gone for some time, but evidently they did not find conditions in the mountains and along the river conducive to a successful settlement. What they did find was plenty of gold ore and placer gold, and they amassed a considerable amount of it for transport to the mother mission in lower Sonora.

They had started upon their return, passing through the Rincons, with the gold packed upon the horses, when they were attacked by a band of Apaches, hereditary enemies of the Pimas. The Apaches had no desire for the gold; they had designs upon the horses and the cattle.

Apparently not discerning that the escort of the padres were Pimas, the Apaches assailed the party and drove off most of the horses and all the cattle. The padres and the Pimas were armed and able to defend their lives, though they could not save their animals because of the suddenness of the attack and the greater swiftness of the Apaches. The sight of their enemies aroused the Pimas to fury, and they gave chase, the padres bravely following.

When the marauders saw their opponents pursuing them with superior weapons, they took refuge in a large cave, driving the horses and cattle to the rear, and defending the stronghold with bows, arrows and rocks. Finally the Mexican party was driven off.

Many of the Apaches were killed, falling in the front of the cave. Some of the animals were within range of the Mexicans' ricocheting fire and dropped where they stood. Some of them, it is likely, escaped, to be picked up by roaming redskins.

The padres and their Pima allies reached their headquarters in the Altar Valley of Sonora, safe though empty-handed, and related these experiences for the record. They knew that the Apaches had no use for gold, and that it would remain where it fell in the cave; but they were never able to return and retrieve it.

Many a Mexican has planned long and talked much of hunting the cave in the Rincons where the padres' gold is lying on the floor, amidst the bones of animals, waiting to be picked up; but it is foreign to the nature of a Mexican to take what the dead have left, unless he has positive assurance that it is meant to be his.

The trip from Benson to the Buckhorn Ranch is an adventure in itself. From the ranch, go by horseback to the foot of the Rincon Mountains. Where the mountains are the steepest, on the ranch side, look for the thickest growth of manzanita, growing closest to the cliff-like rocks. Search in the steep mountainside back of the manzanita trees, where the mouth of the cave could be concealed.

11. What About Waybills to the Lost Dutchman?

Nearly everyone who can read English, especially those who read the Sunday supplement features, is familiar with the story of the Lost Dutchman mine, a deposit of gold in Superstition Mountain, central Arizona; found and lost; found and lost again. Thousands have hunted for this lost treasure, and thousands more intend to do so, as soon as they can get an afternoon off.

Maps to the Lost Dutchman are hard to come by. Men

have been murdered for the maps they were thought to possess. Many have made the search without any map at all. Who can deny it would help the treasure hunter to know what kind of rock the gold is in? The searcher would then know what geologic formation to look for.

It is not difficult to find old-timers in the Salt and Gila Valleys who claim to have samples of ore from Old Dutch Jake's mine. But they are never willing to give a description of it, for they expect to go into the mountain any day now, and find the mine for themselves. Advanced age and diverse physical disabilities have in no way diminished the gleaming hope of wealth and adventure; and these will hold to their last breath.

Public information about the variety of rock the gold was in is meagre indeed, though if one would join the vast number who have had a go at it, this knowledge would be of prime importance.

When Jake paid the shoemaker, Charlie Rodig, with ore for mending his shoes, he paid him with gold in pale yellow quartz. The ore he gave to Julia Thomas to pay the mortgage on her house, was gold in white quartz. He was known also to have had wire gold in black quartz, and nugget gold in pink quartz.

When Jake died, in 1891, some rich pieces of ore were found in a small chest under his bed. These may have come from his bonanza, but there is nothing to confirm this. The ore disappeared the day of the funeral, and no description of it was made known to the palpitating, prospecting public. Reinhardt Petrasch, Jake's closest friend, had seen the ore and he was often questioned. But Reinhardt had hopes of finding the gold deposit himself, and gave his information only to his father and brother, his partners in hunting the lost mine, after Jake's death. Reinhardt died in 1943, after a half century of search.

It is not generally known that upon the few occasions Jake made reference to his bonanza mine, he called it The Quartz Mine, to distinguish it from his placer mine nearby, and from his Number Two mine, in the region of Goldfield.

Some of the old-timers who were personally, though only slightly, acquainted with the secretive old German, believe that the mine he called his Number Two was afterwards filed upon and developed as the Mammoth mine of the Goldfield group, in the foothills of Superstition Mountain.

"The ore was exactly the same as that in the Mammoth," said Curt W. Miller, pioneer editor and publisher, of Tempe.

When the well-known Black Queen mine was discovered at Goldfield, a woman claiming to be co-discoverer, exclaimed:

"I've found 'Uncle Jake's' gold mine!"

This was denied on the ground it was not rich enough to be the Lost Dutchman.

"Why, woman, that won't prove over $10,000 to the ton!" she was told.

"I watched Dutch Jake with a spyglass, once, out in the Superstition foothills," related Steele Pearce, an aged pioneer of Mesa, who has long since passed on, "and I saw him sitting on a red rock with a goldpan in his hands."

The writer of this volume has some extremely rich gold ore from Superstition Mountain which can be accurately described as "red rock," but is confident it is not from the Lost Dutchman; for even though it is heavily charged with gold, it still is not rich enough.

Ore described as brecciated rhyolite, brought to this writer from the vicinity of Weavers Needle, in Superstition Mountain, said to be the landmark for the locale for the lost mine, is charged with having been taken from the famous Vulture mine in Wickenburg, and planted in the canyons of Superstition for promotion and publicity purposes.

In view of the numberless rumors and reports that have been circulated in the West, from Texas to Washington, and from Sonora to Alaska, about this famous lost treasure, it is not strange that among these reports is one that some years ago the Phelps Dodge Corporation took appropriate action to prove whether the Lost Dutchman was fact or fiction: this mining company sent a party of prospectors and geologists into the Superstitions to report on the possibility there of such a vein as the Lost Dutchman is said to be. The report made by this party to the corporation has never been made public.

Lest one be tempted to believe, considering the variance in the ore which Dutch Jake had, that there is no Lost Dutchman mine, and never was, one should give heed to the manner by which he came into possession of the differing specimens of ore. By his own admission, he never went near his rich Quartz mine after 1877, fourteen years before he died. Why did he stay so long away, and where did he get the ore he commonly used for money?

He was then too old to go alone into the rugged mountain so far from his home. He feared to take any companions, lest he be double-crossed and euchered out of his possession. He was in deadly fear of Apaches and white outlaws. He had no need for great wealth because of the extreme simplicity of his life, and his ambition was rapidly fading away.

The conditions which surrounded him in pioneer Phoenix were often so distasteful to him that to get away, he went alone into the foothills, and when upon these trips he sometimes found small veins and pockets of gold, which he took home and used as money, making unnecessary the more difficult trips to his richer mine.

The variations in the rock naturally gave rise to many questions as to the nature of the ore of his secret deposit of richest gold, and as naturally diverted the questions from the truth. When the bonanza is found, if ever, it will be virgin gold in white quartz, a vast vein concealed in a narrow canyon with steep sides, and nowhere near Weavers Needle. Don't be misled by the other varieties of rock.

11

Lost Gold in Texas

A MONG MODERN YOUTH whose favorite sport is hunting lost treasure, it has become the custom to do considerable historical research to authenticate the original adventure and to look for clues to the right personalities and locations. Believe me, this has become stereotyped procedure. For it has happened many times that these factual tales, when told around campfires and in bar-rooms, have been bent far from the facts, and if accepted in this inaccurate form, would be useless for charting a route for a search.

Therefore for those who would like to hunt for the Sublett lost gold, one of the many traditional treasures of Texas, making the point of departure in some one of the many small cities near the Pecos, I here set forth some facts to render it difficult to confuse the historic Sublettes of Wyoming with the Subletts of Texas, an error which in recent years took a careless but earnest adventurer very far afield.

The story of Sublett and his lost gold is one of the favorites in West Texas, and I am permitted to include this account by courtesy of the editor of *Ghost Town News,* now out of print, for whom I had first written it. The Wyoming angle will, I think, open up your eyes to the certainty that all our states have tremendous hidden values, only awaiting the enterprise of those who dare, and you will be assured that those who say we have reached our last frontiers are talking in their sleep.

So before we start on our quest in Texas, let us do the honors to Wyoming:

In the 1820's, the five Sublette brothers in Wyoming were fur trappers with the Rocky Mountain Fur Company, in which William Sublette (spelled with a final e) was a partner. In later years, this company was taken over by Milton Sublette with Jim Bridger, of celebrated memory, and others. Sublette County in Wyoming was named for these brothers and Pinckney Sublette is buried there.

It is not likely that the Sublette boys ever knew that in 1830 a new metal was discovered, eventually to be known as vanadium, and destined to be of vast future importance to the world. No one could then have imagined that in Sublette County there were huge deposits of this potential wealth. The timely discovery of this new field of vanadium in Sublette Ridge, as announced by the United States Geological Survey, in February, 1943, will make this country independent of foreign vanadium and be of great value to our national defense.

Many times since the turn of the century a search for traditional lost treasures has led to the accidental discovery of new and unsuspected mineral deposits, such as the vanadium in the Sublette Ridge. It could easily happen in a renewed search for the lost gold mine of "Old Ben" Sublett (no final e) in West Texas.

1. Sublett's Lost Gold.

Old Ben, nickname of William Colum Sublett, was apparently no relation to the Sublette brothers of Wyoming. Starting from Missouri to go gold hunting in the West, he landed in West Texas, making temporary home at various points along the route now known to the world as the Broadway of America. He was accompanied by his wife and child-

138

ren. Along this route he engaged in prospecting in the near-by mountains, and had he been a trained metallurgist, and had such scientific aids as are available today, this would no doubt have proved a highly profitable scheme. Sublett, however, limited by the era in which he lived, missed out on finding anything worthwhile.

His wife, not able to withstand the continuing hardships, died, leaving several small children to his care. He settled the children in Odessa, Texas, among kindhearted neighbors, while he put into execution a plan for hunting a gold deposit he said a White Mountain Apache had told him was in the Guadalupe Mountains, a considerable distance to the west.

After some years of hardship, ridicule, and snubbing, Sublett did find a source of pure gold. He appeared in Odessa with large nuggets purer than the gold coin of any earthly realm. Whereupon he gave up all semblance of labor, developed a suspicion of all his old friends, and imagined any new arrival in Odessa had come to find out the location of his gold mine and filch it from him.

He apparently had no idea how to develop his mineral wealth without partners, and he was afraid to trust anyone with his secret. Consequently he was unable, or perhaps unwilling to use his fortune to alleviate his humble condition or to give his children the comforts and luxuries to which they were entitled. At intervals, he would disappear from the town, and after a brief absence, would return with a large amount of virgin gold, much of which he spent splurging in saloons.

Expecting that he would be spied upon, followed, tricked, and trailed, he was equal to the cleverest pursuit, and evaded every ruse to uncover his secret.

When Ben's son, Ross, was only nine years old, Ben took him to his secret gold mine and showed it to him. Old Ben believed the boy was too young and his powers of observation too undeveloped to enable him to divulge the secret of the mine's location. He was right.

After his father's death, in 1892, at the age of 80, Ross at-

139

tempted, times without number, to spur his memory to recall the route taken when he accompanied his father to the
mine. He never could remember the exact direction, distances, and landmarks, but often described his recollection
of certain scenes connected with the mine as pictured in his
childish mind.

Sublett is said to have broken down on several occasions,
when badgered beyond his endurance, and to have consented
to take a companion to the mine. But always something in-
tervened to make it impossible for the other to go. It was
useless, Sublett said, to try to point it out from afar.

Tradition tells that one man did get to Sublett's mine
and brought out a sack of ore; but the trip was devious, the
labor arduous, and the whiskey he took for a pick-me-up
when he returned to town drove out of his mind all recollection of the distances and landmarks along the way into
the mountain.

Sublett and his secret gold became well-known across the
nation. Much in legend and tradition has grown up around
his name, a fact that, in itself, points to a base of authenticity
for at least some of the superstructure. Many men knew Old
Ben personally and had seen the large nuggets of pure gold
which he used for money; they were not depending upon
hearsay for their assurance of his hidden mine. But thanks to
his suspicious mind, they had little to guide them when they
set out to locate the secret place.

For half a century, prospectors have hunted over half of
Texas for Sublett's gold, sometimes getting far afield — even
as far as Wyoming. But the treasure has always stubbornly
eluded them.

There is plenty of testimony that the Guadalupe Mountains are richly endowed with valuable minerals. In this volume mention is made of treasure found and lost there. The
Mescalero Apaches, on their reservation north of the Guadalupes, admit the presence of precious metals in those
mountains, but because of their centuries-old tradition of
trouble between white men and red, occasioned by greed for

140

gold and silver, they do no mining in the mountains and discourage all others from doing so.

An ancient document, alleged to have come into the hands of General Lew Wallace, when governor of New Mexico, gave an account of Spaniards mining gold in the Guadalupes prior to 1680. There is no reason to believe Sublett's lost gold is a myth. And there may be other minerals in those mountainsides, elements not known in former times, useful in modern warfare, that would rival the vanadium in the Sublette Ridge in Wyoming.

In the southern end of the Guadalupes, on the east side, is a canyon like a chasm, sheer on both sides, accessible only by a rope. It varies in width from 50 to 100 feet, and is perhaps 75 feet deep. In the wall, near the floor of the canyon, is a shaft, like a cave. In the cave, according to the recollection of Ross Sublett, is the deposit of gold.

2.   Silver in the Shaft.

A fourteen-year-old Mexican boy, in 1825, was permitted to engage in an adventure that would delight the heart of any modern Boy Scout, little dreaming that it would involve him in a mystery which for more than a century would remain unsolved. Anticipating only the pleasure of setting out upon a romantic trip, the little Mexican could not foresee the tragic end and the intensive search that was to follow.

The boy, Pedro Gomez, was allowed to join a company of Mexican men and women who were about to make an exploring expedition into the strange, wild, unsettled country north of the Rio Grande, where the group expected to settle if they found either mining prospects or good agricultural land.

A scout from Boston may roam over this region today and find it strange to him because of the idle oil derricks here, but he will not find it wild or unsettled. It is now Caldwell County, a part of the rich empire of Texas and it may yet become of industrial consequence in our national commerce. In 1825, however, it was infested by hostile Indians.

The exploring party discovered a deposit of medium grade petanque, a compound of silver and copper known to Americans in pioneer days as silver glance. They immediately set about mining the glance, and built a smelter-furnace and reducing pot of native stone, working with such prideful care that their handiwork, though now crumbling and weather-stained, is still recognized as an exemplary piece of masonry. Near the smelter is the old glance vein, still showing a trace of copper.

After working the glance for a few weeks, the mining party found a vein of high-grade silver on top of a nearby hill, and they promptly began to work the richer vein. When they had smelted and molded forty-three bars of silver, they were assailed by a large force of Comanches.

Looking out from the hillside on the surrounding plain, the Mexicans saw the band of hostiles approaching in the distance. Realizing a stiff battle was imminent and that they were greatly outnumbered, the miners hastily hid the silver bars in the shaft near the hilltop.

Like a whirlwind the redskins came and went, leaving all the Mexican party dead, with the single exception of Pedro, who had saved himself by lying close to the ground in the shadow of some boulders. He got safely away.

Through the years of changing sovereignty and uncertain boundary lines which followed, he remained in Texas, where he grew to manhood, married, and had a family, always too absorbed in immediate problems to pursue a search for the silver bars.

In the summer of 1875, tragedy overtook Pedro, then an old man. His youngest son was struck down by an assassin. The murder of the boy nearly prostrated the father, who burned with desire for revenge. When he learned that the murderer had escaped across the Rio Grande, into Old Mexico and out of reach of the Texas Rangers, his grief and desperation knew no bounds.

One day, Pedro approached A. S. Lowry, of the Rangers, then living in Caldwell County, and told him he would make him a present of a large fortune in silver if he would capture the murderer of Pedro's son. Lowry thought the offer was merely idle talk from a father overwhelmed by sorrow for the loss of a beloved child. The Ranger promised to do what he could to get the felon back into Texas where he could be taken.

Shortly afterward, the murderer was enticed across the river to join in a celebration of Mexican Independence Day, September 16, observed in Texas as well as Mexico. When full of *aguardiente* and off his guard, he was captured.

Having seen the murderer tried, convicted and stowed away for a life term in the penitentiary, Pedro again visited Lowry to make the promised pay-off. He told Lowry the story of the silver bars and presented him with a map marked with an X to show the spot where the silver is hidden in the hill.

Of course, Lowry hunted for the silver. He told others and they have hunted. When his nephew, Harvey L. King, grew to manhood, the Ranger promised him a half-interest in the cache if he would help find it. The search has been going on since 1875, but the silver is still where the exploring party placed it, under the observing eye of 14-year-old **Pedro.**

Deep in the sandhill region of southeast Caldwell County, Texas, is the hill having the shaft near the top, with the cache of silver bars. Caldwell County is northeast of San Antonio, with Lockhart the county seat. So many men have searched for the silver, and so many tales have been told of it, almost every man in Lockhart, especially the old-timers, know where the old shaft and smelter-furnace are situated. Harvey L. King, Caldwell County rancher, inherited the map Pedro gave to his uncle, A. S. Lowry. The map is private property. But one can work without the map. Find the old crumbling smelter, and with that as a point of departure, locate the small hill nearby. Near the top is the shaft with the cache of 43 silver bars.

3. The Indian Curse on $20,000,000.

Gold bullion worth $20,000,000 buried on private property can cause more trouble than the tax collector. And old man Trouble surely reared his ugly head, a few years ago, when it was noised around in Central Texas that this immense amount of values in gold was buried somewhere in Bell County on privately owned land.

It all started away back, as do most buried treasures in America. More than a hundred years ago, according to a tradition of the Texas Indians, their forebears were taking free gold from an exceedingly rich mine and amassing it for exchange with the pioneer Spaniards. When they had accumulated enough to be worth $20,000,000 by white men's standards, trouble with the Spaniards and other white men arose, which caused them to wish they had never taken the gold from the ground. Activities on the warpath were indicated.

They placed the great mass of bullion back in the mine shaft and covered it, sealing it securely, in Indian fashion. Through all the years that passed, they never disturbed the treasure, and their lips were mute. Their descendants, however, knew of its whereabouts, its value, and its importance to white men.

The present century was young when an Indian, in a moment of weakness, disclosed the old secret to a white man for a sizable supply of firewater. The white man — fool that he was — let the news leak out. Then trouble started. Many prospectors, amateur and professional, began a search for the gold-filled shaft, which continued throughout a quarter of a century.

At last a group of Texans believed they had located it, in Bell County, near the town of Belton. But alas! the location was on privately owned land.

Usually it is fatal to attempt to grab treasure to the tune of $20,000,000 from under a man's nose on his own property. But peaceful means were devised, and in 1928 a stock com-

144

pany was formed to explore the property, under an arrangement with the owner.

In the hill country, "on a rugged plateau," 18 miles southwest of Belton, county seat of Bell County, where the remains of an old mining shaft were discovered, digging was started, and a mining camp was set up. Digging stopped intermittently, resuming at unexpected irregular intervals. Each time it stopped, rumors circulated that the gold had been found; each time it resumed, the former rumors were denied. There were those, of course, who knew the truth of the matter, but the facts were kept secret from the public to discourage the curious. Thus the venture dragged on for ten years.

Then in 1938 all work at the mine was halted by court order. At that time five persons were on the property, three of them as guards at the mine. On October 14, a call was sent in to Sheriff Bigham, who responded immediately with his deputy, Ralph Jeffers. At the camp they found young W. F. Moore, a guard, had been shot and killed the previous night.

The four others were questioned, and they told the sheriff they were seated in the cook tent when suddenly Moore stumbled out of his tent with a pistol in his hand, and advanced about 40 yards from his tent before he collapsed, dead, shot through the heart.

This is not intended to be a murder mystery story. The county records of Bell County give all the facts of the killing, and a rapidly growing local legend gives more. But the $20,-000,000 in gold bullion has never been recovered.

In this case, our advice is: Leave 'er lay. The Indian sign is on this gold and the time is not ripe for the taking. Find it and you will be paying for atom bombs.

But lest you be disappointed, I am at liberty to tell you it is known there are more than one hundred other Spanish mine locations, in this same county, each with its own legend and store of lost treasure.

4.   Buried Loot Near Weatherford

During the years of the great depression — the 1930's — the boys in the Civilian Conservation Corps did not expect treasure hunting to be a part of the routine program of their service. The boys in Corps No. 877, however, were luckier than many others, for they found an engaging lost treasure mystery right at their door.

Corps No. 877 was located on the outskirts of Weatherford, Texas, an ideal situation in more ways than one. The camp had not been established long when the boys became familiar with the local tradition of the buried treasure, and were eager to search for it. They had learned of it from the old-timers around Weatherford. The boys explored the terrain surrounding their camp and nearby areas, and found old diggings and other evidence that previous searches had been made for the treasure, over a considerable period of time. They proceeded on the theory that the legend was factual and not merely an old windbag's tale.

The story dates from 1840, a time when Texas was but sparsely settled, and the ranchers were continuously fighting to protect themselves not only from hostile Indians but also from marauding Mexican outlaws. In that year, a band of raiders repeatedly attacked the colonists for miles around Fort Worth, making themselves especially pestiferous in the vicinity of Weatherford. Naturally, they were hounded down by the Texans. .

The leader of the band escaped, and not to be hampered in his getaway, he buried his loot, said to be largely nuggets and gold bars, in the outskirts of Weatherford. He found refuge with a Mexican family living not far away. While he was in seclusion, he drew a contour map of the place where he had cached away his valuables, and true to form, marked the spot with an X.

Before he could recover his treasure, he became sick, and as he thought he was going to die, he gave the map to his host in payment for his keep. After the bandit was buried, the new owner of the map studied it and prepared to go after the loot, but before he could act on his plan, he was picked off by a stray bullet in a gun fight, and the map fell into the hands of his wife.

The widow neither knew nor cared what it was all about, and she gave the map to a Mr. Curtis, who spent the next twenty years searching for the buried gold. Now, note the details very carefully, for it is by errors that proper lines for future action may be deduced.

The treasure area, as it appears today, is made up of eight shafts, varying from 25 to 75 feet deep. From the bottom of these shafts tunnels have been dug in all directions, large enough for a man to walk in — a prodigious amount of work, for they total at least 300 linear feet. There is nothing to indicate that any gold or other loot was ever buried there. Some say Curtis found gold and removed it; others say nothing ever was found.

When everything is considered, it is most likely nothing was found, and the outlaw's gold is still where he placed it.

Anyone who has lived some years in Weatherford can point out the location of the old CCC camp, and many can give specific directions for the old Curtis diggings. When you have found the diggings, imagine yourself in the skin of the outlaw, and consider what your course would be. Imagine the law is on your trail and you must get away with all speed. You must get rid of your loot for it hampers you. You bury it quickly in the dead of night. Do you have implements and time to dig deep? Would you want to throw up a lot of fresh soil, a sign that recent digging had been done? No; you would have to risk preparing quickly a fairly shallow hole, place your stuff in it, hurriedly scrape some soil over it, perhaps add a rock or two, and be on your way. If in sand, the wind would soon blow the topsoil about, so the ground would look stale. But certainly there would be no 20 or 30 feet deep digging.

Mr. Curtis undoubtedly made an error by digging too deep, unless he had some information which does not appear in the long current version of the legend. Some day some smart young man with a modern mineral locator — say an army "mine" finder — will find the gold much nearer the surface.

12

Treasure Strategy of the Big Chiefs

IN PIONEER DAYS the Indians had little concern about
money. Yet they were the key to much of the material
of which money is made. They were not often willing to give
precious metals to white men, except upon such occasions as
when pressed by extreme hunger and there remained no
alternative but to buy food from a white man's store. Or
when the desire for fire water overcame discretion. At such
times, virgin gold and silver were money, without mintage.
And if they never had a minted, dated dollar, it was no cause
for repining.

It will be seen from the following tales that the "heap-
big-chiefs" held gold and money in contempt. Well, well,
you say — Yes, I know what you are going to say, but let
that pass. Hunting the chiefs' gold or other treasure may
be a happy device for getting away from it all. For though
the big chiefs are gone, the sources of the Indian gold are
still elements of challenging mystery.

LOST MINES and HIDDEN TREASURE

1. The Lost Gold of Pia Machita's Tribe.

How often it happens that an age-old tradition or legend seems entirely forgotten, or dead, and then something occurs which brings it suddenly to life!

When World War II was in its infancy and Father Roosevelt was calling all young men to his colors, old Pia Machita, chief of the Papago Indians, and long past 80 years old, was arrested by United States Marshal Ben J. McKinney, and committed to prison in Tucson, Arizona, for assaulting and resisting an officer.

Then along with Pia Machita, came out of obscurity a revival of the history of the treasures of his tribe, forgotten through many years — the story of the lost gold at the red mesa, and the most recent search for it by a modern Papago, shortly before gold became political contraband.

But before we proceed to the red table mountain, let us first consider Pia Machita, patriarch of his people, who have lived peacefully for centuries in their homes along the border and have no wish to be disturbed too much by white men and their ways.

When the Great White Father in Washington undertook a war in Europe, Chief Pia could not see that it in any way concerned the young men of his tribe. When the long arm of the white man's law reached into the Papago reservation to take them for the white man's army, old Pia counselled them not to go. For inspiring them to resist the draft, he was charged with an offense against the government.

United States officers attempted to arrest him, taking him from his bed, in the middle of the night. He resisted, with assault, even as you and I, in his place, might conceivably have done. Before he could say knife, he was in the Tucson jail. Tried, convicted, and sentenced, he was, at the time of my inquiry of him, February 11, 1942, still in prison, cheerful, and enjoying excellent health, though not disposed to a loquacious interview.

Old Pia Machita is full of secrets; secrets of buried gold, of carefully concealed mines, of the old Papago gods, of Montezuma, and of tribal history of long ago. But what he

150

desires most, and values most on earth is peace among men. White men will fight for gold, so all knowledge of it must be kept from them; and never a word will he speak to disclose the whereabouts of precious metal. It was a kinsman of old Pia who figures in the following story:

Many years ago when white men were beginning to settle in southern Arizona, an old Papago had a secret gold mine in a little valley east of Ajo, long before Ajo became a town. With his characteristic Indian indifference to gold and silver, he went to this mine only on the rare occasions when he was forced to get something he could use for money to buy food at a white man's store.

Into a small leather bag, he would put a few mesquite bean cakes, and with this supply of food under his arm, he would set out, in a sort of dog trot, eastward, to his secret mine. When taking out the ore, he broke it up as fine as he could, ground it on a metate, so the small leather bag which had held his food was large enough for the amount of pure gold he took away with him to pay for the corn and beans at the store.

So thorough was he in separating the gold from the dross, the merchant never had a chance to see the kind of rock the gold had been embedded in.

Just before the old Papago died, knowing that in the future as in the past, there would be times when water for the crops would fail, he told the secret of his mine to his grandson.

"The mouth of the mine," he said, "is covered with a large flat stone."

The young Papago did not regard this legacy as of much importance, and for several years he made no attempt to find his grandfather's treasure. But the time came, as his grandfather had foreseen, when the rains failed, and the Papago crops died for lack of water. Many Papagoes died, too, for the squash, melons, and beans which they could water from the greatly diminished springs were insufficient to give them strength to hunt for game. The animals had left the Papago range for greener fields, and the hunting trips took the Indians too far from home.

The grandson was hard pressed for food, along with all the others of his tribe. Then one day he remembered his grandfather's secret gold mine as a means of buying food from the white men. Though weak and thin, he followed the instructions bequeathed to him, and went several times to hunt the mine. He never could find it.

When the rains came at last, as they always do, and the Papagoes had food once more, he resolved to find the mine and so be prepared when the lean years came again, as he knew they surely would.

A mining engineer at Ajo had been a close friend to a Papago medicine man, and to this engineer the young tribesman went for help in locating the deposit of gold. Hunting a lost vein was duck soup for this mining man and he readily agreed. Accompanied by an aged relative of the grandson, thus making a party of three, they set out to traverse the distance of 75 miles eastward across the Ajo Valley.

Then they followed an old tribal trail, up the first mountain ridge to a waterhole near the top. From there the trail led on over the top and down on the other side into a valley. In the middle of this valley is a flat-topped red mountain with an ancient Papago burial ground at its foot; for this valley was once the largest summer ranchería of the tribe, who were long noted for a plentiful supply of gold. Near this red mountain the search for the mine was made.

On the west side of the table mountain a large gold-bearing rock was found, weighing more than 25 pounds and containing several hundred dollars' worth of gold. But the mine itself was not found, nor did they learn where the large rock — known in miners' lingo as "float" — had come from.

The young Indian, however, said the information he had received from his grandfather convinced him the mine was somewhere near the base of the red flat-topped mountain, in the midst of the valley below the ridge east of Ajo.

In the Papago Indian Reservation, east of the famous copper town, Ajo, southern Arizona, close to the western edge of the Santa Rosa Mountains, at the northern end of the Santa Rosa Valley, will be found the flat-topped red mountain where the old Papago's lost secret mine is said to be.

"Table mountains," high and rocky, with flat surfaces and steep sides, such as the flat-topped one in Pia Machita's ancient rancheria are frequently the remains of lava floods from which the soil by which they were surrounded has been washed away, leaving the basalt towering above the adjacent country. These table mountains have often been found to have areas in them of gold-bearing sand and gravel.

2.   Cochise Steals the Strongboxes.

Cochise, chief of the Chiricahua Apaches, was nobody's fool. He was quick to learn; just as quick to learn from a crook as from an honest man. He was especially apt at acquiring all the tricks of the trade of the white outlaws.

In the course of his contact with the white race, Cochise learned that, in attacking the stages for the purpose of taking the horses and killing the passengers, it was also a part of the regular procedure to steal the money and the strongboxes of the Wells, Fargo Express Company. Why the Indians should steal the bullion, cash, and money chests, no one can say, for they did not need money nor understand the value of it. And certainly bullion was no treasure to them.

An occasion arose in the late 'sixties, which gave Cochise and his friend, Chief Mangas Colorado (Red Sleeves) an opportunity to rob the Butterfield stage and steal two of the express company's strongboxes filled with money and gold.

As the stage rolled along toward Dragoon Pass, Cochise and Red Sleeves, with a party of their tribesmen, bore down upon the stage. The ruckus they raised, whooping, yelling, and cavorting, frightened the stage horses; and, by throwing fear and confusion into the passengers and guards, created the right frame of mind for the white brethern to act as if bereft of good sense. Before they could recover their civilized wits, the Indians were far on their way toward their hideout in the Dragoon Mountains.

153

Some of the whites were dead, the guards scared stiff, and the strongboxes gone.

How the Indians transported the two heavy chests into the almost inaccessible recesses of the Dragoons is a mystery; if, indeed, they did so. It is known to the Apaches of today, however, that the two chiefs took the chests to a rendezvous in a chosen spot where one can go only on foot or with a burro; and that they buried the plunder, covering it securely, with no idea of ever retrieving it.

As it was stolen purely for spite, and was of no use to them, they never touched it again. Their tribesmen today believe they buried it in a canyon contiguous to Cochise's cave. Some think it was buried within the cave.

Get yourself a map of the Coronado National Forest, 1927. Note Township 17 S., R. 23 E. Find Stronghold Canyon on the eastern side of the Dragoon Mountains. This canyon is so named because Cochise used it as a hiding place, and he is buried in a secret place at the canyon's mouth. At the upper end of the canyon is an auto park and public camp ground, named by the U. S. Forest Service, "Cochise Memorial Park."

Many persons think it is not possible to find Cochise's cave, but it is not so difficult as all that. In 1940, John D. Mitchell, noted treasure hunter and author, told this writer that he had recently found the cave and entered it, taking special note that the cave had a floor of soft dirt. The cave is twelve miles southeast of the town of Dragoon, he said, in Dragoon Pass, Cochise County, Arizona, in the Dragoon Mountains, not accessible to an automobile.

3.   The Gold Trap of Chief Red Sleeves.

Mangas Colorado, which when translated into English, is Red Sleeves, was known in select Apache circles as a trusted pal of Cochise and Geronimo. He was frantic with irritation and annoyance when white miners moved in and began operations in the Santa Rita Mountains in New Mexico, his favorite stamping ground.

Of the two hundred Americans there engaged in the gold and copper mines, in 1861, one hundred fifty were hard-boiled, experienced, fearless Indian fighters, with no compunction in shooting a hostile at sight, and to them all Indians were hostiles. Many of the miners were sharp-shooters, having had long service in the United States Army, some being veterans of the Mexican War.

Mangas Colorado itched to get every white man out of his country, but they were too many for his forces to kill, and too smart to be overcome by Indian strategy. It would take a long time to kill them one by one, but there seemed no other way. In the course of nature, he could not expect to live long enough to see it accomplished. Nevertheless he apparently spent much time figuring upon how it could be done.

It dawned upon old Mangas one day that the white man's besetting sin was greed for gold, combined with a dislike for hard work. Mangas had several gold mines in the Guadalupe Mountains, lying near the boundary between New Mexico and Texas, and he had no use for the gold at this time, though he later learned to trade it to the American soldiers for commodities not common in Indian economy.

Playing on the white man's greed, he reasoned if he could take their leaders into the mountains, one by one, on a pretext of showing them where they could get more gold with less work, he could dispose of them, one at a time, leaving the others to guess what had become of them.

Selecting the more important men in the camp, according to Capt. John C. Cremony, who is quoted here, Mangas approached each one privately, Cremony being one, and said:

"You good man. You stay here long time and never hurt Apache. You want the yellow iron. I know where planty is. You go with me, I show you; but tell no one else. Mangas your friend, he want to do you good. You like yellow iron? Good! Me no want yellow iron. Him no good for me; can no eat; can no drink; can no keepee out cold. Come! I show you!"

155

But alas for Mangas and his secret schemes! The miners compared notes, discovered the old rascal's duplicity, and concluded it was a trap to kill them at retail, and they refused to fall into it.

Later when he tried the same trick with American soldiers in the forts in Arizona and New Mexico, they, too, saw through the scheme and gave him the "brush-off."

Mangas never told the white men where his gold mine was, but it was observed that when he came into Fort Sumner (the old Fort Sumner) to trade his large nuggets of gold to the soldiers, he came straight from the Guadalupe Mountains, where Geronimo also had a secret mine, and where John Cremony found incredible deposits of native silver.

The preceding paragraph gives the clue. The treasure hunter can trace the location of the gold trap of old Chief Red Sleeves by drawing a bee line from old Fort Summer, New Mexico, to the northwest slope of the Guadalupe Mountains. The treasure is a vein of gold so pure it is almost like bullion.

4. Where Is Geronimo's Lost Gold Mine?

"I am planning to spend my vacation in the hills," a young man writes, "and a friend who is going with me thinks it would be interesting for us to hunt for Geronimo's lost gold mine. Are there any clues to point out where we should look for it?"

There is plenty of proof that Geronimo knew a source of gold, for he sometimes used it as a medium of exchange. He much preferred, however, to take by trickery or by right of conquest, when not able to cajole or prevail by chicane. The fact is established, by the numerous occasions when he gave gold ore in exchange for something he desired, that he knew gold and its uses, and had access to a supply of it.

There are several "clues," and up to this time none of them has been followed to its ultimate conclusion. Many who have hunted for the Dr. Thorne mine believe it was the mine Geronimo so often promised in return for his free-

156

dom, when he was a captive, or for some other favor.

Dr. Thorne, who had been taken to the mine blind-folded, and brought away in the same manner, so that he never really knew its location, said he believed it lay in a deep canyon somewhere within a triangle whose three points were Red Mountain, (at Granite Reef), Four Peaks, and Weaver's Needle. Such a triangle can best be discerned, in these days, from the Harvey Bush Memorial Highway, beyond Stewart Mountain Dam.

Others hold the opinion that Geronimo's gold mine lies along the Verde River, not far from where will be found deposits of copper. Considerable evidence, dating from old Fort McDowell days, sustains this theory. Others think the old chief had access to a vein of gold in the proscribed inner reaches of Superstition Mountain, where other Indian tribes were traditionally afraid to go.

Geronimo and his small group of Apache lieutenants were widely traveled, always on the warpath, and when on their forays into western Texas, they found, so it is said, deposits of gold in the Guadalupe Mountains, described by Geronimo himself as the richest gold mines in the country.

The story persists, though it would be difficult to prove, that Geronimo made a deal with a United States Army officer in which he was to disclose the location of his gold mine in return for his freedom, when he was imprisoned at Fort Sill by the federal government, deprived of nothing but his liberty. As the chief was to show the mine, and not merely to tell where it is, there was no action. For though allowed to travel and to visit various fairs and expositions while a prisoner, Geronimo was never permitted to go on prospecting trips, and died in prison.

Some of his kinfolk still live in the wild Sierra Madre, that rugged mountain range which lies along the boundary line between Chihuahua and Sonora, known to be the locale of gold deposits surpassing in richness the ancient mines of Nayarit. When hard pressed by American troops, under Lieutenant Britton Davis, in 1885, Geronimo took refuge with his people in these mountains, inaccessible as the nests of eagles. Here any amount of gold would have been at his command.

Geronimo's descendants live today on the Mescalero Apache Indian reservation, in New Mexico, within sight of the Guadalupe Peaks, and only a few hours' ride from them. Two of his sons, educated and holding positions of influence and power in their tribe, certainly know how gold can be used to arrive at any desired goal. Who can guess whether they know the secrets of their tight-lipped, self-willed old father as to the gold of Guadalupe and the Verde River Valley? But if they know the whereabouts of the precious rock, they do not avail themselves of that knowledge.

In the first months of 1938, two Mescalero Apaches accompanied Dr. Helge Ingstadt, Norwegian explorer, on a visit to the Apache tribe in the Sierra Madre of Sonora, separated from contact with the outside world for generations, their primitive ways uncontaminated by current "progress." Dr. Ingstadt's purpose in visiting this isolated tribe was to study their language for comparison with the language of the Indians in the Arctic regions.

Into the country of the famous Lost Tayopa treasure he almost penetrated, seeing a few Indian women, indistinguishable as to tribe; and then his two Mescalero Apache guides gently but firmly steered him again into civilization. Who can say it was not by design that the net result of the expedition into Geronimo's gold country included neither language nor treasure?

Gold has a way of falling into the hands of those who cannot use it. In the region around Winkelman, land was once assigned to Geronimo for his reservation, though rumor says he scorned it. The area is mineralized, and it is a fair speculation that more of the old chief's gold lies there. It is in the same general locale as the famous lost gold deposit known in Arizona tradition as "Yuma's Lost Gold," fully told in this volume under the title, "Squawman's Fateful Gold." One hunting Geronimo's gold here has a double chance of finding a lost lode.

TREASURE STRATEGY OF THE BIG CHIEFS

Look first in the canyons of the Verde River. Look also in the beautiful Aravaipa region immediately south and east of Winkelman. Look for free gold in white quartz, and in pink quartz, near a spring.

13

Lost Treasure in Colorado

COLORADO surpasses many another state not only in magnificent scenery but also in mineral wealth. It is inevitable that in addition to the many rich discoveries of precious metal that have occurred there, adding immeasurably to the wealth of the nation, there have been other worthwhile finds, kept secret, for a multiplicity of reasons, and knowledge of their location lost before they could be put on a profitable basis.

Colorado, therefore, has its share of tales of lost treasures, including perhaps the most horrendous of all known to America — the story of the leader of a gold-hunting party in the mountains of southwestern Colorado, who, before the treasure was found, turned cannibal and ate up all the registered Democrats in Hinsdale County.

No; I'm not going to tell that one in an election year, but I am going to relate three that are more pleasant, which, while they might tempt you to make a lawful hunting expedition, will not lead you into anything wrong. But, of course, it won't hurt you to know that in the place in the

160

San Juan Mountains, towards which the cannibal and his trustful party were headed, an important discovery of uranium was made in 1951, announced, apparently with glee, by the United States Department of the Interior.

1. Gold Mystery on The Mountaintop.

Everybody in southern Colorado, through five generations, has heard of the rich lost gold mine high in the nearby mountains. The tellers of tall tales say that Spaniards came up from Mexico, a few years after the American Revolutionary War, and discovered, in a rugged mountain peak, somewhere near what is now the state's southern border, an immensely rich deposit of gold. It was, they say, west of Trinidad.

The Spaniards began preparations for mining, timbering a shaft, making melting ovens and a cleaning trough, so the story goes. They had little more than started taking out ore, when something, never explained, occurred to call them away. They ordered their peons and Indian slaves to cover the mouth of the shaft and remove all evidence of their labor. Then destroying their trail down the mountainside, the Spaniards and their train of horses, mules, and servants left that region forever.

There is no question that the mountains and mesas of Colorado are teeming with gold, but of the hundreds who have heard this legend, many have not believed it, thinking it wouldn't hold water. According to tradition, the Spaniards discovered the gold by accident, under conditions in which they were not equipped to undertake extensive and long-continued mining operations.

Why, ask the scoffers, would a train of Spaniards be high on the mountainside? If they had any sense, they'd go round the mountain rather than over it. And, anyway, would smart men, as the pioneer Spaniards certainly were, lug a lot of stuff up a mountain for no definite purpose? If they found the gold by accident, then mining was not the purpose. What, then, was their purpose? Even if they knew positively there

161

was gold up there, how were they to get it down for transportation to a seaport? There were plenty of other difficulties, too, in those far-off days, the scoffers say. No, no; the treasure was only a myth!

But on the other hand, many were ready to believe that a vast amount of precious ore was lying, lost, up there in the heights. And faith made it as certain as a mathematical fact. Naturally, every man of them hoped fate would give him the time and opportunity to reconnoiter and spy out the long forgotten locale of the coveted gold.

Hundreds of men, singly and by twos, have sneaked off on a brief respite from their everyday vocations, and have gone up into the mountains, seeking, seeking . . . Others by scores have gone well organized, with carefully selected pals, and have used as much prospecting science as they could muster. But never, never, solitary or in company, did any one of them return with incontrovertible evidence that he had at last found the old lost Spanish diggings, which certainly are as rich today as the day of the initial discovery by adventurers from far distant Iberia.

Among the many whose faith in the legendary mine established the treasure as fact in his burning imagination was Manuel Torres. Manuel was convinced that the lost lode was in Culebra Peak, an elevation in Costilla County. He went many times up the sides of the peak looking everywhere the earth showed the slightest sign of mineralization. He believed that, finally, if he kept on looking, he would, by the process of elimination, find the Spanish gold.

One day in 1939, when taking a vacation from his job as an employe of the city of Trinidad, Torres went again into the mountain pursuing his favorite project: looking for the elusive lost gold. He kept on ascending by a circuitous route, up Culebra Peak, until he was a mile above timberline. There on the north side, he discovered the mouth of a mine.

Noting a huge rotting timber in among a mass of rocks, he knew at once that the wood had been transported up the mountainside from some remote place, and laid there for some special reason. Why? When? And by whom? These questions did not seem important at the moment.

He began to dig away the rocks to see what lay at the other end of the timber. As he kept on digging, water burst through among the rocks. Following through to where the outburst began, he found a mine drift which extended about 300 feet into the crown of Culebra Peak. Torres was convinced that at last he had found the long lost Spanish mine!

Investigating further upon the surface he found a rock dump, rather far from the mine mouth. At about three miles from the mouth of the shaft, he found some smelting masonry and cleaning troughs.

Shortly after his discovery, Torres filed the neccessary papers with the authorities to secure ownership of the mining land. But if he ever found any rich ore in the old mine, the fact was never given any wide publicity. All queries as to the results of assays of ore from the mine were turned aside, and it can only be conjectured as to what Torres really had in his discovery.

It is safe to assume that Torres did not find the legendary gold deposit of the Spaniards, found and lost 150 years ago. That mystery still remains to tantalize the eager prospector hoping for easy riches.

What Torres found was perhaps the remains of a more recent venture, a mine which was abandoned because it filled with water and was — may be — not promising enough to warrant transporting the necessary equipment for pumping, considering the difficult mountain terrain and the distance involved.

Most old-timers who have hunted this lost lode believe it lies in the rugged peaks rising west of Trinidad as the southern point and Walsenburg as the northern point. Trinidad is in Las Animas County; Walsenburg is in Huerfano County; Torres' discovery in Culebra Peak is in Costilla County. Where these three counties come together lies Santa Isabel National Forest, in which are East Spanish Peak and West Spanish Peak, having elevations above 12,000 feet. Only

163

God knows what values lie therein, and it might pay to look the ground over. But bear in mind there's many a treasure in the ground besides gold. Uranium, for instance.

2.   Three Skeletons Guard Lost Gold.

A solitary prospector came into Durango, Colorado, one day in 1905, bowed down by the weight of a sackful of extremely rich gold ore.

He was in urgent need of ready money and could not wait for the ore to be smelted and returned from the Denver mint as coin. After having specimens of the ore assayed, he showed the assayer's reports and offered the sackful of ore for sale. While displaying it to possible cash customers, he related how he came by it:

When prospecting in the Bear Creek region, of the eastern Nettleton district, he said, about thirty miles from Durango, he had accidently found the tunnel of an old mine. He realized some mystery hovered over the mine, for there was evidence that it had been abandoned suddenly, and probably involuntarily, many years ago.

The timbering had rotted and was falling away. All around on the floor, and on the ground outside the tunnel, were heaps of gold ore, of the same kind he had in the sack. The ore was very high grade, and the vein, which he had not taken the time to locate, being then short of food, must have been only a few feet away.

Inside the tunnel were the skeletons of three men, bleached snow-white, though covered with dust. All mention of special landmarks as a trail back to the gold was cagily avoided.

The prospector was eager to sell the ore quickly so he could return to the mine with an adequate supply of provisions and the necessary equipment to make a thorough survey of the extent of the gold vein. He hoped to find it sufficiently extensive, he said, to interest some big mining corporation.

In those days, many of the large corporations employed

prospectors to search out mines for them, and they frequently purchased discoveries made by independent miners. Free-lance prospectors often made a quick turnover on lodes of gold and silver, and now and then on other metals. Every man jack of them was equipped with a durable hope of making a strike he could sell.

In a few days the stranger had sold the ore. He imme-diately departed from Durango, and never came again.

In the late spring of 1918, Pedro Martinez, not eligible for service in the army, visited Durango with a quantity of the same kind of ore, teeming with gold. He had the same story to tell: By accident he had found the mine. He described the tunnel; the falling timbers, the heaps of ore outside and on the floor, the bleached bones, with the three skulls. He re-ferred respectfully to the three skeletons as *los tres padro-nes,* and indicated the mine's location as in the same general area, the Bear Creek region.

Before Martinez could return to the mine, or file a claim on it, he fell ill of the flu, which was prevalent at that time, and died, silent on the subject of a waybill.

In the fall of 1938, a sheepherder brought into Durango a sack of gold ore which was recognized by old-timers as the same sort of rock as that brought in by Martinez. The sheep-herder, too, told the same tale, identical in all details.

Local people decided that a story checking three ways and standing up through so many years must have some basis in fact. Even the doubters could not explain away the ore. Several townsmen grubstaked the sheepman to lead them to the Three Skeletons mine. The expedition was quickly be-gun and as quickly abandoned: the guide could not find the way back. The three skeletons guarding the heaps of gold are doubtless still guarding.

Who were the three men who once animated the skele-tons? Who killed them and how, while they were at work? How long ago? Why were they not missed and their fate dis-covered? If they were killed by assailants, why did not the murderers return for the treasure? The fellow who redis-

165

covers the Three Sekeltons mine may also find the answers to some of these questions.

Go to Durango; follow Bear Creek where it flows through the eastern Nettleton district, about thirty miles from the town. Then seek the mineralized area along the creek. Gold is where you find it, and some other metals now equally valuable may be there, too.

3.   The "Buttinski" Lost Gold Strike.

Many a young fellow, during the years of the great depression, not being able to find a paying job, went out prospecting — in a hope, perhaps, of moving from rags to riches. Among them were, of course, many who knew nothing of ores and minerals.

One such well-intentioned young innocent played in magnificent luck, in 1934, only to have his achievement dashed to pieces by the ill-timed meddling of an old know-it-all prospector who "butted in" at just the right moment to throw an immense fortune out the window, and give rise to a baffling mystery which may never be solved.

One afternoon, in Durango, Colorado, an honest-faced young man walked into the Newton restaurant and asked to see the proprietor. He wasn't looking for a job, he said; he had a business proposition for Mr. Newton. Upon meeting the cafe proprietor, the young man, without any preliminaries, laid his proposition on the line.

"Mr. Newton," he said, "I've been out of work for several months and have nothing in sight, so I have decided to go out prospecting. Will you grubstake me? If I find anything, we'll split 50-50 on it, whatever it may be."

Mr. Newton looked the young fellow over and liked his looks. He thought he would be a good risk and consented to take a chance. He bought the boy some camp equipment, and a few of the essential mining tools, and furnished him with enough provisions to last two or three weeks.

With his prospecting outfit packed upon a burro, the

young man left the town, giving no hint of the direction in which he was headed.

About two weeks later he returned. He went into the Newton restaurant at the lunch hour and showed Mr. Newton some large pieces of white quartz heavily shot through with great veins of a yellow metallic substance.

"I have found a place where truckloads of this stuff are lying right on the top of the ground," he told Newton. "All I have to do is pick it up. It's half yours."

Mr. Newton was much impressed. Some of the customers also looked at the rock, bug-eyed. It certainly looked good. Might be an easy fortune in it. Some of the customers began to eye the boy as if deliberating whether to try making a deal with him when Mr. Newton wasn't looking.

At a nearby table, an old prospector sat leisurely picking his teeth, after eating a beef stew. Suddenly he arose from his chair and ambled over to the counter where the pieces of quartz were lying. Picking up one rock, he squinted at it, turning it over in his hand.

"Nuts!" he snorted. "Taint gold! Just iron pyrites. Ain't worth picking up. It's rightly called fools' gold because nobody but a fool would take it for gold." With that he stalked out.

Nobody likes to be ridiculed, especially before strangers. Mr. Newton and the boy were no exceptions. They turned away crestfallen. The boy went out. Mr. Newton laid the rocks on a shelf back of the counter and went on with his work. He thought no more of the yellow metal in the white quartz, even failing to note that the boy had not yet told him where he had found it. The old prospector went his way, confident, no doubt, he knew all about ore and couldn't be mistaken, and had, therefore, saved Mr. Newton from pouring money down a rat hole.

A month went by. Then a mining engineer, who apparently knew his groceries, happened in to the restaurant for a late breakfast. He saw the rocks lying on the shelf behind the counter.

"May I look at that quartz rock?" he asked. Mr. Newton

167

placed the rock in the mining man's hand. He turned it over and examined it from all sides.

"Do you know where this ore came from?" he asked. "It is one of the richest pieces of gold ore I have seen in a long time. It wouldn't take much of that to make a fortune."

Mr. Newton drew a long breath. Who was right, the old prospector or the mining engineer? Inclining to trust the judgment of the scientific mining man, Newton sent the quartz to an assayer. It assayed better than $5000 to the ton.

The boy, however, had disappeared.

Now this is a case that is wide open. But the point of departure must be Durango, a typically western town in the southwest corner of Colorado, near the New Mexico line. The source of this rich quartz was evidently only a few days' travel by foot and burro out of Durango, and there's not much else to go by. But it's a safe bet the boy went into the mountains northwest of the town. In the foothills there you would expect to find values. Better get a hunter's license and go in the hunting season, combining business with pleasure.

14

Treasure in Utah

UTAH is one of our states which still has considerable
unexplored territory. Thousands of square miles of
virgin wilderness — desert and forest — where, as the Irish-
man said, "the hand of man has never set foot," still beckon
the adventurer and the scientific pioneer.

But this will not be for long, for the discovery of uranium,
that precious element so essential for blowing man down as
well as up, has inspired the building of new roads and the
development of old trails into highways. Much magnificent,
hitherto hidden, natural scenery is being brought into view.
And here the geologist, the mineralogist, the oil prospector,
and the seeker after gems and precious metals, may find their
goal.

The hardships which usually accompany treasure hunting are being reduced or eliminated, but it will be some time
before these new moves affect the two diverse areas of Utah
in which lie the values I shall outline in the following two
tales:

LOST MINES and HIDDEN TREASURE

1. The Lost Ledge of Truelove Manheart

Away back in 1885, an old prospector, known by the romantic name, Truelove Manheart, reckoning that his years were numbered, settled down in Park City, in the northeastern part of Utah, near the Wyoming line.

He intended to do some leisurely prospecting in the direction of Hayden Fork, with Park City as a home base, before his prospecting days should be over. He had been told by an old crony of his younger days, who had since died, that in the Hayden Fork country there was an exceedingly rich gold vein, "where you would least expect it." He meant to go after it in a manner befitting his years — by taking it easy and not staying out too long at a time.

As he expected this to be his last fling in search for treasure, he took the precaution of making a friend of an assayer in Park City, in whose assays he could have complete confidence, and whom he could trust to keep his secret when he at last made the great strike. Secrecy would be imperative to protect him from claim jumpers.

The old man had luck. Sure enough, after a few days' search, in the Hayden Fork country, he discovered a very rich ledge of gold; and sure enough, just as he had been told, it **was in a rock formation in which you would least expect it.**

With a good supply of the ore, he hurried back to Park City, in a high degree of excitement. Forsaking his usual caution, when he handed over his samples for assay, he told his friend the whole story: in what direction he had gone; how long he had been out, and just how the ledge of ore lay. The tests were made without delay, and the assayer announced that the ore specimens showed $50,000 to the ton!

Pending the filing of his claim, Manheart started immediately to assemble supplies and equipment for returning to the ledge and working the mine. Meanwhile his assayer friend, who must have been related to a woman, lost no time broadcasting the news. Though nobody among the local populace could believe the region could have ore so rich, a

170

stampede began to sprout. Suddenly — and literally out of a clear sky — a great emergency halted the gold rush.

A forest fire, rapid and intense, moved up in the area between the Hayden Fork country and Park City, threatening the town with destruction. There had been no rain for many months, making the dense, dry vegetation an invitation to flame. All hands were necessary as firemen, to avert immediate disaster. Gold-hunting became of secondary importance.

When the fire was brought under control and Park City was safe, the gold ledge of Truelove Manheart became once more the talk of the town, mulled over in every saloon and at very bar. Many schemes were laid for chiselling in on the treasure.

But where there had been green vegetation, majestic trees, rocks in the colors of nature, and other landmarks, nothing now remained but charred and blackened stumps, burnt-over hummocks, soot-covered stones, and ashes of shrubs. The landscape, ordinarily of rare beauty, now had the gloom of funereal desolation. Nothing remained to mark the way back to the lost gold ledge of Truelove Manheart.

In time, new growth covered the ground. But the big trees were gone; the great stones, split and fallen in pieces. The region would never again look the same.

Time after time, Truelove Manheart attempted to retrace his steps in the unfamiliar scene, seeking to orient himself by time, distance, and direction. But never, never, could he bring himself again to the place where the gold ore lies. His disappointment at failure to retake the fortune that had once been within his grasp hastened the death of the old man, and the last regrets of Truelove Manheart were for his lost gold ledge.

Many others have searched in the Hayden Fork country for the rich ore. In 1935, a trio of Park City residents, Tom Chrysler, Marion Lewis, and Dell Redden, prepared to spend the summer prospecting for the gold .They planned to go over the Hayden Fork district, once and for all, inch by inch, and find the vein if it was there. They went — and returned. If they found anything it was not the lost ledge. The golden treasure is still hidden — since the day Truelove Manheart left it.

Before going to Park City, make inquiry at the United States Land Office, in Salt Lake City, for the exact location of the forest fire, about 1885. Then locate that portion of the devastated area lying between Park City and the Hayden Fork district. Somewhere in the edge of that region — about where the Hayden Fork section begins — you will find the lost gold ledge of Truelove Manheart, in a rock formation which rarely has gold.

2.   The Rattlesnake Mine.

Andre Knuts, known to his friends as Gus, was working alone in an old zinc mine in Milford, Utah. Knuts, a 40-year old Finnish prospector, had leased the mine in 1941, and apparently was barely making a living, for he was not spending freely. Quiet and close-mouthed, he kept his affairs to himself, a dangerous course to pursue, as it proved, for it led to the conjecture he was hoarding considerable wealth.

On November 18 of that year, his body was found in an old abandoned shaft, where it had been thrown, his throat cut from ear to ear. Investigation proved he had been killed in his little cabin, his body dragged to the shaft and flung out of sight.

No motive for the murder could be shown, and finally the officers concluded he had been killed for refusing to disclose where he had concealed the money received for the sale of his zinc ore. Wherever he had concealed it — provided he had any to conceal — there it is today, for nothing tangible indicated he had been robbed.

The mystery of the Finn's murder served to bring Milford once more into the headlines. The discovery of tungsten ore north of the town had brought in a sudden influx of population, creating a small boom after its long obscurity as a ghost town. The Pearl Harbor incident, a few days later, put the finger on the mines of Milford to furnish strategic metals for the second World War, as they had done also for the first.

"In 1918, before the close of Mr. Wilson's war," said Edward C. Whalin, ex-Cripple Creek gold miner, "I was operating a mine at Milford, Utah.

"Maybe you don't know where Milford is. It's south of Sevier Lake, northwest of the Mineral Mountains, and on the Union Pacific Railroad, in the South Star district. Quite a town Milford used to be, and for a long time an overnight stop of the gold freighters,

"Our camp cook was a Chinaman, and naturally we called him Charlie. He was very punctual and neat, and very satisfactory as a culinary artist, but he had one terrible fault: he was always looking for some sideline, outside of his kitchen, by which he could make some extra money. And he had more schemes for making profit out of junk than a dog has fleas.

"And speaking of fleas, Charlie could have cooked up a scheme to make money out of them. He knew more about bats, bugs, and snakes than any college professor you ever saw.

"One day there came to our camp a young Swede, not long out of Sweden. He could hardly understand a word of English, and of course, he couldn't speak it well, either.

"He didn't seem to think much of our mine, but he stayed around camp for two or three days, and got quite friendly with Charlie. Suddenly he announced his intention of going out to look around for a good gold mine for himself. Taking a couple of men with him, he went prospecting south from our camp, evidently expecting to turn up a rich mine, with a mere sandwich and a bottle of pop for a grubstake.

"A few miles south of us there really was a good gold mine lying idle. Few knew of it, for it had been abandoned by its owner a long time before. It had a splendid vein of gold, and was not hard to work; but it had been a sanctuary for rattlesnakes to such an extent that more time and energy were consumed in killing the snakes than remained for taking out the ore. So the owner simply turned the mine over to the snakes and quit.

"Yes, you've guessed it: the Swede and his two compan-

173

ions stumbled by accident upon the rattlesnake mine. Seeing several piles of slag about, they rummaged around until they found the timbered shaft. Everything looked as if the mine had once been a good paying proposition, and they wondered why it had been so completely abandoned.

"The Swede said he would go down the shaft and see what conditions were below ground. Accordingly, down he went, taking a candle and a few matches.

"As he slowly descended, those watching from above saw him put out his hand on the wall of rock, near a crevice, and pick up a rattlesnake, stiff as a poker from the cold. The snake was too cold to bite. The Swede threw it down as if he believed it harmless, and said:

" 'He no bite.' "

"He continued on his way down into the mine. When he was within a few feet of the bottom of the shaft, his eyes popped out; giving a great scream and dropping his candle, he started up out of the shaft, raving and gibbering. When he got to the surface, he tried to tell what he had seen, but, as I told you, he couldn't speak English very well. From his incoherent ravings, his companions gathered that he might have been suffering from too long continued imbibing of some cups that cheer more powerfully than tea.

"He had reached a part of the mine where the cold did not penetrate, and there in that equable temperature, he had seen a huge moving mass of rattlesnakes, coiled together and writhing — a mass as large as a hogshead. The sight and smell of that concentrated coil of vipers in that subterranean corner were too much for the young Swede. He came up from the mine a maniac.

"His two companions brought him back to our camp, but we could not do anything for him. The shock had unseated his mind, which was probably about ready, anyhow, to be toppled over. He did not regain his sanity and in a few days he was taken away to the state insane asylum.

"The fate of the young Swede was a real grief to Charlie, who, however, was made of sterner stuff. He could not understand how the sight of a few snakes could so thoroughly upset a man. Far from being upset, Charlie knew how he could make some money from such a situation.

"The more often the story of the snakes was repeated, the larger the number of them grew, and the more pensive and absent-minded Charlie became. At last he asked for a few days' vacation, and we arranged for an understudy to take his place until his return.

"Taking a huge black iron kettle, Charlie departed for the rattlesnake mine. No, not for the ore; the gold meant nothing to him. He was after the snakes.

"Charlie collected the rattlers, one by one, and took out their venom, which he saved in bottles. Then he put the bodies of the snakes into his big kettle and boiled them down for their grease. As they boiled, he took off the scum; that was the cream, so to speak, of the oil. Then he boiled them some more and obtained a brew somewhat less powerful, but nevertheless, as he claimed, full of curative properties.

"The venom, which Charlie said was worth four hundred dollars a pint, he sold in San Francisco, to be used in making serum. The grease he sold to be used in making a cure for rheumatism. The fame of rattlesnake oil for this purpose is world-wide.

"Charlie came back to his kitchen, richer, gayer, more interested in sidelines, and less in biscuits than ever before.

"So you see," said Whalin, "what'll drive one man crazy, will get another fellow several thousand dollars."

Charlie so completely denuded the gold mine of rattlesnakes that the owner resumed mining operations soon thereafter, and eventually worked the mine out.

"There are still some good prospects in that vicinity," concluded Whalin, "and if you want a waybill, don't hesitate to ask."

North of Milford are the tungsten mines; south are the gold mines. Mining engineers say the rocky hills in this region are highly mineralized, charged with tungsten, zinc, lead, horn silver and gold. Try east and west; also southeast and northwest, and see what happens.

15

Mountains of Silver

THE DISTANCE of the silvery moon from the earth
is only small change: somewhat less than 250,000 dollars — pardon me, I mean miles. Pluto, however, is in the
folding money: more than 3,700,000,000,000 miles away, and
takes more than 250 years to pay off — I mean to complete
his orbit around the sun.

The reader, gentle or furious, may be surprised to learn
there is more than enough silver on this continent to make
a silver dollar for every mile from here to Pluto. Those
who doubt it may rally round and read here the factual
stories of mountains of silver, waiting, waiting; here in
North America.

To realize how stupendous a mountain of silver can be,
consider Cerro de Potosí, in Bolivia. This mountain, 5,000
feet high and containing more than 5,000 shafts, yielded to
the king of Spain a total of $15,791,000,000 from 1545 to
1825. This would be about 200 billion dollars today. And
while the interval of time may seem over-long, remember
the mining was done practically by hand, by peons and en-

slaved Indians. Henry Ford, Thomas Edison, Charles Steinmetz, and other master minds who have given us the terrific tempo of today, were still in the ethereal world, waiting for their time to come.

1. Silver Mountain in Chihuahua.

Nearly a hundred years ago, reports of the vast mineral wealth characterizing all parts of Mexico were circulating around Europe. Stories were told of the immense silver deposits in the mountains of the Santa Eulalia district, in the environs of Chihuahua City. The French government, in need of money to support its overseas army, sent an expedition, under its most famous mining engineer, to verify the rumors about the richness of the Santa Eulalia mines. The Frenchman invited an American, General Lew Wallace, to accompany him, and it is to Wallace we owe the amazing description of the Santa Eulalia silver.

These mines constitute a *real* (a district of mines of gold or silver; the literal meaning of *real* is "royal"); so many of them that they were never counted, and there is no complete record of them. The deposits of silver are in strata, Wallace reported, "not so rich as abundant and inexhaustible . . . the oblong mountain in which we find the San Jose, Parcionera, Negrita, and Santa Rita mines is a kind of mother-mountain, or silver core, from which the metal radiates in all directions, growing less rich according to the distance from the center . . . 5,000 men might pick and dig and blast away at it for a hundred years, and at the end of that time, the yield would be as rich if not richer than when they began."

An understanding of this condition is further glimpsed in this exchange between an American prospector and a Mexican, meeting by chance on the mountainside:

"Is it worth while to prospect here?"

"Yes," replied the Mexican. "It is not rich but certain."

"Are you following a vein?"

"No; there are no veins here."

"You work then, where you please?"

"Yes; the mountain is all alike."

The discovery of the silver came about through vice and crime; but the precious metal was subsequently, in part, used for the glory of God and has served Him through two-and-a-half centuries.

In 1700, when Chihuahua City was not much more than a mission surrounded by large country estates, a trio of bandits, aware that justice was on their trail, fled into the Santa Eulalia Mountains. Their hideout was known and they were compelled to change base frequently; a hardship, since it was necessary to make each new secret camp near a source of water, an essential not easily found.

While moving from ravine to ravine, and from hillside to hillside, they discovered outcroppings of silver everywhere. Because of the incredible plenitude of the silver, the bandits knew they could soon change their status from that of outcasts to that of nabobs. After much discussion among themselves, they decided their first problem was to readjust themselves to the world of honest men, and it seemed they could do this quickest and best through the priest. Accordingly, one of their number went, sneaking by night, to the mission, with a proposition to the padre.

"If you will hear my confession, Padre, and the confessions of my two *amigos,* and will give us absolution," the outlaw proposed, "we will repay you with enough silver to build the grandest cathedral in the New World."

Fair enough, thought the padre. So he went into the mountain under cover of darkness, and met the outlaws. They confessed and were absolved of ther sins. Through the influence of the priest, they were restored to security and good will among their fellow citizens, and they kept their word.

The Santa Eulalia mines were developed, though by primitive, wasteful methods, and their fame spread over the world. Miners from north and south rushed for a share in the wealth and fame. Population and trade followed.

The cathedral was built at a cost of a million dollars. The sum was accumulated from the twelve-and-one-half cents given from every $8.00 of silver taken from the mines, or 0.015 per cent of the production at that time. The cathedral now, after 250 years, is still beautiful — as beautiful as a mountain of silver.

For more than 150 years, the Santa Eulalia mines were worked in the haphazard manner of the *gambucinos;* that is, by individual miners, picking and digging by hand, taking only the rich pieces, disregarding all low grade ore. In recent years, organized capital has been at work retrieving the silver by modern methods, and two companies are operating in the district; the Potosí Mining Company, and the Compañia Minera Asarco, local subsidiary of the American Smelting and Refining Company.

But who knows in what recesses of the mother-mountain the *gambucinos,* as of old, may be still picking and digging by hand at the silver riches stored by Nature in the rock and soil?

If you should ever find yourself in the Santa Eulalia Mountains, dig, wherever you may happen to stand, for the chances are 100 to 1 you will find silver.

2.   Silver Mountain in the Reservation.

As far back as the early 1850's, the region of the Gila River had a reputation among the natives of Sonora as being what they called a hotbed of silver. By that, they meant that silver was created there, and no matter how much was taken out of the ground, more silver would be formed. The idea was the same as that, by picking flowers out of your garden, more flowers will bloom.

In 1872, an aged but agile Mexican left his home in Sonora to hunt for precious metals along the Gila River to the north. Near the headquarters of the United States Indian agent of the San Carlos Apache Reservation, he discovered a tall peak which seemed to be shot through and through with silver.

As he described it, the silver ore was nearly the same type as that found in the celebrated Silver King mine, which

179

was found several years later in the Pinal Mountains, just north of the Gila.

The peak was marked by a network of silver veins in red, green, and black, he related, and nuggets of native silver were to be found everywhere upon the ground.

The old man returned to Mexico, intending to inform himself in regard to the United States law for staking a claim, and to get the necessary equipment for setting up a mining camp, to concentrate the values without having to transport the ore to Mexico.

Before he could complete his arrangements, sickness overtook him, and he saw that he would never be able to carry out his plans. He made known to the men of his family the huge value of his discovery and described to them its appearance and location, advising them to make an attempt to attach a legal claim to it, and to work it for their joint benefit.

"There is enough silver there," he said, "to make every member of our family plenty rich."

After his death, his kinsmen and friends formed a party to go into the United States and establish their right to the mountain of silver.

With a sizable *conducta*, well equipped with provisions and the necessary mining tools, and bearing a certificate of their proper peaceful purpose, signed by the government authorities of Sonora, they followed the route north, as instructed by their departed kinsman.

Arriving at the San Carlos reservation, they identified themselves as peaceful legitimate prospectors. They were told by the official Indian agent that if they made any discovery of metals upon the reservation, they could not be allowed to set up camp and do any mining. If they made a strike, however, outside the reservation boundaries, then the Indian agent had no jurisdiction, and they could stake a claim and take out ore . . . The Mexicans agreed to abide by the rules, and proceeded upon their errand.

After several days of search, the peak was found. To

their dismay, they learned it was barely within the reservation, at the extreme southwestern corner.

In keen disappointment at finding the vast silver deposit within the proscribed territory, the party returned to Sonora, keeping their knowledge of the silver bonanza a secret within the family. Later, a female member of the family married an American and the secret was slightly unraveled.

The mountain of silver remains intact, for modern Apaches are not concerned with precious metals; they have become an exclusively agricultural people and build up their bank accounts from grain and cattle. Since the time of the second discovery of the silver, efforts have been made to obtain enactment of laws reopening Indian reservations to entry for mineral rights.

First, request from the United States Indian Service, in Washington D. C., a map of the San Carlos Apache Reservation. This may cost you a few cents. Study well the elevation as indicated on the map, at the extreme southwestern corner. When on the ground, bear in mind the silver peak is "barely within the reservation."

3.   Silver Mountain in Northern Arizona.

When Captain W. H. Hardy founded the now forgotten town, Hardyville, on the Colorado River, in 1864, he had one eye on the river trade, the other on the precious metals which were known to abound on both sides of the river.

Gold and silver were known to be in the mountains, north, south, and east. But the chance that the prospector, with several arrows in his back and his scalplock missing, would be found by casually cruising buzzards, was a constant damper to the spirits of both professional and amateur prospectors.

An optimist by nature, Captain Hardy had set up a mill for crushing ore. Some gold and silver in quartz had been brought in, but because of the unremitting rampages of the Indians, the mill was mostly idle.

Many inexperienced men came to Hardyville, from

New York, Pennsylvania, and other eastern states, lured by reports of gold and silver in the mountains, and with their concepts of the noble red man gleaned from the works of fiction then current, glorifying "Poor Lo."

It became a serious problem to Hardy to keep tender-feet from going off into the dangerous country without adequate protection. Many of them disappeared, after buying a small grubstake at the Hardy store, and were never seen again. Now and then one returned with specimens of gold or silver ore.

One day in 1866, a straggling prospector applied at the store for enough food to see him through a brief expedition into the mountains. Having loaded up his burros, he headed east. In about two months, he came again, bringing some unusually good specimens of copper and silver, an ore that Americans call "silver glance," and Mexicans call *petanque*.

He asked for Captain Hardy and showed him the ore. Hardy examined it and realized its value at once. Where was this found? That was the question.

"Up near the mouth of the Litte Colorado River," said the prospector, "is a mountain of this stuff. The whole mountain is made of it."

"This ore would assay at least $7,000 to the ton," said Captain Hardy. "Is it all as rich as this?"

"It's all just like that," replied the prospector.

"And you say it's at the mouth of the Little Colorado?"

"Yes, right near the mouth of the river."

The ore was weighed, and Hardy gave the prospector its value in money. The stranger promptly bought a ticket for the trip down the Colorado River, as the steamboat was then waiting at the pier, and he passed from the Hardyville scene forever.

Captain Hardy showed the *petanque* around among the local mining men and told them of the mountain of silver — enough to keep his mill busy for a long time. He had no trouble in organizing a party to hunt for it. Many men offered themselves and he selected those known to be able Indian fighters, as well as familiar with ore. With their pack mules loaded with supplies, they took their course as straight as topography would allow, to the mouth of the Little Colorado.

They had the samples of ore with them, and they searched thoroughly over a wide area on both banks of the river. They not only could not find the mountain of silver, but they could not find the place from which the prospector had taken the ore, assuming there was less than a mountain.

Suspicion came into Captain Hardy's mind that the prospector did not intend him to find it. But some of his companions, well supplied with confidence in the mineral possibilities of Arizona, thought the mountain of silver was on some other river and the stranger had made an honest mistake in naming it. "Perhaps," they said, "it was the Santa Maria." Anyway, they found nothing to put in the Hardy mill.

In Coconino County, Arizona, near the mouth of the Little Colorado, which joins the Colorado at Cape Solitude, Grand Canyon National Park. Or perhaps farther south where the Santa Maria joins the Bill Williams River. Look on both banks of the river, near the confluence.

16

Treasures Hidden in Compostela

NAYARIT, a state on the west coast of Mexico, is a choice place for treasure hunting and prospecting. Rich in minerals, its climate is ideal, and little science has been brought to bear to disclose its treasures. Though one of the first states to be settled in Old Mexico, it is still waiting, content to have its development come on gradually. A paradise for those who desire to escape the faster tempo of the north, and yet exercise the mind on the glamourous mysteries all around them here.

Nayarit's most charming city is Compostela, site of some of Mexico's most antiquated Spanish architecture, and point of departure for relocating the lost treasures described in this chapter.

1. The Cockroach Mine.

Wind, water, heat, hunger, thirst, and mystery often stand, singly or in combination, between man and the treasures of the earth. But nearly always something less formidable adds to his difficulties when in search of the Golden Fleece.

Upon occasion it has been insects, poison ivy, and snakes which have reared barriers insurmountable by any but a Jason or a Hercules. The many stories of fauna in the gold mines will surely persuade the treasure hunter that he requires a knowledge not only of geology, geography, astronomy, and paleontology, but of zoology and entomolgy as well.

In 1914, a Lieutenant Davis, ex-officer of the United States Navy, became involved in the then contemporary Mexican revolution; and finding himself on the losing side, he was compelled to hide out for a while, to avoid being a victim of the god of war.

He concealed himself in the old cathedral in Compostela, Nayarit — one of the oldest cathedrals in Mexico. He was found there by a kind-hearted padre, who connived at his concealment, and not only permitted him to remain there in hiding, but brought him food and water.

While thus secreted from his enemies, Davis amused himself by studying the old church records, and in them he read of an ancient gold mine, fabulously rich, which had been worked by the early Spaniards.

The time came when it was safe for him to leave his hiding place and go about without fear. He immediately went on an intensive prospecting tour, knowing the entire State of Nayarit to be highly mineralized in the precious metals. He succeeded in finding a splendid outcropping which he thought would be profitable to exploit.

He thereupon left Nayarit and went to San Diego where he purchased considerable mining machinery, and took it by boat down the coast to Rosario, a little town near the Nayarit line in Sinaloa. His friends say he took out vast quantities of gold, amply justifying his judgment as a prospector.

But in the midst of his success he could not forget that the mine he had found was not the *antigua* he had read about in the old records in the cathedral in Compostela. He craved the satisfaction of rediscovering those old workings, to finish what the Spaniards had begun so long ago.

Taking a few of his *mozos* — Mexican men servants — he

went on a prospecting trip to make a more careful search aided by those who, he felt, must be familiar with every foot of ground in that vicinity.

At last, in the heavy subtropic undergrowth, they found what looked like an old abandoned mine shaft, with every indication of great age. It seemed not to have been disturbed for a long time.

The *mozos* cut down the surrounding brush, cleaned some of the top soil away, and opened it up so they could look down into it for some little distance. The shaft was very deep, and Davis saw that it would be impossible to descend into it without help, and then only by going down on a rope. He was determined to go down, let come what might.

Providing himself with a stout rope and carrying a carbide lamp, he ordered the *mozos* to lower him slowly down the shaft.

As they let the rope out, inch by inch, and he went deeper into the earth, he noticed the color of the rock which formed the walls of the shaft. As he proceeded farther from the daylight, he observed the color changed, taking on a peculiar tone such as he had never before seen in rock; a phenomenon he could not explain.

Just then the rope swayed and his knee and elbow touched the wall of the shaft.

Instantly the brown wall began to move, with an indescribable, faint squeaking, crunching sound, the like of which he had never heard. Immense brown cockroaches darted in all directions; hurrying, skurrying, full speed ahead, and to the right, the left, upward, downward, and sidewise, but mostly down toward the floor of the shaft. Thousands, millions, innumerable myriads of cockroaches moved on down into the mine, swarming, covering the entire inside surface as far as the eye could see.

The impossibility of making even the wildest estimate of the vast number of the repulsive insects struck the mind of the mathematically-inclined lieutenant with such force that he dropped the light and yelled at the top of his lungs.

The Mexicans hurriedly drew him back up to the light

186

of day, and he told them what he had seen. They laughed.

"*La vieja mina de las cucarachas,*" they said, with characteristic lack of enthusiasm. The old mine of the cockroaches.

The cockroach mine was known to the Mexicans from the days of the pioneer Spaniards. It had been ignored for so long that it had become a mere tradition. It was known to be very rich, *muy rico,* with an almost inexhaustible vein of gold, but the legend persisted that it was impossible to work the mine because of the vast number of abominable cockroaches which had preempted the place. For that reason the Spaniards, and later, the Mexicans, had been compelled to abandon it. They had lost all recollection of its location, and the story of it had passed into their folklore.

"No one wanted La Cucaracha mine," the *mozos* told the lieutenant. "Since the days of the *antiguas,* the cockroaches have ruled the mine, and no one cared or dared to dispute their sway. The mine devil preferred the cockroaches to the Spaniards; and the padres, many generations past, had given the mine over to the insect pests. Let them have it."

Lieutenant Davis calculated that the astronomical number of insects in the mine could be accounted for only by an inconceivable number of generations of them, and he felt inclined to believe what the *mozos* told him. Recognizing the futility of attempting to conquer that horrendous horde of insect life, he surrendered to its superior force and gave over all hope of developing La Cucaracha into a paying property.

And to this day, the gold is in the possession of the cockroach corporation. Some day a party of entomologists, canny enough to make pals of mining engineers, will take large dividends from the treasure of La Cucaracha mine.

Plan to spend your next vacation in Compostela. Early in your stay there, annex the ear of an old-timer among the Mexicans, treat him to a few quick ones at the best pulquería and then ask him about La Cucaracha mine. He will tell you the best and shortest route to the mine and the cockroaches. And may God go with you.

2. Countess de Miravillas' Secret Silver.

Scornful mention is often made of the "idle rich", but never of idle riches. It is the idle riches that become the lost treasures, and by doing so give rise to vast tapestries of tradition, hung upon a fine grey hair of history.

It is solely because the riches of Countess de Miravillas were completely idle that they took their place among the missing, and have remained lost through several generations.

Down in Mexico, in Nayarit, formerly known as the State of Tepic, somewhere near the old cathedral at Compostela, are the ruins of the ancient hacienda of the countess. Dating back to the time of the pioneer Spaniards in Mexico, nearly three-fourths of the high adobe walls are still standing, though as each year passes and the occasional rains fall, they become a trifle more diminished.

To begin at the beginning: History does not tell how the countess — then a plain *señora* or *señorita* — happened to be in Mexico, at that time so wild and unsettled, and so unsuited to a woman alone. Tradition does not account for her father, her husband, or her son; nor suggest any hereditary domestic background for a character so remarkably typical. Anyway, there she was, and there, in the richest mineral area in the world, she had a prodigiously rich silver mine.

Having the genius for organization common to all true children of Spain, she organized and systematized the work of mining her rich holdings. Had business management then been reduced to a scientific formula as it is today, she might have been dubbed Countess of Efficiency instead of Countess of Wonders, (Miravillas).

Every day she sat at the gate and watched the peons bring the bullion from her smelter and place it inside the wall. There she checked it, lifted it, estimated its weight and value, and instructed her confidential servants to cache it away in her secret vault, while she entered a record of the day's production in her book.

It was necessary, of course, for her to pay the royal fifth to the treasury in Spain and her tithes to the church in Rome.

188

But her production of silver was so vast that the immense riches left for her own coffer was far more than she could ever have had any reasonable need for, even had she been an open-handed spender.

One day she conceived the idea of having a special gift made for the king. It must be all of solid silver and it must be something so distinctive that he would hesitate to throw it into the general treasury to be melted down for coin.

She called in one of those extraordinary clever Aztec silversmiths — never surpassed in any age or country — who was practicing his art in Mexico City. To him she gave orders and designs for a beautiful silver hen, each feather made separately, a dozen solid silver eggs, and a lovely nest made in exquisitely wrought filgree, all of the purest Tepic silver from her mine.

So remarkable was the skill displayed and so perfect the fine detail that these few words can give no idea of the exquisite beauty and daintiness of the whole conception. Suffice it that the gift, when received by the king, was so pleasing to him, he made his loyal and devoted subject a countess, and she was thereafter known as *la condesa de Miravillas,* or the Countess of Wonders.

During her long life, she sent many another splendid gift to the king, but none of them so pleasing to the Spanish fancy as the beautiful hen sitting in the nest upon solid silver eggs. Somewhere in Spain they may still be in existence today. In Mexico their beauty and charm have passed into deathless tradition, preserved in the equal beauty of the Castilian tongue.

Through many years the *condesa* continued to dwell in her hacienda and to engage in mining, keeping the record of her silver in the pages of her endless blank books. When at last she died and was buried in the nearby *campo santo* (consecrated ground) in Compostela, a great quantity of fine jewelry was buried with her.

Upon her death, the peons promptly ceased to produce the daily quota of silver. The detested enforced labor which the countess had so rigidly imposed came to an abrupt end.

189

The mine was covered and concealed. The location of the secret cache was forgotten. The silver treasure, abhorred as the cause of their slavery, was scorned. The hacienda fell into disrepair, and rank sub tropic weeds and brush grew up about the place where her miners and peons had been wont to toil. But the old countess and all her ruthless works were neither mourned nor forgotten.

The old *campo santo* where she is buried, has, after so many years, fallen into decay, Sun, rain, and wind have slowly worn away the protecting adobe wall which once surrounded it; its consecrated character utterly disregarded, the sacred ground is used as a corral. There the horses and burros rest in the mesquite shade and there they sleep the nights away.

Some years ago, a map showing what purported to be the location of the secret treasure and the mine fell into the hands of a descendant of an old Spanish family once on close terms with the countess. No member of this family had any success in tracing the mine or vault, and with the disintegration of the hacienda, the self-appointed legatees lost interest. The map eventually became the property of the Menchaca brothers, of Compostela.

These brothers are of the working class, but considerably above the peons, and they have very clever commercial minds. They determined to try to find the lost treasures of the *condesa.*

By working and saving, they acquired means enough to buy the hacienda. After cleaning away the vegetation and debris, they set up a small store nearby and began to make money. With the profits they bought cattle and stocked the land; they acquired more land, enlarged their store, and opened several mines.

Industrious and honest, the brothers have become wealthy; but never for one moment have they relinquished the desire to find the Lost Condesa mine, for which they have searched so unremittingly.

Always in their employ are from fifty to sixty peons whose job is to look for the lost lode and the ancient overstocked treasure vault. It is told that the brothers maintain a laboratory, with the latest modern equipment for assaying, and if the Lost Condesa vein is to be found, it is probable they will find it.

They have no need for the ancient riches, but having once started on the trail of the golden hind, never while life lasts will their hearts give over the search; for the pleasure is in the chase and not in bringing the game to earth.

If you must go down to Nayarit to hunt the Lost Condesa mine and treasure vault, go to Compostela and ask the padre at the old church. He has heard the story probably a thousand times and can tell you in what direction to look.

17

Black Gold in Fumes of Death

S EEMS AS THOUGH the more hellish the region is, in which to hunt a lost treasure, the more fun it is to hunt it. Surely the area in Southern California, where Pegleg Smith searched for the lost black gold, is hellish enough to suit the most exacting. And the happy hunting has continued through more than ninety years.

One day in June, 1934, my neighbor, Charles Edward Whalin, an erstwhile miner and retired railroad man, about sixty-five years old, walking with a cane and nearly incapacitated because of a chronic heart ailment, called at my home. He was carrying a small piece of paper in his hand.

Seating himself and taking a long breath, he asked:

"Have you got a friend who has an airplane?"

"Certainly I have," I replied; "many people have planes now and some of my young friends are good pilots. What's on your mind?"

"I want to get someone with a plane to take me to look for the lost Black Gold in California. Did you ever hear of it?"

192

"Yes, I've heard of it. But I'm not going to help you get anyone to take you hunting it, with your weak heart. Why, man, the excitement would kill you! But tell me what you know about it."

Hoping that I was letting myself in for a nugget from Whalin's great store of bizarre western lore, I grabbed up a pencil and placed a notebook under my hand.

"I know just where this Black Gold is," he said. "If I had an airplane, I could go right to it. You can't get to it in any other way."

"How come this Black Gold is lost? And why is it black? And how did you hear of it? And what do you know about it, anyway?" I asked. So he told me.

It was James Smith, known in California tradition and history as Pegleg Smith, who first reported the finding of the Black Gold. He had spent many years hunting the precious metals, and at the time of his search for the mysterious gold deposit he was about fifty-two years old.

In 1859, Smith, with a couple of Mexican mules, was prospecting for gold around the thousands of little cones which cover the landscape for miles around in Southern California, south of Barstow. He had heard a great deal about gold in this locality from other pioneer prospectors, and he was moved to this adventure especially because of curiosity, aroused by certain tales told him by an Indian whom he frequently employed as a prospecting companion.

Though Smith had never discovered any trace of either gold or silver when in the Indian's company, he never charged his failure to any guile on the tribesman's part. A man of unusual character and intelligence, he brought to Smith several stories, all more or less vague in detail, of a curious black gold to be found among the sterile, arid, cone-shaped peaks which thickly stud the country south of the Panamint Mountains and Death Valley.

In those days, Indians were not able to recognize gold unless it showed bright and yellow; they knew it only as "the pretty yellow stone." That this Indian should know it in some other form was somewhat surprising.

Smith questioned him and tried to pin him down to specific information as to where this queer form of gold was concealed. But true to his tribal teaching, the red man was reluctant to disclose the secret, for his ancient tradition forbade it. Finally he did indicate some rather hazy and indefinite directions for finding the dark rock.

Because of the Indian's negative attitude, Smith determined to hunt the treasure alone. With his two Mexican mules, he casually strayed off without mentioning any destination. When he had proceeded for some miles on what he conceived to be the trail designated, though he was gaining only a little in altitude, he began to have difficulty with his breathing. Also he noticed that the mules were coughing and sneezing. Something was wrong, but what it was he did not know. They slowed down their pace and pressed on.

Finally he noticed that all the rocks lying around upon the ground were very dark-colored, and he came upon a pile of bones conspicuous in their whiteness. He recognized them as human bones. Beside them were some small piles of black stones.

The coal-black stones looked out of place upon the ground where they were lying, and he picked them up and carefully examined them, noting how extremely heavy they were. Too dark to be gold, he thought; maybe some worthless substance just covered over with a dark film of manganese. But heavy enough to be high grade gold.

He struck them upon the metal in the front shoes of his mules, and as he pared them away upon the iron of the mule-shoes, he saw the stones change color, getting lighter and brighter as he got farther from the black surface of the stone. He recognized the metal as gold.

But where had that long-departed human brought those stones from? How far from the source was the ill-fated man when his doom overtook him?

Smith went no farther. Loading upon the backs of his mules the black stones — which when milled later gave $19,000 — he retraced his steps and sought the Indian. Somewhat annoyed that Smith had been on a still hunt for the mysterious Black Gold, he churlishly responded to Smith's questions:

"Yes, I know where those black stones came from, and my father knew, and my grandfather, and his father before him. But I shall not tell you. You cannot go there."

"Why not?" asked Smith. "If I can get some of that rich ore out and have it milled, I will give you a share, too."

"That makes no difference. You cannot go there. You will die; the death fumes will kill you."

"The death fumes?"

"Yes. They will kill the mules, too. The mules will cough and sneeze and their eyes and mouths will get sore, and they will die. No bird ever alights there; no lizard, no scorpion, no centipede ever runs there. Not a blade of grass, not a bush of greasewood or sage. No living thing can come out of there alive. Even the buzzards will not . . ."

The Indian would not pursue the subject and he discouraged all further questioning from Smith. But Smith was not easily turned aside from an idea once fixed in his mind. He persuaded a friend to join him in trying to find the source of the black stones. When Smith died, in 1865, or maybe 1866, they had not yet found it.

Many men attempted to find the alluring Black Gold after Smith's day. In later years the Indians, perverted from their tribal teachings by the white men, told of a vast amount of the black stones in a huge hollow hill which, from their description, the white men knew to be an old extinct volcano. And they told of members of their tribe who, when sent into the hill by white men, reached the floor of the crater but died on their way out.

Numerous white men, they say, who have tried to reach the gold, have never been seen again. The Indians believed the poisonous fumes were the breath of the gods, determined that none should rob them of their gold. The way is strewn with bones of animals and men, bleached to the whiteness of snow, lying beside empty water bottles.

The blackened, heat-ravished, earth-torn rock is thirty-five miles from the nearest water. Fumes rise from the ground so heavy with elements destructive to life, that going in and coming out alive is impossible. The fumes have a deadly, disintegrating effect upon the flesh of both man and beast, so it is said. This effect has been described as much the same as that which the world now knows to come from radium — a form of decay for which there is no remedy but death.

"Engineers tell me those fumes arise from some compound of arsenic," Whalin said.

"But why is that gold black?"

"Well, I don't exactly know, but the books say that when gold is ground to a fine powder it is black or garnet color; and if it was ground to a powder by some of the mysterious processes of nature millions of years ago, and then welded together by a high heat, such as volcanic heat, it might still be black. Who knows?

"Only two men have ever gone in there and come out alive," Whalin continued. "They spent a long time getting ready, scheming ways for caching a water supply and for getting out fast, once they got in. When they did come out they told of an almost limitless amount of gold ore in nuggets and flat chunks, stained black, they said, as if heavily plated with manganese. Fifteen hundred tons, so they said, were there in sight, sticking out of the ground.

"Why, the Santa Fe hasn't got an engine strong enough to carry it from Los Angeles to San Bernardino!

"These two brought out all they could carry, hampered as they were by the necessity for haste in getting back to pure air. One of them died shortly afterward, and the other took his $65,000 worth of ore and bought him an orange grove, and lived in it for quite a few years, but his health was never any good after that.

"The assay, they said, showed not only gold, but platinum, beryllium, and bragduchuite."

"What's bragduchuite?" I wanted to know.

"Better look it up in the encyclopedia. But wait until I show you this." Whalin referred to the piece of paper in his hand.

Taking the paper from him, I read this tabulation:

Value of one ounce of ore, the gold at $24.50.

1 lb. Troy			$290.00
10 ” ”			$2,940.00
100 ” ”			$29,400.00
1000 ” Avoirdupois			$393,000.00
2000 ” ”	(1 ton)		$786,000.00
1500 tons			$1,179,000,000.00

"That's a lot of money," I said, giving the paper back to him.

"And you don't think that's worth going after in an airplane? Well, some people are funny."

Whalin never did go after the Black Gold in an airplane. But in 1936, two young men from Phoenix came to ask what I knew about the Black Gold. They had an airplane and one of them is an expert pilot. They believed they could find the crater of the gold. I sent them to see Whalin.

"Fly along the highway out of Parker, Arizona, to Barstow, California," Whalin, then ill in bed, told them. "Or go out of Yuma, Arizona, to Indio, California. Examine the area lying between Barstow and Indio. Especially notice around Amboy, southwest, toward Virginia Dale. If you're thorough, you can't miss it."

The two young aviators circled over the area indicated by Whalin, flying as low as safety would permit. But they could not find the crater of the Black Gold. Nor from the air could they distinguish the large number of small cones from the surrounding flat desert ground. They accordingly returned to Phoenix, convinced that to locate the treasure from the air, more information would be required.

Whalin, who died shortly afterward, was greatly relieved when he learned they had not found it.

"Go to Mecca, California, and take the last road out into the hills. There's only one road that goes there. Before you

197

come to the end of the road you will find two old prospectors who have been there for years, prospecting in the nearby Chocolate Mountains. They can tell you how to find the Black Gold."

18

Treasure on the Shore

EVEN THOUGH treasure hunting may be your favorite
outdoor sport, ten to one you've never once thought of
hunting treasure at the beach. Most people think of this fascinating avocation as connected with the deep sea, or the
mountains, or the desert. If you are one of these, I have
some new ideas for you.

No, it's not about some pirate treasure washed up by the
waves. The treasures I'm going to tell you about in this
chapter have no tradition of blood and murder, though the
oldest of them may have been ancient loot. These treasures
are, rather, involved in history, geology, and the atom bomb,
in three widely spaced periods of time, and yet they may all
be available to any adventurous spirit who will seek them.

Here I give you three different choices of treasure on the
shore, hunting any one of which would be a thrilling venture if taken singly. I am here laying all three on the line to
make it easy for you to figure out a way for having a go at all
of them in one short summer vacation. One is somewhat
scientific and the other two are, though simple, expeditions

199

to bring the past into the present, though not extended greatly in geography. Let us take the oldest one first, and let the third be the one which had its first public notice in 1951.

1. Strange Treasure at Gold Beach.

From the town of Gold Beach, on the coast of Oregon, forty-three miles north of the California state line, comes a tale of lost and buried treasure, among the most interesting and myserious in all America.

A few years ago, a farmer living near Gold Beach was plowing his field. The point of his plow went unusually deep and turned up a large number of beautiful, strangely-made silver ornaments and other small silver objects whose use could not be even guessed.

Several local archaeologists, invited to examine the relics, declared the trinkets did not resemble anything they had ever seen before. They would not hazard any opinion as to the period, country, or culture that produced them.

It was made known at this time that two other similar caches of strange silver gadgets had previously come to light at Gold Beach.

After much speculation and fruitless inquiry, someone in the town was inspired to question the local Indians. Yes; the Indians knew something — but not all — about it.

Long, long ago, they said, a group of strange men came to the coast of Oregon, and for seven suns they buried much treasure in secret places in the land. They went away and never returned. The Indian tradition says there were five of the caches, of which three have been found. But there is more — a great deal more — of which the Indians know only that it required days of labor to conceal it.

The strangers were not Indians, they said, nor were they like the present day white men of Oregon. But what race they belonged to, where they came from, and where they went, the tradition does not reveal. Nor can the Indians tell whether the strangers came overland or by sea.

One day I was pondering this engaging mystery while doing some historical research. My eye fell by chance upon an arresting sentence which ran something like this.

In 1579, a ship bearing the name *Golden Hind,* and carrying a cargo of gold and silver looted from the Spaniards, sailed out of San Francisco Bay, up the coast of California to Oregon, after its commander, Sir Francis Drake, had ceremoniously taken possession of the land in the name of Queen Elizabeth of England.

My mind immediately seized upon this sentence, like a terrier upon a rat. With a mental running jump I landed smack upon the conclusion that here was the answer to the Gold Beach puzzle. In my elation I failed to remember the exact words, so the above is not verbatim, nor have I remembered the author's name. Could be, I thought, that Drake and his merry English sailors cached the silver trinkets at Gold Beach. The strange designs of the ornaments and the inexplicable purposes for which the other oddities were created might be owing to the fact that they were the work of ancient Peruvian silversmiths, made to serve some special uses of the Incas, from whom the Spaniards had taken them.

If Sir Francis had met a situation which called for a change in space or weight upon his ship, and he found it necessary to shift his loot, he would be likely to discard silver and retain the gold; for his sovereign, Queen Elizabeth, the First, expected her buccaneers to return to her ports with the richest of cargoes.

The burial of the booty would indicate an intention to visit again the Oregon shore and reclaim the treasure. Since Drake had, as he thought, taken possession of the continent in the name of his queen, he certainly must have believed that he, or some other English commander could and would recover the plunder.

What the undiscovered caches may consist of is a fascinating mystery, but it is logical to assume, whatever their shape and purpose, the objects are made of gold or silver.

The discovery of the two remaining caches is an adventure of greater moment to the archaeologist and historian than to the Get-rich-quick Wallingford, for the antiquarian value of the artifacts may be more than their mere intrinsic worth.

The prospector around Gold Beach need not long remain empty-handed, even if he fail to find the mysterious treasure. That region is very richly mineralized.

When metals of all kinds were vital to United States defense, the citizens of Curry County (Gold Beach) were eager to make an intensive development of their mineral resources. Meeting with little response from state and county authorities, the citizenry, in protest, appointed a three-man committee to investigate the possibility of seceding from the state of Oregon and joining the state of California. All of which points to the authenticity of the claims of mineral riches in the county, and the seriousness with which they are regarded by the community.

For the two as yet undiscovered caches, it might be best to look in a line rather north and south of Gold Beach, instead of farther inland from the coast. That is, unless radar or other scientific aid indicates otherwise. Gold Beach can be found on any map of Oregon. The town is on the Oregon Coast Highway, U. S. 101.

Now let us move down a short distance from Oregon into California, and try to prove that we of this century are smarter than those who preceded us. We can at least prove that we have better equipment and are more advanced in our approach.

2. Gold at The Bluff

The California gold rush, when two years old in 1851, pressed hard upon the water's edge of the Pacific. In that year, a rush to the beach at Gold Bluff took place; it came to nothing and was forgotten until 1867. Then once again great excitement arose over the discovery of gold in the sands at Gold Bluff.

On the Pacific shore, at about latitude 41, between the present towns of Trinidad on the north and Arcata on the south, is a high hill of gold-bearing formation. At the foot of this hill is a wide beach of sand which, in spots, is very rich in gold.

This sand has for countless ages been shifted around by a heavy surf, so that the gold upon the beach today may be at the bottom of the sea tomorrow. But the golden sand that is washed away by surf and tide may be returned in the same way, and the beach always offers a possibility of finding gold.

In 1865, a miner, prospecting atop the bluff, failed to find surface evidence of gold. He looked down upon the beach below and concluded that, if there was gold in the hill, it would probably show in the sand at the bottom. He went down and gave the beach the "once over", running the sand through his fingers, examining it under his glass, and finally trying it out with his pan. He found it teeming with free gold.

He kept his discovery a secret for about two years, while vainly attempting to make satisfactory arrangements for mining gold. His efforts to get financial backing were kept as quiet as possible, for he feared to have his project come to public notice. But eventually his news leaked out, and for the second time — just as he had feared — a gold rush started at Gold Bluff.

The agents of a big mining company recorded its claim to a part of this beach. The company's secretary, described in the records of that day as "a gentleman of much intelligence," examined the beach, and sent some of the sand to the company's metallurgist for an assay. Basing his estimate upon the metallurgist's report, the secretary informed his company that if the sand proved to be only one-tenth as rich as that examined, each member of the corporation would receive at least $43,000,000.

His remark was quoted from Alaska to Sonora: Gold

seekers rushed in and staked all unclaimed portions of the beach. Assaying of the sands raged like an epidemic. They found that the gold content of the sand was extremely variable. They were born too soon to know of Tom Sawyer's trickery with Aunt Sally's spoons, or they might have observed that what the sea laid down today, it would pick up again tomorrow.

Interested only in what would pay sure and prompt dividends, the mining company abandoned its hope of millions from the beach and turned its attention to other developments. The sea, however, went on endlessly washing the golden sands both in and out, and does so still. Meanwhile the hill which was feeding the sands with gold still stands and will doubtless continue to make a placer field of the beach until the bluff itself is washed away, or is reduced to rubble by an atom bomb.

On the Pacific shore, near latitude 41, in Northern California, between Trinidad and Arcata.

3.   Uranium in the Beach Sands

No tradition and little glamour and romance are inherent in the search for uranium, though considerable excitement usually ensues when a discovery is made.

Now comes Dr. Colin O. Hutton, professor of mineralogy at Stanford University, with the alluring statement that deposits of low grade uranium "are contained in common beach sand available on every California coastal beach." Dr. Hutton recently found such a deposit near Half Moon Bay, and in his enthusiasm he disclosed his finding to the press early in 1951.

The learned professor regards his discovery as highly important since most uranium used in making the atom bomb is extracted from very low grade ore. He believes that the deposits of black sand found at Half Moon Bay originated in the high Sierra and were washed down by the rains and the melting snows, flowing on to the sea, halting on the shore. One ton of the thorite black sand, he says, will produce one pound of pure uranium oxide, the "trigger" within the atom bomb.

This is worth looking into, and is a logical diversion after the search for the strange treasure in Oregon, and for the gold in the sand at the Bluff. No waybill is necessary. All you have to do is move right on down the coast. Have you never heard that one thing leads to another?

19

What Treasure in
Death Trap Mountain?

THE FORCE that can be used to split uranium into two differing elements where but one element was before, is very mysterious to most of us. But one thing we can readily understand: prospectors will be as glad to find a deposit of uranium as they were previously happy to find gold.

Prospectors and adventurers in the future are likely to be men of science with college degrees. Many an old prospector who could neither read nor write found gold and lesser minerals, but to locate uranium requires specialized knowledge. Now, with science brought to bear, conditions hitherto inexplicable may be made clear in terms of radioactivity connected with uranium or radium, or some similar rarity in the mineral world.

Radioactivity from some such element may be the answer to a long-forgotten tradition of the Hualapai Indians, of Arizona, brought into public notice in 1895, and ignored ever since.

206

WHAT TREASURE IN DEATH TRAP MOUNTAIN?

A few miles north of the rugged mining town of Kingman, in Mohave County, Arizona, an inexplicable form of natural power expresses itself in one of the most baffling phenomena known to man. The manifestation was known to the Hualapai Indians for centuries. They were content to recognize it as the power of the gods. The erudite white doctors of science cannot designate more definitely than by calling it radioactivity.

Because of its sure fatality to its unsuspecting victims, the Hualapais named it the Death Trap. The peak whereon it glows was known to them as Death Trap Mountain.

The Death Trap is in a narrow gorge, a little pass in a rugged and almost inaccessible mountain in the Cerbat range. The locale is of great interest to hunters and prospectors, for this mountain is the hide-away of antelope and big horn sheep, and lies in the gold and silver country.

Without obvious lure, the Death Trap is an immense jagged volcanic rock, so heavily charged with some nameless force that it deals death to any living thing which touches it — according to the claim of ancient tradition and more modern testimony. The stone has been described by those who have seen it as bursting up through a mass of shale and reaching to a height of about seven feet on the mountainside. Over the top a sharp ledge projects, making a three-sided tunnel about ten feet long and perhaps five feet wide.

The rock is described as having the luster of blue metal. It is seamed and ribbed as though by the action of flowing lava. At certain hours of the day when the sun shines directly upon it, the stone takes on a pale blue tint; at rare times it becomes almost colorless, and then, so say the Hualapais, it is perfectly harmless.

As the sun moves away from the mountain pass, the stone becomes darker and darker; when night comes, it glows with the steady, cold brilliancy of modern neon light. On moonless nights the stone shines the brighter and becomes a fascinating magnet for the wild animals inhabiting that region. The light can be seen for considerable distance at certain points below, where no other mountain masses obscure the view.

Though the tradition of the Death Trap was known to the Hualapais from prehistoric days, the stone was not known to white men until 1883. It was discovered by the men working on the Santa Fe Railroad, which, in that year, was extended across the Colorado River at a point nearby.

The railroad men, taking a holiday, went hunting in the Cerbat Mountains, about fifty miles from their railroad camp at Topock. They spent the night at a point from which they saw a bright, unflickering light up on the mountainside. Though curious about the light, they did not approach it. When they returned to their work on the railroad, they mentioned it and made inquiries. The Indians told them a a little about the power in the rock, but in keeping with the natural reticence of the red man, they withheld the complete tribal tradition.

In February, 1895, a small party of hunters from Pennsylvania, visiting in Arizona, went into the Cerbat range, hunting mountain sheep. Having no guide, they strayed farther from their base camp than they intended. Late in the afternoon, in the vicinity of the Death Trap, they started a sheep from the brush below. The sheep in its fright ran blindly into the narrow gorge beneath the overhanging ledge and, to the great surprise of the hunters, who had as yet not fired a shot, it fell dead upon the rock.

They moved forward to inquire into the mystery, when suddenly an old Hualapai came noiselessly out of the brush and halted them. By his words and gestures, they understood him to say:

"No, no, stay. You will be killed. You will die. Go no farther. The god in the stone will kill you, too."

The sheep, he made them understand, had stepped upon the Death Trap, and the hunters, if they followed after, would die, even as the sheep.

Under the influence of the kind demeanor of the white men and of their gifts of tobacco, the old Indian told them about the Death Trap, as he pointed out the vast number of

208

whitening bones lying in the gorge, fallen from the deadly stone and blown by the strong winds to the sloping mountainside.

While they stood gazing at the spectacle, a rattlesnake crawled out from a crevice in the mountain and approached the darkening rock. Mounting the edge of the stone, the snake writhed, coiled, raised its head, and fell lifeless.

The hunters thanked the Hualapai for saving them from a dreadful fate, and expressed their regret at losing the sheep, for the day was almost gone and sheep were not plentiful. The old man then removed from his middle a lariat of woven horsehair, and with a gentle whirl, he flung it up under the ledge, around the head of the sheep, without touching the rock, and quickly dragged the animal within reach of the white men who eagerly desired it for their evening meal. The tribesmen, he said, often drove animals upon the rock to lasso them for their flesh and fur.

The sheep was borne away to the hunters' camp and the Indian was invited to accompany them, to share their supper of fresh mutton. In camp that night, calling their attention to the brilliant light which could be seen from their campsite in the moonless dark, he told, in halting phrases, the timeless legend of the stone and its inexplicable power.

Long ago, even before the memory of their oldest grandfather, a stranger came to the Hualapai tribe, asking for food and shelter. His head and face were of a singular blond beauty, but his body was small, shrunken, deformed. His eyes were large, brilliant, blue as the sky, such eyes as were never before seen by the Hualapais. Though using no medicines, he had strange powers of healing the sick and injured — sometimes merely by fixing those large luminous eyes upon the patient. Even the wild animals loved him, and forsaking their natural ferocity, followed him about.

Having proved him, the chief of the tribe held the stranger in such trust and affection he made him a tribal medicine man. During the many years he remained with them, time had no aging effect upon him. Others grew old and the children matured, but the blond, blue-eyed, hunchbacked medicine man changed not.

The chief's son grew to manhood and was about to marry. The most beautiful of the Hualapai maidens was to be his bride. The marraige day was set and all was ready for the ceremonial rites. When the hour came to array the betrothed in garments fitting for the consort of a chief's heir, she could not be found. All search for her was vain. Gone as if she had never been!

Deep gloom settled down over the tribe. The day set aside for rejoicing became one of heaviest sorrow. Finally an old woman, withered and toothless, approached the chief and told him their beloved blond medicine man had, by his magic, taken the bride away. This the chief could not believe, for the medicine man had never betrayed their trust. But at last he was forced to believe.

Because of their love for the blue-eyed stranger, none would consent to see him killed, but all were agreed they must drive him away. Twelve of the braves were selected to see that he left the Hualapai region forever.

At sunrise they told him he must go. Giving him a fair start, they swiftly pursued. On and on they went. As time passed, they found themselves following, not chasing. He was leading them on, and as if drawn by some irresistible magnet, they could neither halt nor retrace their steps. When the chief sent runners to bid the braves return, they gave no ear to the commands.

On and on; looking neither to the left nor to the right; seeing only the once-loved figure before them. The hour of sunset near, they still ran without pause.

As the red sun reached the far horizon visible through the mountain pass, the chief's couriers, following the twelve, were spellbound and stood like statues, seeing the dozen braves fall, one by one, dead in their tracks, as they stepped upon the parted segments of a huge blue stone — the medicine man no longer visible.

And the Hualapais say the strange blond medicine man invoked into the stone forever the fateful power of the gods,

210

to frustrate pursuit of him and his stolen Hualapai bride.

White men tell that they have seen the stone and know that on moonless nights it shines with the cold steady glow of a neon light. They say any living thing contacting the stone, dies. But they do not tell how the rock became so charged with deathly power. No man knows.

Either Kingman or Topock will serve as a point of departure into the Cerbat range. Topock, a very small town on the Colorado River, is not so well known as Kingman, which during World War II was a great aerial military encampment.

It will be difficult to find the Death Trap, without first studying the Cerbat Mountains from the air, as was done with the celebrated Superstition Mountain by airmen from Williams Field. Since the time when the railroad men saw the glowing rock in 1895, much water has passed under the bridge, and it is impossible to say to what extent trees and shrubs have grown up, obscuring it. The Death Trap will probably be discovered by accident again, when hunters or prospectors come upon it unexpectedly. It cannot remain hidden forever.

20

The Lost Nail-keg of Gold

DON'T BE FOOLED when someone tells you Arizona, New Mexico, and Texas have all the lost mines and hidden treasures; Missouri comes up as a close contender for first place.

Of all Missouri's good stories of buried gold, among the most shocking is the history of the lost nail-keg of gold money buried on the old home place of Dr. Talbott, in Nodaway County — a nail-keg full of United States gold coins: half-eagles, eagles, and double eagles. What a furor would be created if that nail-keg should suddenly be found! And do not deceive yourself; though the gold has been lost for 80 years, it may yet be discovered. Modern science is wonderful!

In the northwest corner of Missouri, bordering on Iowa, is Nodaway County, with Maryville the county seat. Near Maryville is Barnard, a small quaint town, such as you often find described in old novels of England and America. Barnard was settled before the Civil War, and the descendants of the pioneer families still live in this region — the kind of

212

people among whom Americans from any state can easily feel at home.

Since Barnard is where we are going on this trip, you will want to know it is on U. S. Highway 71, straight north of St. Joseph, Missouri, and just a nice trip north from Kansas City, Missouri; it is also on the best of highways east and south from Des Moines, Iowa.

An increase in population after the Civil War brought into this area the professional people essential in every well-rounded community, and among these was Dr. Lynn Talbott. The doctor was badly needed, for there was much sickness in Nodaway County, and he became very popular, both as a doctor and as a public-spirited citizen.

He prospered from the start, and he acquired a fine home a few miles north of Barnard, on the Stagecoach Road. His home was known far and wide as the House of Seven Gables, after the novel by that name which had enjoyed great fame for two decades.

In this luxurious home he established his beautiful wife, and there they reared their two sons, Charles and Hugh. These made up the Talbott household, with the addition of Jamie, the hired man.

It is important to the outcome of this story to take note of the fact that the Talbott home was well furnished with all items of household gear and ornament regarded as essential to luxury and comfort at that time. The furniture was in the dark heavy style, and the windows were draped with heavy lace curtains, very modish then, but now looked upon as in bad taste for any period.

In those days the people of small towns did not have ready access to banks. The use of folding money and checks was not so common as it is today. Gold money was in circulation everywhere, conveniently carried, easily kept, easily passed from hand to hand, and accepted with no fear that some economic instability affecting the nation's banks would render it null and void.

Dr. Talbott's practice grew apace and his patients paid their debts in gold, five-, ten-, and twenty-dollar gold pieces.

213

When the time came that his family did not require all the income, the doctor began tossing his spare gold pieces into a nail-keg. He kept this up for years.

One day when adding a handful of coins to the keg he noticed that it was almost full; he decided to put it away and start filling another. For safekeeping he concealed the keg somewhere about his home place, and told no one where he had placed it. He did not say he had buried it, but his family assumed he had done so.

The gold in the nail-keg would never have entered the roster of lost treasures, had it not been for the terrible tragedy in the Talbott home on the night of November 12, 1869.

It was a moonless night, and snow was falling. The doctor had finished his supper; his wife was busy in the kitchen, and the two boys were supposed to be engaged with their own avocations somewhere about the house. Jamie, the hired man, was in the barn, taking care of the doctor's horses. The light from his lantern could be seen from the kitchen.

The doctor, wearied from his day's work, went into the parlor, drew aside the lace curtain and looked out at the falling snow. To assist the draft in the fireplace, he raised the window a trifle, and then, letting the curtain fall back into place, he sat down near the window to read. The light from the lamp in the center of the room rendered him easily visible from outside, even through the mesh of the curtain.

As he sat reading, relaxed in his heavy armchair, a bullet zinged into the room from the direction of the window, and buried itself in his head. The good doctor, Barnard's most valued public servant, and the only man with the key to the keg of gold, was dead.

Now this is a story of buried gold and not a murder mystery. But you will note that, somehow, gold and crime seem to go together. Certainly you will want to know about the murder.

Mrs. Talbot had heard the shot and ran to the kitchen door, seeing Jamie's lantern in the barn, where he was giving the tired horses their evening meal. The boys ran into the parlor and found their father — dead. Jamie, more shocked and excited than the others, rode immediately to Maryville for Sheriff Toel. The sheriff came at once to the House of Seven Gables, horrified and distressed at the murder of the well-beloved doctor.

Carefully the sheriff went over the scene of the crime several times, pulling aside the lace curtain and noting the snow as it filled up the tracks outside the window. The staggering question was not only *who* killed the kindly doctor, but also *why* was he killed? He had no known enemies, but he was reputed to have a nail-keg of gold money hidden somewhere on his home place. Was money the motive for the crime?

When the sheriff left the House of Seven Gables, he had no clue; but he did have a well-defined theory to work upon. He had concluded it was an inside job, and he prepared to work upon the members of the Talbott household.

Two nights passed. Public feeling in Barnard was strong, demanding police action to find the murderer. The Talbotts, downcast and miserable, sat at dinner in the kitchen in the warmth of the big stove. Answering a rap at the door, Mrs. Talbott admitted a young man they had never seen before. She asked him in to warm himself by the stove.

The stranger told them he was looking for a job. Did they have any work he could do? Charley and Hugh took him out to the woodyard where they had been cutting firewood. That work was agreeable to him, and for several days the three young men worked amicably together and in short order the two Talbott boys became very intimate with the stranger, who told them his name was Chandeler.

The two young Talbotts noticed that Chandeler behaved very oddly when anyone came into the woodyard where they were working. He would turn his back, or step out of sight around the corner of the tall woodpile. Finally Charlie asked him:

"What makes you act like you're afraid when you see anyone? Is the law after you for something?"

"Well, I don't know; might be," said Chandeler. "You

215

see, I killed a man back east where I come from, and I don't know whether they'd look for me so far west."

"Don't you worry," said Charlie. "You're safe here. Hugh and I killed our dad for his nail-keg of money, and they'll never in the world suspect us. Help us to find that keg and we'll give you a share."

Toward sunset that day, Chandeler quietly took one of Dr. Talbott's horses and rode away from the House of Seven Gables, hurrying along the Stagecoach Road to Maryville and Sheriff Toel. Imagination might say that, as he proceeded along his way, the lace curtain in the Talbott parlor was swaying in rhythm to the words: "Murder will out; murder will out!"

Soon after sunup the following day, Sheriff Toel appeared at the Talbott home, and took the two sons away to the Nodaway County jail, charged with the murder of their father.

After a delay of almost a year, their trial began on September 9, 1870. On the testimony of young Chandeler, who proved to be a private detective from Kansas City, the two boys were found guilty and convicted. Judge Lafe Dawson sentenced them to be hanged.

At the last moment, the boys confessed the crime. When asked their motive, they admitted it was to get possession of their father's keg of gold. When questioned as to what they had done with so much money, they stated they had never been able to find it.

It was the lace curtain that solved the murder. Sheriff Toel noticed the curtain was in perfect condition; not damaged in any way, with never a thread broken nor a trace of powder burn. He knew that one person must have held the curtain aside while another shot through the open window.

The questions that remain unanswered through the years are: Where is the nail-keg full of gold coins? And how much money was in the keg?

When I discussed this case with an old-time police detective, he told me the following, and I can't do better than to pass it on:

"I think the keg was nearly full of coins," he said, "and that would be a lot of money. The doctor probably began to save the money for his sons when they were yet little boys, intending them to have it at his death. Had he not been murdered, I believe he would have left a clue, or have told his wife where it was."

"Where do you think he could have buried the keg?" I asked.

"Well, after some study into the known facts," the old-timer replied, "I reconstruct the situation like this: On a bright spring day, some years before the crime, the doctor went out his back door, toward the barn, to work among his shrubbery. He took a spade, and maybe to strenghten the deception, he also took a trowel. On the pretence of improving some of the shrubs, he dug around the roots. I think the shrubs were near the side of the barn where the horses were kept.

"When he had dug enough around the bushes to make it appear that this was his sole interest at the moment, the doctor made a hole deep enough to take his keg of coins, close up under some overhanging branches. Such a place would be safe, as Jamie, a trusted servant, went in and out of the horse barn many times a day, and would notice any prowler around the barn, or the boys if they were digging around there.

"The shrubbery would grow from year to year, and the branches would hang closer to the ground, always improving as a guard. The shrubs are probably no longer there, not even a sign of them. I'm not sure the barn is still standing, but it would not be too hard to find out where it stood."

Go out along the old Stagecoach Road until you come to the site of the old House of Seven Gables. Now, heeding what the old-timer said, the first thing to do is to find out where the barn stood. Mark the outline of the walls. Then with your mineral locator, go all around where the outside walls stood, at a distance of six or eight feet. If this reconstruction is right, the gold will be found.

217

The keg has doubtlessly rotted away, and the coins, having been soaked by the many snows and rains of eighty years, are perhaps well-encrusted with soil. But gold never rots, never rusts, nor evaporates. So, happy hunting for the nail-keg of gold money. If you find it, don't forget your Uncle Sam, that famous coin collector.

21

Lost Gold in Iron Pots

FEW PEOPLE KNOW anything about money except that it's a handy thing to have around the house. Money changes in value for reasons which are not readily understood. Many things can happen to paper money, but metal money is permanent. Gold and silver will still have value long after the stamp and image upon it have passed away.

This was illustrated a few years ago when a farmer, plowing his field, somewhere in Yugoslavia, turned up an old earthen pot containing several hundred ancient silver coins. Not able to read the inscriptions on the coins, he took them to a local antiquarian. The savant reported that the coins bore the imprint of a kingdom and a ruler which had not been known in Europe for 600 years. Whereupon the farmer exclaimed:

"The king is gone; the kingdom is gone, and the people are gone, but the money is still silver!"

It almost seems that many people crave to hide money away in pots, and in 1951 the entire population of Belgium took up this pastime in a big way. In that year, the Belgian mint issued 38,000,000 silver coins, and by Christmas time every one of those coins had gone into retirement. What had become of them?

The Belgians are a thrifty people and they had stowed the hard money away for safekeeping, while the paper money, in which they had less confidence, passed from hand to hand for what it might be worth from day to day. Someday, perhaps many centuries hence, iron pots full of silver coins, may be dug up almost anywhere from the soil of Belgium.

In that same year, British workmen, laying a cable in the main street of Chester, England, turned up a large earthenware pot containing a hoard of Saxon silver ingots, bracelets, and other silver artifacts, buried more than 1000 years ago, an item to prove the lasting value of pots as a safety vault.

When in the course of American events it became necessary for our early pioneers to hide hard money away in pots, they could always find an iron pot around handy. And if the Confederate money had been hard money, a few iron pots could have preserved some of it up to now, and it would still have value. Whereas Confederate folding money is a mere memento or curiosity, iron pots, when buried in the ground, north or south, will keep a long time, in damp soil or dry.

While apparently there is no bank like an iron or earthenware pot, yet banking in buried pots has presented one serious drawback: Oftentimes it has proved impossible to identify the exact spot where the pots were buried, and consequently many of them have never been found. Absorb the following data of lost gold in iron pots, study the terrain, and you may be able to find one or both of them.

1. The Iron Pot With $50,000

There's a lot of history tied up in this story of lost gold in an iron pot. In fact, readers who follow stories of lost mines and buried treasures, if only for the glamour and romance of them, acquire a vast amount of historic lore. For the old valuables, lost and found, are part and parcel of the history of settlements, industries, folkways, and sometimes of the pursuit of science such as archaeology and geology.

In tracing the "why" and the "how come" of the lost iron pot with its $50,000, buried long ago, near the foot of the Estrella Mountains, in central Arizona, one gets a hint of the everyday dangers and the importance of the white settlers' drawing together in permanent settlements; and of the conditions in the raw desert country north of Tucson, subject continually to the depredations of hostile Indians and other outlaws in those times.

This episode shows the stern necessity of uniting for safety in traveling that wild country. Had the wagon trains not been reduced in number, the battle with the Apaches might have been averted, and the iron pot never buried in the ground.

In 1870, William Simmons, a Texan transplanted briefly to Prescott, Arizona, returned to Denton County, Texas, and as he had become well acquainted with general conditions in both Arizona and Southern California, and knew the roads, trails, and short cuts in that region, he was prevailed upon to act as leader in a covered wagon train of Texans who wished to remove to Southern California.

The party set out and all went well until the wagon train was somewhat west of Tucson. Simmons, it seems, had often spoken in high praise of the new settlement, which became the town of Phoenix, and of the promising future of the Salt River Valley, where the climate was free from frost and snow, and where, because of the infrequent rains, water was being brought to the land by way of canals.

When past Tucson and the journey's end still seemed far away, some of the party, wearied with the many days and nights of travel, decided to proceed to the Salt River Valley and try their luck homesteading near the new settlement. The rest of the group, now about one-half the original number, continued by a northwest route to California, passing north of the Gila in order to cross the Colorado River near present Blythe.

The Apaches, who were making their seasonal journey from the Gulf of California to the Superstition Mountains,

221

became very troublesome, making it necessary to keep extra guard and to be especially alert in protecting the animals. Also the Texans had reason to suspect they were in grave danger from white outlaws.

With their number reduced by the splitting of the party, it was necessary to revamp all their plans for safety and to make longer marches. They had not meant to camp near the Estrellas, but night overtook them at the southernmost end of the range, within view of the beautiful profile known as Montezuma's Head, and there they halted.

As they were short on men to handle firearms, the party made the traditional circular rampart of their wagons, placing within it their horses, mules, and cattle. Also as a safeguard against white renegades, they pooled all their gold and silver money, their watches and other jewelry, to the value of about $50,000, in a black iron cooking pot, and buried it in the middle of the circle, the soil padded down upon it by the trampling feet of the animals.

The night passed peacefully, but at daybreak the party was attacked by Apaches, trespassing in the region of the peaceful Pimas. After a furious fight, with casualties on both sides, the Indians were beaten off, but not until the savages had stolen several horses and set fire to some of the wagons.

When the Apaches withdrew, the caravaneers who remained buried their dead and piled the graves with stones. In great haste to leave the scene of the disaster, they hurried on their way toward California. In their confusion and excitement, they forgot to dig up the black iron kettle of valuables.

Some years later, one of the party returned to the scene of battle, and tried to find the spot where the iron pot had been buried. Having been a mere boy when with the wagon train in 1870, he could not remember the detailed landmarks, and his efforts were fruitless. Where the caravaneers placed it, there it remains today.

The iron pot with its $50,000 of ready-made values has been more coveted than many a lost mine and has never been forgotten through the years. In September, 1941, Master Sergeant John Falk, of East Greenwich, R. I., and Private

John Carrara, of Bethel, Conn., were stationed at Luke Field, near Phoenix, from which they could at all times view the Estrella Mountains. They undertook a prospecting trip to these mountains one afternoon, underestimating the disance from the Field, as most easterners are apt to do, who have no acquaintance with the difficulties of negotiating the desert. As time passed and they were unaccounted for, planes were sent out to hunt them. They returned under their own steam, empty-handed, exhausted, and footsore. But wiser.

Whether they sought the pot of gold, or the lost treasure of Ortega, mentioned in another chapter, or the deposit of ilmenite known to be in that region, they did not disclose, and their experience was a warning to others at the Field not to go treasure hunting on foot in the desert unless well prepared and desert-wise.

The antiquarian may find other treasures at the foot of the Estrellas. In April, 1946, some Pimas, hunting in an unfrequented corner of their reservation, at the foot of the range, found an old buckboard wagon, at least 70 years old. The skeletons of two horses with Spanish bits still in the jaws, were hitched to the buckboard, plants and trees growing up through the floorboards. The horses were facing a tall cactus which had apparently been their hitching post. Ten feet above the ground was the mark of a rope or strap which had tethered them to the cactus, showing the growth since the day the team was tied. Roundabout were remnants of harness and bridle, and coins dated 1865. The relics were removed to a mission on the Pima reservation, but the story will remain another desert mystery.

The Spanish bits and the absence of horseshoes hint that this was a Texas or Mexican outfit, and it is fair to guess the driver was looking for the cave with the Ortega treasure.

At the south end of the Estrellas, below Montezuma's Head, in a level campsite, with a small butte on the east side, some say not far from Telegraph Pass, nearby in the mountains. In fact, some old-timers call this "the lost treasure of Telegraph Pass."

2.   Tragedy Marks Dutch Oven Gold.

If you were to find an old Dutch oven or an iron pot full of gold coins or other valuables made of gold, you would, of course, be under legal compulsion to take it to a bank and turn it in. But your generous uncle, Señor Sam, would give part of the value back to you. At least he would give you back the oven or the pot.

A Dutch oven full of gold was recently found in California, after having been lost for several generations. A Dutch oven full of gold money is still lost in Oregon, and you know of the iron pot with $50,000 still lost near the Estrella Mountains in Arizona.

The old Dutch oven or iron pot named in this report, however, was buried in Kansas, and though hundreds of treasure hunters have searched, none is known to have found it.

Many years ago, some say in 1865, a caravan of covered wagons was returning east through Kansas from the California goldfield. They had some gold, but not as much as the size of the party might lead a seasoned outlaw to expect.

On the way through Ford County, in the sand dunes, about ten miles southwest of the present small town of Offerle, the caravan was attacked by Indians. The travelers saw the redskins coming from afar off, and realized that some of their number were likely to be killed. They pooled their gold money, what watches and gold jewelry they had, and placing them in a Dutch oven, buried it in a spot known to them all, so that those who might survive could recover and claim it.

No one, however, escaped the terrible slaughter by the Indians except one little girl whom they carried away with them, as was their custom to do with children, and sometimes with women.

The scene of the massacre was stamped indelibly upon the child's mind. The whooping and yelling of the redskins; the firing of the guns by the whites; the bows and arrows; the stampeding horses; the blood flowing from the killed and wounded, and all the horrible detail of such an experience could never be forgotten. And with it all she vividly remembered an old gnarled and twisted tree as an outstanding feature of the landscape.

The child lived with the tribe for several years, but as the white population of the Middle West increased, and life became increasingly hard for the Indians, she escaped and rejoined her own race. When she grew to womanhood and married, she often told her family and friends of the battle and the Dutch oven with the gold money. Finally she desired to return to the scene of the massacre and once more view the place where she had lost so much that was dear to her. She thought she might find the old Dutch oven and take the gold as an inheritance from her parents.

She found the place with ease, but she did not find the oven. The old gnarled tree, pieces of the wagons, human bones, arrows, and various items of old metal convinced her she was not mistaken in the place, but she could not point out the spot where the treasure had been buried.

The sand dunes have been searched over and over. Nearly every man, woman, and child in Offerle, which has a population of about 500, has at some time hunted for the Dutch oven, but in vain. Residents of Fort Dodge, less than 50 miles away, try their luck also, but the shifting sands of the dunes have foiled all comers.

Some of the local residents think the winds blowing upon the sands have uncovered the oven and that it has been secretly taken away, but this is doubtful. Gold is heavy and sinks farther into the ground with each passing year, and in all likelihood the oven is now at a depth beyond the shifting sand, and will be uncovered only by some human agency.

Go ten miles southwest of Offerle, in the sand dunes, a favorite afternoon drive for the young people of the town, each of whom hopes someday to stumble upon the iron oven that holds the gold. Look for the old gnarled tree, or the place where once it stood. Not far from where the old tree once had its roots will be found the pot of gold at the end of the rainbow.

225

22

The Belle McKeever Gold

THE KIDNAPPING of a beautiful young girl in pioneer days set in motion an Apache hunt in Arizona that resulted in the finding and losing of a valuable deposit of pure gold, the search for which, renewed intermittently through the years, has not ceased to this day.

In 1869, Abner McKeever and and his family, which included his beautiful daughter, Miss Belle, were settled upon a ranch in the big bend of the Gila River. Living in peace and friendship with the Papago and Pima Indians, the McKeevers, like the tribesmen, were compelled to be constantly on the alert against the roving hostile Apaches.

The Papagoes were living south of the river, and the Pimas on the north side, peacefully engaged in their ordinary agricultural pursuits, but with a weather eye always out for their hereditary enemies, the Apaches.

The truculent Apaches frequently sneaked through the territory of the peaceful tribes, and sometimes went through brazenly as a challenge to them when on the seasonal trips which the Apaches were wont to make from Mexico to Superstition Mountain and return.

The town nearest to the McKeever ranch was Colorado City, that being then the name of the present town of Yuma. Across the Colorado River from Colorado City was Fort Yuma, where United States troops were garrisoned.

Not far from the McKeever ranch, though some little distance from the bank of the Gila, Abner had a rich placer mine, at which all the members of the family worked from time to time. The labor was not extremely arduous, since it consisted mostly in merely digging in the sand and panning for the "colors." McKeever's daughter, Belle, sometimes took her turn at panning.

One hot summer day, when several members of the family were spending the day at the mine, they were attacked by a sizable party of Apaches, coming up from Mexico, en route to Superstition Mountain for the annual saguaro apple harvest. A battle ensued, too sudden to permit the McKeevers to call upon their Pima and Papago friends for help.

The Apaches, having all the advantage, seized Belle McKeever and made off with her. Knowing from previous experience that they would be pursued, the savages separated into several small bands, each band racing from the scene in a different direction.

Word of the attack and the kidnapping was immediately sent to Fort Yuma, and United States troops were dispatched to the Gila River region to overtake and punish the Apaches. When the troops who arrived at the scene of the battle had observed the lay of the land and mapped out their campaign, the soldiers separated into small companies in the same manner as the Apaches, each company "lining out", according to the several clues, after the redskins.

The time required to carry the word of the attack to the fort by horseback, and for the troops to reach the McKeever placer mine, from which to trace the Indians' trail, gave the tribesmen a chance to put considerable mileage between themselves and their pursuers. The soldiers, therefore, found the trail somewhat cold.

The lieutenant in charge detailed Sergeant Crossthwaite

with Private Joe Wormley and Private Eugene Flannagan to take a slightly northwesterly course, in the belief that the band with Belle had taken that direction.

Without pausing to give their horses the proper rest, after the forced march from Fort Yuma, the soldiers struck out immediately upon the lieutenant's command. They were without adequate rations, and with a very limited supply of water — in the shadeless heat of an Arizona summer.

Ere long their water was gone; then their food supply gave out. Two of their horses dropped dead from heat, thirst, and fatigue. The soldiers had not yet come upon any trace of the kidnappers and the captured Belle.

The trio halted long enough to cut up one of the dead horses and refresh themselves with horsemeat. Packing some of the steaks upon their one remaining horse, they took time out to make a search for water, striking more directly north into what was to them a totally unknown country, believed afterwards to be the foothills of the Granite Wash Mountains.

Their need for water hourly becoming more acute, in a temperature producing constant and profuse perspiration, finally grew so pressing that Wormley became delirious. Near nightfall, on the steep southern slope of a hill, they found a spring of cool, clear water, just in time to avert a greater catastrophe to them all.

That night, exerting their little remaining strength they built a small fire beside the spring and in the embers roasted some of their horse steaks. Then, somewhat revived, they fell into a refreshing sleep.

In the morning, squatting at the edge of the spring to take water for washing their begrimed faces, they noticed the spring was completely lined with gold nuggets. In the hillside, above the spring, were two veins of quartz, "one narrow, the other sixteen feet wide," (on the word of Col. James McClintock, Arizona historian).

The quartz was so richly gold-bearing that the soldiers dug the gold out with their knives, and loaded about fifty pounds on their only horse. Pursuit of the Apaches and recovery of Belle McKeever having passed out of their minds by reason of their exciting discovery and their physical unfitness for further hardships, they purposed to retrace their steps to the Gila River and report to the lieutenant.

Sense of direction and locality completely failed them. They wandered about for three days, and then were shocked to a sense of reality when their one and only horse dropped dead. Though unaware of the fact, they were then less than a day's journey from the Gila River.

Unable to agree as to the general direction to the river and the shortest route to it, the three soldiers separated. Each proceeded alone, but their paths were not far apart.

Wormley reached the river first, weak, emaciated, and still somewhat out of his mind. Though able to give a sketchy account of what had happened, he could not guide a searching party back over his trail.

And is it strange that his story of finding the gold superseded in public interest his account of failure to recapture Belle McKeever from the hands of the barbarous Apaches?

A party was made up of about a dozen men to "line out" in the general direction indicated by Wormley, in desert and hills, to aid Flannagan and Crossthwaite, if they could be found. They found Private Flannagan, exhausted and helpless. His story checking exactly with Wormley's, some of the men took Flannagan into camp, while the others went on in the hope of rescuing Sergeant Crossthwaite.

But the once-doughty sergeant had not survived. His body was lifeless when the searchers found it. In his pocket was a small roughly-drawn map, made with a match stick, showing the springs, the hill, and the two veins, but naturally lacking all data of directions, distances, and identifying landmarks.

Again the searching party divided, some to take the body of Sergeant Crossthwaite to camp, for disposition by the army, the others to go on and, if possible, to find the golden spring.

A little farther north the searchers found the dead horse, less than one day's journey from the river. The gold ore was

229

still in the pack securely strapped to his back. Not only tradition but written history records that the fifty pounds of ore carried $1800 in gold. From that day to this the riches in the spring have been known as the Lost Belle McKeever mine.

In time, Eugene Flannagan recovered his health. But he never recovered from his fear and horror of the desert. He lived in terror of ever again meeting with a shortage of water; and not for all the gold in the world could he ever again be induced to go on an overnight journey away from the river.

He made several half-hearted attempts to relocate the spring, but his fear of again undergoing the terrible suffering occasioned by lack of water, under the hot summer sun in the Arizona desert — or some other unknown fear — precluded his following through to a reasonable conclusion. He never, however, deserted Arizona, and died in Phoenix in 1880.

Was the golden spring ever rediscovered? If so, it has never been announced to the public. But in the general direction of the three soldiers' expedition, several golden bonanzas have been discovered and worked out. This is not saying, by any means, that no more gold deposits lie there under the surface, or in the recess of the now unknown spring.

And what of Belle McKeever? Was she ever retaken from her Apache captors and restored to the bosom of her family? No record of her recapture is to be found in the writings of Arizona historians. Some of the old-timers or their descendants may remember, but all researches into Belle's fate made by this author, through a period of years, have failed to solve the mystery. History and tradition make no further mention of her.

Get a map of Arizona. Find the big bend of the Gila River. Draw a line west but slightly north. Figure out about two-and-a-half days' travel on a tired horse. Then draw a line north toward the Granite Wash Mountains, but still in northern Yuma County. Now you're getting warm.

Do not confuse Granite Wash Mountains with Granite

Mountains. Granite Wash Mountains are in Yuma County, and there is no wash close roundabout to give them that name. They comprise a small range running north and south, north of Salome and in the Harcuvar region, where several bonanzas were once in operation.

23

Nellie Cashman and the Lost Gold

PERHAPS NO WOMAN of the pioneer West was better known, better liked, and more respected, up and down the map, than was Miss Nellie Cashman, whose experiences in the raw and rugged frontier ranged from mid-Mexico to northern Alaska, and beyond the Arctic circle.

It is not generally known that she once hunted a lost gold mine in Baja California, which still remains lost, notwithstanding some heroic efforts to find it.

Now let's get this straight about Baja California. There's no comma between Baja and Califonia, as is so often seen when this region is named in the American press. Baja (pronounced báh-hah) means "low" in Spanish; the name is therefore used to mean "Lower California." This mysterious, long, narrow peninsula belongs to Mexico, and geographically has nothing to do with the U.S. state of California, except to border on it, making a part of the boundary between the two republics. Let this be grist to your information mill, for some day in the not far distant future, Baja California will be rich and famous because of its great abundance of natural resources, its delightful climate, and its strategic location for sea and air movements in a global war. But at present, what a wonderful place for a hide-away or for treasure-hunting adventures!

Baja California abounds in legends and traditions of ancient lost treasures, not only precious metals in the ground, and secret caches of coin and gold, but also ancient art in paintings and architecture; also in deeply intriguing stories of the Spanish padres who founded the now forgotten missions. Nellie Cashman did not know about these treasures and the missions when she went on the gold hunt. She was wiser when she returned, but what she had learned remained closely guarded behind firmly sealed lips.

Miss Cashman was born in Queenstown, Ireland, and with her sister, she came to this country soon after the Civil War. Landing in Boston, she was among the first to make the trip from sea to sea by the first U. S. transcontinental railroad, arriving in San Francisco in 1869. The sister married Thomas Cunningham, but Nellie, by choice, remained a spinster, to become "Aunt Nell" to five little Cunninghams, whose care she assumed when the parents died; the marriage, the five births, and the two deaths all occurring in the short span of fourteen years.

A beautiful woman, with raven black hair, bright, snapping black eyes, fair and delicate Irish skin, and a figure a Powers model might envy, Nellie Cashman endued everything about her with the quality of drama: she was a dramatic figure in a dramatic setting, and the wonder is that no playwright has ever written a stage or screen drama around her.

If ever a human being loved action, adventure, emergency, and crisis, it was Nellie Cashman, and in 1877 she joined the stampede to the Cassiar gold district in the far north, an enterprise promising all the action and adventure her heart could desire. There in the land of perpetual cold and snow she made a reputation as the champion lady musher; distinguished herself for ability as a prospector, and carried her devotion to the Catholic faith throughout every day and hour. She became known far and wide as a doer of good deeds and a rescuer of those in distress. In fact, her life was one long saga of acts of charity and mercy.

It is well remembered to this day that by sheer force of personality — without an iota of properly constituted author-ity — she accomplished one thing never before heard of in northern Alaska, in a period when airlift belonged only to the realm of the Arabian Nights:

She compelled the delivery of potatoes and other fresh vegetables to the miners in the far-off Cassiar gold diggings — brought in through special arrangement by express, with priority over almost every other commodity. The miners were saved from scurvy, and blessed the name of Nellie Cashman.

The following year Nellie returned to California, and af-ter a brief visit there, she cast about for a suitable place to go into business. Concluding that Virginia City and Pioche, Nevada, were nearly worked out, she decided to settle in Tombstone, Arizona, where the silver mines were in bonan-za.

Thus it was when "the town too tough to die" was in its rip-roaring, quick-trigger heyday, she was conducting the "Delmonico" restaurant in that town, and acting as foster mother to the five orphaned children of her sister.

Never one to resist the call of adventure, Nellie pricked up her ears when a gold stampede took place in Baja Cali-fornia, across the gulf from Guaymas. Tombstone was a silver town; gold was something else again.

One day in 1884 a Mexican came to Tombstone from the new gold field, and showed a collection of large pure gold nuggets, a great mass of which, he said, was to be had for the taking, just outside the town of Mulege (Mulega), on the east coast of Baja California, easily reached from southern Sonora.

A small select group of Tombstone men, including M. E. Joyce, one time supervisor of Cochise County, and Mark A. Smith, later United States Senator from Arizona, undertook to go down to these gold fields and stake out claims. Most of them were experienced in mining and familiar with gold ore. They felt confident that, with their knowledge of gold-bearing rock, they could not miss the new gold field so vividly described to them.

Persuaded perhaps by her irrepressible love of adventure and risk, or perhaps lured by nostalgia for a repetition of her gold-hunting days in Alaska, Nellie Cashman joined them. She dressed for the part in levis, soft-collared flannel shirt, and Stetson sombrero.

Old-timers in Tombstone never tire of telling of that day when the gold-hunting party, with Nellie the most colorful figure among them, left the city, in the famous old Modoc stage, bound for Guaymas, a formidable trip in those days. Most gold-hunters go quietly; but not this party. As the stage stood in front of Nellie's restaurant, taking on the passengers, the populace lined up as if for a circus parade. As the stage finally started, hats and handkerchiefs waved to them, hail and farewell, and they were off.

In Guaymas they chartered a boat for the trip across the gulf to Mulege. On foot they trudged many weary miles from the town, through wild desert country. Making camp in a flat, dry place, they set out to examine the terrain, after the manner of prospectors. The men scoured the areas of sand and gravel, looking for placer. Nellie, however, started out alone, going farther inland among the mesquite, ironwood, and other desert growth, no doubt trying to apply her gold-mining lore learned in Alaska.

None of them discovered anything of value, and day after day they returned to camp, fatigued and disappointed — all except Nellie, who, in the face of everything, remained vital, cheerful, and confident.

Thinking, time after time, that they would surely find the bed of the big gold nuggets the next day, they stayed longer than they had planned. True to form, their water supply gave out. The men went out from camp in different directions to find a spring or a stream of fresh water, for without an immediate supply their lives would be endangered. They seemed to have lost calculation of how far they were from Mulege, where water might be available. One and all, they returned to camp empty-handed, despair and failure written in their faces.

Nellie, who had often returned from her solitary sorties with no gold but with no dismay, became impatient with the ineptitude of the men. Making a show of desperation at their terrible plight, she finally said:

"Now I'm going out to find water — and no fooling!"

Waving a playful goodby, she disappeared to the southwest among the mesquite in the hot silence of the desert.

Guided by a sense seemingly not possessed by the men, she found her way to a small Catholic mission, where she could get water in plenty. With goatskin containers filled with water, on the backs of burros, in charge of a servant from the mission, she arrived in camp, light-hearted, assured, and nonchalant. There she found the men frantic with thirst.

When the burros appeared in the camp with their life-saving water supply, with Nellie in the lead and the servant bringing up the rear, the Tombstone men could scarcely believe their eyes. Were they seeing a mirage, or was all this real?

Marvelous that they could be so dense as to assume that Nellie Cashman, who could, in the wilderness, find a mission, servants, burros, and water, could not find gold in the adjacent dry terrain, after all her prospecting experience in Alaska. They did not realize that Nellie had something which she valued far more than any gold she might possibly discover anywhere this side of Kingdom Come: her faith, and loyalty to those serving her faith.

The party returned to Tombstone, shamefaced at having failed to make a gold strike, though assured the gold was there, that little-known country being notably gold-bearing.

Nellie Cashman said little about this adventure. It can easily be discerned that at the mission she acquired some special information which greatly impaired her desire to find a gold mine in that particular locality:

A group of foreigners mining in that region would be a disruptive influence in the peaceful life of the mission, and

236

Nellie's sympathies would naturally rest with the bearers of the Holy Faith, for whom she would be content at any time to forego a fortune. She made no plan for a second try at the gold, and so far as we know, the padres and their mission continued to live in peace.

With a radius of about three miles, circle Mulege, on the gulf, in Baja California. The gold, both placer and vein, will likely be found to the southwest. And don't forget you are an alien in Mexican territory. If you are supplied with proper credentials for entry into Mexico, and you find any valuables, you will be entitled to your half-share, on the same basis as a Mexican citizen.

24

Nigger Ben's Lost Mine

ONE OF the richest gold mines ever discovered in Arizona is located in Yavapai County, in the north central part of the state. The mine is now known as Rich Hill, but as far into the past as eighty years ago the Indians were calling it Little Antelope.

This mine and the neighboring gulches have produced more than twenty million dollars in placer gold, we are told. More than $780,000 have been picked up in large nuggets from the surface upon the top of Rich Hill, so report says. Turning over a single boulder would often disclose nuggets worth $5,000 and $6,000 of almost pure gold. These statements are all a part of Arizona tradition.

Alleged records are mentioned in published accounts of this placer mine as proof that in 1862 and 1863 more than half a million dollars in nuggets were picked up from a single acre on top of this hill.

A. H. Peeples who came into the territory with the famous Walker party, is said to have taken a fortune in placer gold from Little Antelope, and since he liked farming better than mining, he acquired a ranch in what is now known as Peeples Valley. On this ranch he had a number of employes, and among them was an industrious, intelligent, and well respected Negro, called by all who knew him, with no intent of disrespect, Nigger Ben.

There is often a peculiar bond of sympathy and understanding between Negroes and Indians, and Ben was on the friendliest terms with the Indians who frequented the Peeples ranch. One Indian in particular attached himself to Ben and passed a great deal of time in his company. Their devotion to each other implied the trust without which friendship is impossible.

The Indian was aware that Ben had dreams of some day discovering a rich gold mine all by himself, which he could claim for his own. The Indian had had enough experience with white men's ways to know that Ben could protect such a claim by pursuing a certain course with the United States government, which would give him the same security it would give a white man. Then Ben could build a fine house, marry, and, like a white man, entertain his friends with lavish generosity.

One day Ben's Indian friend confided to him the astounding information that, not far from the Little Antelope mine, there was another hill, surpassingly rich in gold; in fact, it was so much richer than Little Antelope that the Indians called it Big Antelope.

Ben was fired with immediate interest and excitement. He immediately envisioned all his wildest dreams come true.

"Who owns the Big Antelope mine?" he asked, calmly.

"The Indians own it," was the reply. "But they keep the gold a secret. They have no use for it themselves and it makes big trouble when they do business for it with white men. So the Indians let it be, and white men have never found it."

There are several likely looking hills not far from Little Antelope, but how could one tell which one the Indian had in mind?

For some months Ben pondered on this. He studied the possibilities of making contact with the mine without the

Indian's knowledge. He thought he might at least look at it and see for himself whether the Indian was telling the truth. Heretofore they had treated each other square, but this sounded so big that Ben's confidence in the tribesman seemed about to give way under the strain. After studying the matter from all sides, he decided to abandon the idea of finding the mine alone.

Finally, though not implying any doubt of the Indian's story, Ben asked him to guide him to the hill and let him see for himself the Big Antelope with its fine store of gold. The Indian refused.

"No," he said. "We are getting along all right as we are. Why bring down trouble upon our heads by not letting well enough alone. The gods do not like the Indians to give away their secrets to the white men — or to black men, either, for that matter."

But Ben harped upon that one string for so long that eventually he wore down the Indian's resistance. He consented to be Ben's guide to the farther hill where he said the treasure lay.

They set out. When they arrived at Sycamore Springs, the Indian's manner underwent a sudden change. He dropped his friendly attitude, and his demeanor became sullen, cold, even hostile.

"The mine is near here," he told Ben. "You must look for it yourself."

It was more than mere superstitious belief that serious misfortune would overtake an Indian who led a white man to any concealed treasure. Battle, murder, and terrible death had so often followed such disclosures that it had become a part of the duty every Indian owed his son, as a form of life insurance, to teach him that the wrath of the gods would overtake the Indian who made known to a white man the whereabouts of "the pretty yellow stone."

Though Nigger Ben was not white, his Indian friend was acute enough to realize that Ben was as covetous, and therefore as dangerous as if he had been as blond as the hunters' moon. The fact that Ben was neither red nor white added another element to his thought, no doubt, and so confused the Indian's simple mind that he was overruled by fear of his tribal gods' revenge.

While they rested at Sycamore Springs the Indian remained stoically indifferent to all persuasion. He sternly declined to open Ben's eyes to whatever gold may have been lying before him. He insisted that while Ben could search as much as he pleased, it would have to be without aid from him. Meanwhile, he would wait there, he said, until Ben either found the mine or satisfied himself that he could not find it. Then Ben was to rejoin his waiting friend and they would return to the pleasant Peeples Valley together.

Ben struck out alone, leaving the Indian at the springs. He searched for three days. He had been with A. H. Peeples in 1862, when Peeples, Paulen Weaver, and Jack Swilling discovered the gold mine known as Weaver's Diggings, and he knew gold when he found it. There can be no question that he was not deceiving the tribesman when he returned to Sycamore Springs and reported failure.

Together they returned to the Peeples ranch, and Ben spent several months studying over the matter. He respected the Indian's reluctance to guide him to the mine, for he knew the tradition forbidding it. Since many particulars pointed to the red man's good faith, Ben believed it was merely his own luck or carelessness that had caused him to fail in finding the gold.

Some months later he prepared to make another search for the Big Antelope. Again he induced the Indian to accompany him as far as Sycamore Springs. Before setting out he called Mr. Peeples aside and to him confided his plan. He named a date for his return and said:

"If I have not returned to the ranch by that time, Mr. Peeples, will you send to Sycamore Springs to look for me, or will you come? If I haven't come back by that time, it will be because something has happened to me. If the Indian shows me the gold, he may afterwards kill me."

"Now, Ben, don't be foolish," said Peeples. "Stay here on

the ranch. Don't go running off on some fool chase with an Indian. You ought to know better."

Ben, however, was not to be dissuaded, and Peeples gave the desired promise.

The time passed and Ben did not return. Accompanied by two of his ranch hands, Peeples hastened to Sycamore Springs. There they found the body of Nigger Ben. He had been murdered. The Indian had disappeared and he was never seen in Peeples Valley again.

Peeples and his companions examined the body carefully before they buried it. They concluded that death had occurred only a day or two before. In Ben's pockets they found large nuggets of yellow gold. They were convinced he had been successful in his search; he had found the Big Antelope and was on his way back to the Peeples ranch.

What took place between Ben and his Indian guide, they could only guess. It is likely that when the Indian learned or suspected that Ben had actually found the Big Antelope, he became fearful that the wrath of the gods would alight upon him for having been instrumental in the discovery. In order to halt the merited vengeance from heaven he may have attempted to avert his fate by the only means he knew, and "wiped Ben out."

Peeples afterward stated to James H. McClintock, Arizona historian, that it was possible Nigger Ben was not murdered; he might have died in the desert from thirst.

In 1891, Ed Schieffelin, discoverer of the Tombstone silver, with a large party of prospectors, examined the entire region indicated by Nigger Ben's experience, but they found nothing, outside the then well-known recorded claims.

No gold was ever found at Sycamore Springs, and the Big Antelope mine is still undiscovered.

This lost lode is in the Weaver gold mining district, in the southwest corner of Yavapai County, east of Congress. But when so near a county line, a vein may run into the next county. Nearby is Antelope Peak, with an elevation of 5,786 feet. In Ben's time there were some waterholes nearby. The gold is in a rock formation similar to the ore from Rich Hill. Go in the general direction of McCracken.

25

Lost Opals – Platinum – Diamonds

MANY PERSONS, sensitive to color, regard the opal as the most beautiful of gems. Many more prefer the diamond. Both of these gems are at their best when set in platinum. Experts say a gold setting diminishes the brilliance of the diamond, while it offers not enough contrast for the flashing fire of the opal; so here platinum becomes the royal metal.

Now what will you say when I tell you I know of a lost opal mine, a lost diamond mine, and a lost platinum mine? And I will go just one step farther — just one, mind you — and mention another lost mine so incredible, that even I, myself, would never believe it, if I did not hold the proof within my own two hands. A lost mine of *yellow* turquoise!

When the gem-lovers and treasure hunters among my friends behold this large specimen of yellow turquoise which I possess from the lost mine, they stand bug-eyed with incredulity. Never heard of it, they say.

Lest it be thought an opal mine, when found, might not pay dividends, it will be worth while to glance at the

244

output of the Rainbow Ridge opal mine, in Virgin Valley, Nevada, owned by G. Keith Hodson, of Mina, a mine noted for its fire opals. This mine, in 1919, produced the famous Robling opal, now in the Smithsonian Institution, in Washington, D. C., and valued by collectors at $250,000. Known as "black opal," the gem weighs seventeen ounces and gives off flashes of red and purple fire. Originally owned by Tiffany, Hodson's mine has produced many exceptionally beautiful gems, the finest being found near the surface.

1. The Lost Opal Mine.

For centuries the superstition has persisted that there is a jinx on opals. Certain philosophers in the occult sciences say this jinx doesn't hold for persons born when the sun is in the zodiacal sign, Libra, which is mostly in October. And it may be that those of you who weren't born under Libra, had better pass this one up.

But it cannot be denied that October would be an ideal month to make an expedition after the lost opal mine, for this mine lies in a region where the summers are very hot, not conducive to strenuous activity; though the other seasons, beginning with October, give the kind of weather you hope you will find in heaven.

In 1879, a party of American prospectors, wandering north from the Mexican border, passed through Tombstone, Arizona, and went northeast, crossing the state line, and proceeding a few miles into New Mexico, about thirty miles west of Lordsburg. There, in a little range of mountains, called the Horseshoe range, because of its semi-circular shape, they discovered a deposit of opals.

They were looking for gold, and though they vaguely recognized value in the gems, opals were not the object of their single-minded search. So they traded their interest in the mine to two prospectors who gave them some gold bullion for a grubstake to continue their search for the precious metal.

The two who acquired the mine from its first claimants probably were not born when the sun was in the sign, Libra, for when they sent a small crew to develop the opal mine for them, the miners were chased away by Indians. The location proved to be dangerously near Chief Cochise's stronghold, and as his Chiricahua Apache tribesmen were constantly on the move, little could escape their eagle eyes.

The owners at this time took a dim view of the prospect for peace with the Apaches, and after a few years of inactivity at the mine, they gave it away to two other fellows, to whom they were in arrears for wages. These two were mining the gems in 1885, when a band of prowling Chiricahuas sneaked in upon them and killed them both. Their birth dates are not known, but clearly the opals were not for them.

The opal mine was never worked after that, and its exact location has been forgotten. However, it can be argued that, like a "fixed star" the opal deposit is today exactly where it was then.

In 1902, the story of the lost opals was revived in the southwestern press. The son of a prominent Arizona pioneer made an attempt in Phoenix to organize a small expedition to go into the Horseshoe range to hunt the deposit of gems. The Indians were then peacefully ensconced on their various reservations, and there was nothing to fear except rattlesnakes, scorpions, centipedes, Gila monsters, mountain lions — and the jinx.

For some reason which the local newsmen could never ascertain, the whole scheme fell through. Personally, I believe it was because the leader was trying to put the plan on foot in the extreme heat of an Arizona summer, when interest in opals is at a low ebb, superseded by a constant desire for shade and a tall glass topped with foam.

Did the jinx fade away when the Indians were pacified, or is it still hovering over the jewel mine? This question cannot be answered until the mine is rediscovered and the gems put to their destined use.

Now, let's see: just where should one look for this mine of opals? If you're sure you want to look, here is your waybill, and all you need besides is a two-weeks' vacation, and an old car or a burro, some bacon and beans, a pick and shovel, and the spirit of adventure.

The Horseshoe range turns in a curve southwest of the little town of Summit, New Mexico, close to the Arizona line. These mountains are about fifteen miles from the Summit railway station, built for the Arizona and New Mexico railroad, which later became a part of the El Paso and Southwestern line.

Viewing Summit from the Arizona side, it lies southeast from Duncan; from the New Mexico side, it is slightly northwest of Lordsburg. The Horseshoe Mountains are said by prospectors to have the appearance of being well mineralized, and probably contain other values besides opals. The next time you are in Summit, ask some old-timer about opals in the Horseshoe range; he can probably give you a better waybill, exact to a gnat's eyebrow.

2. The Lost Platinum Ore-body.

Platinum is now having its little day as a most important element. Though it first became known in Europe in 1741, and had been found in an alloy in a tomb in Egypt dating from 700 B. C., it has been held in high regard only for a century or a little more. In 1823, it was found in gold-bearing sands in the Ural Mountains of Siberia, and that has been its chief source since. Now that Russia has cut us off, we have had to turn to South America and Canada for this metal which has become essential for our military projects.

Military projects, I say? Yes, indeed. Platinum is used in electronics, without which certain aspects of modern warfare would be seriously hampered — not that we'd have to go back to bows and arrows!

Before starting out on the expedition to find the lost platinum mine it is well to know what other elements may be found along with the platinum, in case one of these others should show up first in the test.

The platinum group is made up of iridium, osmium,

rhodium, palladium, ruthenium, and sometimes copper, chromium, and titanium. Any of these may be found in platinum ore, but the most likely, and perhaps the most desirable, in these days of wholesale destruction so carefully designed, is palladium. Don't be downcast if you've never seen palladium; few of us have ever laid an eye on it.

Found in all platinum, so the claim is made, and in some nickel, silvery white in color, palladium does not tarnish and is used now in jewelry as a substitute for platinum. But my "prediction of things to come" is that it will soon pass as an article of jewelry, and will come into strong demand, if the hydrogen bomb is brought to a "successful conclusion," (whatever that may prove to be.) Note well: palladium is capable of absorbing "up to nearly 1000 times its own volume of hydrogen gas," a fact of extreme significance to our top flight scientists. Now let's go and hunt the platinum mine.

One day in 1882, a pioneer prospector, Joseph Yount, was looking about in southern Nevada, for a deposit of copper. He had a development plan already in mind and was somewhat over-anxious to make such a strike. In the side of a small hill in the Yellow Pine Mining District, near the town of Goodsprings, he found what he was looking for. Sure enough, it was copper, though intermingled with some unfamiliar yellowish grey substance.

The copper mine became the property of the Boss Gold Mining Company, a stock corporation, owned by a small group of stockholders, and the mine was known as the Boss mine. The price of copper, over several decades, was very unstable, and the company was sometimes not only unable to pay dividends, but also could not remain continuously in operation. It fell into arrears for current bills and for wages. But since profits depended upon the price of copper, and there was always a chance the market would go up, the stock in the company was well regarded, and was accepted in payment by some of the company's creditors in lieu of money. Among those who accepted stock for wages was the camp cook, a woman from Los Angeles.

248

In an irregular fashion the mine's affairs were kept alive for several decades. When World War I was imminent, a chemist at the smelter, testing the ore from the Boss mine, was puzzled by the strange reaction from some of the ore. Applying a number of tests, he found the answer: the yellowish grey substance in with the copper was high grade platinum, an element he had not previously suspected, as platinum is usually found in auriferous sand, and not in dolomite limestone as was the case with the Boss copper.

When the officers of the company were notified of the chemist's findings, they realized that, ever since they began the development of the mine, they had been throwing away good values into the dump, platinum at that time being priced at from 70 to 90 dollars an ounce. They hired more men and had the dump well worked over, thus reclaiming nearly all the rejected platinum. Also they made the necessary arrangements for realizing on both the copper and the platinum as it came from the mine. A single carload of the ore sold for $135,000 (Old Style dollar value.)

When the news got around, nothing on earth could avert a platinum rush in the area surrounding the Boss mine. All the ground within a radius of a mile was staked and claims filed. Dozens of men, mining engineers, geologists, mineralogists, experienced prospectors, and just plain adventurers made a most careful examination for further deposits of platinum, but no more platinum ore was found.

The copper and platinum in the Boss mine, during all this time of frantic searching by others continued to pay off. The company was out of the red, and had enough earnings to pay dividends. The woman who had been the camp cook in the lean days, was located by means of advertisements in the Los Angeles newspapers, and the earnings from her shares of stock were handed over to her — real money, along with surprise and rejoicing, for nothing is more heartening than unexpected money on the first of the month.

As the mining continued, the platinum suddenly played out. All efforts to locate a continuation of the ore-body failed. The mother lode of the platinum in that area is a geologic mystery. But mining engineers are certain it must be there. The question is: where?

This copper-platinum mine is in the side of a hill rising sharply from the floor of a desert canyon. A short distance above the canyon floor a tunnel was run for the purpose of cutting under the ore-body, to find out if the ore continued farther down into the earth. Cross-cuts were also made, and the exploration was thorough. But no more platinum came to light in the hill.

Metallurgists and geologists hold the opinion that, in the far distant past, a large deposit of platinum existed in that region, and that, through the ordinary processes of erosion, it was washed down, leaving the pockets of platinum mingled with the copper. If this is true — and there is no theory to contradict it — then somewhere buried in the floor of the desert canyon, they say, must be a rich deposit of platinum. A search for the lost ore may be truly rewarding.

Ask in Goodsprings, Nevada, for the resident agent of the Boss mine, though the mine was not in operation as of 1952. He can tell you where the mine is. Then having visited the mine, which, of course, you must respect as private property, study the desert canyon floor, on all sides of the hill where the Boss tunnel is. When you have located the platinum, if the location is not already claimed, the rest is easy.

3. Lost Diamond Mine in California.

When the diamond fields of America are mentioned, most people think of the well-known fields in Arkansas and North Carolina. They overlook California entirely. I would like to remind such persons that, if they have never read the story of the 200-pound diamond found in California, as told by Major Horace Bell, in his titillating book, *Reminiscences of a Ranger*, life has cheated them of chuckles to which they may justly be entitled.

It's no joke, however, that diamonds have been found in California in widely separated areas, and over a long period of time. The California State Division of Mines says diamonds were found in that state shortly after placer mining began, in 1849. In the gold washings of the Mother Lode area, good diamonds were found, though the discovery did not create any widespread interest.

These diamonds were never traced conclusively to their source, but geologists believe they were washed down from the dark volcanic rock in the Sierra, though ordinarily these gems are found in "pipes," that is, round, vertical outcroppings.

Not long after this early discovery, diamonds were found in Cherokee, Butte County, and since the search for them in this proved area has never been wholly discontinued, this county ranks first in the number found.

"Placer deposits elsewhere have also yielded them from time to time," says the Division of Mines. "Their occurrence has not been limited to any one field. No record has been kept of the total number found, but it is probably between 400 and 500. Since all of them are chance finds, there can be no doubt that many more have been overlooked or destroyed.

"A few of the stones found," the statement continues, "are more than two carats in weight and of good quality, but the majority are small and mostly 'off color,' usually with a pale yellow tinge. Most of these diamonds, now in the possession of different individuals, were found during the days when placer mining and hydraulicking were at their height, and since that time diamond finds have been less frequent."

In 1942, a man, on an errand of his own, in the outskirts of San Bernardino, picked up a diamond weighing two or three carats, of good quality and color. His interest at the time did not lie in the direction of jewels, so he gave the stone to a friend and then forgot all about it.

The friend took it to Dr. Thomas Clements, head of the geology department of the University of Southern California, who tested the gem for weight and hardness, declaring it worth about $200 when cut. No one knew, however, where the original finder had picked it up, beyond the fact that it was in the environs of San Bernardino.

When the story of the diamond and its gem quality was made known, a woman informed Dr. Clements, that, some years earlier, her grandfather had found diamonds near San Bernardino, and that she knew approximately where to look for them. No one, up to early 1952, has relocated the field; though it is known to be about one mile out from the town.

Locate a spot about one mile from San Bernardino where the gravel might tempt you to pan for gold. Then forget the gold and look around for diamonds. If you don't find them, remember diamonds have also been found in all the following counties of California: Amador, El Dorado, Fresno, Nevada, Plumas, Siskiyou, and Trinity. Many more fine gems may still be available in these places.

THE END